*A  Rhetoric of Style*

# A
# Rhetoric
# of Style

*Barry Brummett*

*Southern Illinois University Press / Carbondale*

11  10  09  08     4  3  2  1

Library of Congress Cataloging-in-Publication Data
Brummett, Barry, 1951–
A rhetoric of style / Barry Brummett.
    p. cm.
Includes bibliographical references and index.
ISBN-13: 978-0-8093-2858-1 (pbk. : alk. paper)
ISBN-10: 0-8093-2858-5 (pbk. : alk. paper)
1. Semiotics—Social aspects. 2. Style (Philosophy)
3. Language and culture. 4. Rhetoric. 5. Mass media
and culture—United States. I. Title.
P99.4.S62B78 2008
302.2—dc22                          2007046307

Printed on recycled paper. ♻
The paper used in this publication meets the mini-
mum requirements of American National Standard
for Information Sciences—Permanence of Paper for
Printed Library Materials, ANSI Z39.48-1992. ∞

*To Belema Dorlean and Deandre Dorlean,*
*to Khalil Akbar and Makkah Akbar,*
*young people of style and grace, who enrich my life*

# Contents

# Preface: Style and Rhetoric

[S]tyle, in the broadest sense of all, is consciousness.
—Quentin Crisp, *How to Have a Life-Style*, 47

Imagine a gay couple at a table in a busy restaurant. Their waiter, an attractive young man, bustles around with energy and a winning smile. One man of the couple sighs, his gaze following the waiter as he moves around the restaurant.

*"Wow, what a hottie!" he mutters. His partner scowls and casts an appraising glance in the direction of the waiter for a moment.*

*"Give it up, he's straight, you know," the partner murmurs cruelly.*

Surely, this brief exchange or others like it will be familiar to most of you. We can likely all admit to making similar attributions about the sexual identity, class, or race of friends and perfect strangers alike, even if such attributions then turn out to be incorrect. We cross a street or avert eye contact when approaching someone on the sidewalk if we perceive him or her to be poor enough to beg. A tourist from New York is hailed in an Oklahoma panhandle diner with a "You're not from around here, are you?" But how do we make such judgments? Levels of interesting complications unfold if we think about these and similar examples for a moment.

In the case of our gay couple, the polarities of sexuality may be reversed in one's memories of similar incidents, but the point is this: People do make attributions about others' sexualities (and class, places of origin, and so forth) based on nothing more than their publicly observed behavior. Alexander Doty points out that the comedian Jack Benny was widely if tacitly read as gay due to his walk, gestures, and tone of voice (66–67)—yet, how did people get from a gesture to a judgment about sexuality? How did our gay couple know that the waiter was straight with no opportunity to observe his actual sexual practices? If we think more about the example above, we might realize that others in the restaurant may well have been making complementary attributions about the gay couple as gay. The gay couple may know that and may know precisely what it is that they are doing that draws those judgments. Some gay people may sometimes even exaggerate or camp up their gestures, actions, and grooming in full knowledge that those signs will ensure such attributions. In a society that is still significantly hetero-normative, such assertive display of signs of nonhetero sexualities comes at a cost. If we suppose our gay couple knows they are being read as gay but chooses not to forgo gestures, actions, and grooming that draw those attributions when they could do so, then *why* do they not attempt to pass as straight? Why do any of us act and speak in ways that entail social cost when we could do otherwise? To consider this further, might there be some sense in which the gay couple really cannot display themselves other than as they do? Yet, it is entirely possible that the straight people in the restaurant have no more knowledge or control over whatever is read as straight about them than do any of the gay people. Is there some sense in which the waiter is powerfully constrained to give public performances that will cause others to read him as straight? And what of gays who are consistently read as straight or straights who are usually assumed to be gay—have they no options in what they give others to read?

Consider another example. As each election season rolls around, members of the public will be quoted in the media as making their voting decisions based on whether the candidates "care" about them, about their geographical area, their demographic affiliations, and so forth. The public seems to have forgotten President Harry S. Truman's dictum that if you want a friend in Washington, you should get a dog. The public wants a buddy in the White House and seems hardly to care about competence. Hence, perhaps, the loss of the 2004 presidential election by Senator John F. Kerry to the incumbent President George W. Bush, for many people could not get past Kerry's surface of rigidity and low emotional charge. He seemed not to care about Jane and Joe Lunchbucket and was widely caricatured as resembling the Addams Family's moribund Lurch by comedians and wags (although I heard one wisecracker remark that Kerry more closely resembled the cranky, apple-throwing tree in *The Wizard of Oz*). These attributions may have been encouraged by the venerable stereotype of Boston Brahmins as stiff and re-pressed. Yet, how many among the public had any more grounds on which to judge Kerry as cold and uncaring than our friends in the restaurant had to judge one another's sexual identities? Furthermore, given that accusations of a stiff demeanor surfaced early in the campaign, Kerry certainly had an opportunity to perform a glad-handing, big-yucks demeanor, but he did not—or could not. Yet, in what sense was he so constrained?

All of these sets of examples turn on the concept of *style*. Richard Majors and Janet Mancini Billson argue, "Style includes attitudes, assumptions, and feelings about self and others, as they are expressed in language, dress, and nonverbal behavior" (72). Mike Featherstone provides another serviceable list of what might count as style: "[T]he signs of the dispositions and classificatory schemes which betray one's origins and trajectory through life are also manifest in body shape, size, weight, stance, walk, demeanor, tone of voice, style of speaking, sense of ease or discomfort with one's body" and, we might add, use of objects and possessions such as clothing, home or office décor, automobiles, and so forth (20).

Note that these authors connect style to *communication*, and although they do not use the word, they refer to communication that influences others, or *rhetoric*. We use style to make claims about ourselves and others to bring about desired results. When we put on jeans, we are not just clothing our nakedness, we are speaking a language formed in cloth. *Style is a complex system of actions, objects, and behaviors that is used to form messages that announce who we are, who we want to be, and who we want to be considered akin to. It is therefore also a system of communication with rhetorical influence on others. And as such, style is a means by which power and advantage are negotiated, distributed, and struggled over in society.* This claim is supported by Bradford Vivian's argument that rhetorical analysis is especially appropriate for understanding style and aesthetics in social contexts: "Rhetorical inquiry is singularly equipped to account for the nature of the aesthetic dissemination—for the character of the collective vibration, the shared sentiment—by which a particular style is crystallized" (239).

When we make assumptions about others on the basis of their surface appearance, are we employing stereotypes—and aren't stereotypes a bad thing? This is a tricky issue. A lot may turn on what we mean by *stereotype*. Certainly *false* stereotypes are bad, because they do not serve as good guides to behavior. If I entertain the stereotype that all Jews are secretive, rich, and covetous, I will come to grief for it is radically untrue. But we use *true* stereotypes all the time. You did not pick up this particular book, I would assert; you picked up your stereotype of a book. Had you not felt sure you knew how these things work each and every time, you would have had to rediscover this book as well as every other book you pick up each time you try to read one. The journalist Walter Lippmann mentioned the practical value of stereotypes in his trade: "Without standardization, without stereotypes, without routine judgments . . . the editor would soon die of excitement" (222) as would we all—each experience would be as if the world had been born that morning, as if all mem_____ had _____. You may prefer to call these _____ _____, or *generalizations*, but they all reference _____ _____ and linguistic processes. As Edward Schiappa argues, we simply must use categories to be able to think (*Defining*, 13–21). So in our

interactions with others, yes, we employ, and we must employ generalizations, standardization—call them stereotypes if you like. This is as true for
our interactions with people as with objects. As Mirja Kälviäinen put it, "We
look at others, at least on first sight, through stereotypes" (81). The current
volume studies the ways in which such stereotypes work rhetorically in our
use and understanding of style.

But let us also consider what we are saying when we refer to gay styles or
to Boston Brahmin styles. We are not saying that everyone who is gay will
display a "gay style" nor that gays never display styles read as some other
sexuality. We are not saying that those who are not gay do not or cannot
display styles that will be read as gay. What we are saying is that there are
cohesive clusters of style—movement, gesture, speech, vocabulary, decoration, and the like—that will be *read* as gay or straight and that such expectations and attributions *work* at some level often enough to be constantly
used by even the most tolerant and careful social actors. Some stereotypes
may have such power that they call to those people to whom they are attributed actually to perform the stereotype.

I have two purposes in writing this book. First, I want to pull together a
number of observations made by other scholars and critics that place style
at the center of popular culture today in late-capitalist societies globally.
Style is a good construct for understanding *the intersection of culture, commodification, and capital.* Style is a major, perhaps *the* major, way in which
cultures are now formed, and it is very likely the most important engine of
commodification and consumption today. Style is above all systematic and
signifying, and as a system of signification, it gives an angle of approach to
understand preoccupations that are shared around the world.

My second purpose is arrogant, overreaching, indeed, it is impossible,
but I will essay it. Vivian is correct in saying that "for better or worse, then,
modern rhetorical theory lacks a contemporary rationale and methodology
for the study of style" (223). I hope this book develops such a rationale. But
I also intend to offer the rationale of style as the basis for a contemporary
and future rhetoric.

I want to argue that style is the key to constructing a rhetoric for the
twenty-first century. I will not argue that a rhetoric of style completely replaces earlier rhetorics, such as, those of Aristotle, George Campbell, or
Kenneth Burke, which still find broad relevance. But style is in some important ways the name for a system of persuasive signs and meanings into
which nearly everybody, globally, has entered. For a long time, it has been
fashionable to think of societies as so diverse and divided that we need at
least half a dozen rhetorics in our conceptual repertoires, rhetorics that
will help us to function rhetorically and to understand how such functioning

occur in this or that context. But after centuries of increasing fragmentation and decenteredness loosely described as "postmodern," I think we are headed toward a more unified cultural system grounded in late capitalism. If that is true, then what we need is one rhetoric to describe how more and more of us in late-capitalist societies—and that is a greater and greater percentage of the world each year—behave rhetorically. Yes, there are variations of culture, class, race, and so forth that call for rhetorical specialization and sensitivity—but there is also style, an increasingly global terrain of shared knowledge, action, and judgment. Aristotle's rhetoric "worked" because he was writing about a tightly knit community of relatively homogeneous people in ancient Greece. Despite the enormous diversity and fragmentation in today's world, style is what knits the world into a relatively homogeneous system of communication. I, therefore, will end up offering it as the basis for a rhetoric that undergirds today's global culture. *Style is the name of the rhetoric for the social system that we all have in common.* My crime is clearly more likely to be failure than low aim.

There is a key ambiguity in this book, to which I may as well confess now. Much of what I say and much of what the people I quote here will say has to do with popular culture, or a rhetoric of popular culture. Style is so central to popular culture that the rhetoric of style and the rhetoric of popular culture are practically the same thing. One might say that thinking in terms of style is a way to think about popular culture. So I believe it will be fruitful to see those two concepts as highly porous or missible, one to the other. Style may be a special and smaller set of the popular, but it is not much smaller. Style is also an element of popular culture that is extremely demotic, being something everyone engages in constantly, and so may be even more widely relevant to the reader than is the idea of popular culture. One may hold oneself aloof and claim never to traffic with popular culture, but one has a style in doing so.

In pursuit of my overly ambitious goals, my first chapter locates style at the center of popular culture. In that chapter, I explore definitions and basic concepts of style. I urge an understanding of style as a system of signification grounded largely in image, aesthetics, and extrarational modes of thinking. The simulational nature of style is explored, and I look at the idea of homology as a way to understand the cohesion and systematicity holding different styles together.

The second chapter explores the social and commercial structuring of style as its chief handmaiden, and we are all enrolled in hyperconsumption through a preoccupation with style.

The third chapter edges closer to rhetoric, as it considers the political consequences of style. The chapter explores the idea of identity and then argues that identity today is largely structured by style, hence the controversial concept of identity politics. Style and the images it entails are the chief sites of social and political struggle for most people in their everyday lives, the chapter shows. I also entertain some widespread and serious complaints about the involvement of style with politics.

The fourth chapter pulls together the discussion to that point and proposes style as a rhetoric for the twenty-first century. Theoretical and critical tenets of this rhetoric are developed. The chapter offers systematic guides to the understanding of style as today's chief rhetorical system. I offer five major structural components of a rhetoric of style: (1) primacy of the text, (2) imaginary communities, (3) market contexts, (4) aesthetic rationales, and (5) stylistic homologies.

The concluding chapter of rhetorical analysis illustrates the theoretical argument, showing how rhetoric works through style. I explore a style that I believe provides an imaginary core and unity to what is sometimes called the "gun culture" in the United States. Although such a culture is not even close to being the monolithic conspiracy imagined by many on the Left, I think that those interested in guns and their lawful uses are unified by a style and that the exercise of the repertoire of that style has political purposes. I argue that a working-class style, or the image of one, unifies the gun culture. But any ideology, and any style, has contradictions that are key to how it functions politically. Gun culture's working-class style entails two contradictions. The first contradiction is between two great traditions of work, the urban and the rural. Gun-culture style follows rural themes of work, clothing, posture, and speech, yet it follows urban themes of the threat of violence. The second contradiction is a poignancy felt by many who have done factory work, and that is a tension between a yearning for independence and free action on the one hand and deference to authority and power on the other. The chapter serves as an example of how style is political and as an example of how a rhetoric of style works methodologically. The chapter launches the reader into his or her own examination of the rhetoric of style.

We close with a postface. I assert an imaginary etymology, entirely untrue, for the word *preface* and, correspondingly, *postface*. The book closes with a brief consideration of some issues that will likely be troubling to most readers

## Acknowledgments

I want to thank students, too many to name, who have studied style and its rhetorical dimensions with me at the University of Texas at Austin and at the University of Wisconsin at Milwaukee. If that's you, and you are reading this, please know you were an inspiration. I want to thank the on-line magazine *Pedestal* for the original publication of my poem "At the Gun Show." Thanks to Professor Edward Schiappa and Professor Mark Meister for their support and helpful comments. And thanks to Karl Kageff and the staff at the Southern Illinois University Press for a smooth and helpful editorial process.

# 1

# Style at the Center of Popular Culture

> The projection of style can be effected by three principal
> means—our speech, our movements, and our appearance.
> . . . Though it is the least powerful way of communicating
> style, appearance receives more attention than all the other
> means put together. Presumably this is because there is more
> money in it.
>
> —Quentin Crisp, *How to Have a Life-Style*, 63

What do I mean by *style*? Many possibilities come to mind. In its broadest sense, I might use style to mean *the way in which we do something*, including how we speak, act, move, eat, dress, decorate, and so forth. If that sense of the word is impossibly broad, we might still note the way that *style* leans toward breadth and scope. But let me begin more narrowly. Witold Rybczynski explains the interesting etymology of the word:

> The Latin root of "style" is *stilus*. A *stilus* was the sharp-pointed tool used to write on wax tablets and, by inference, *stilus* also referred to the way that something was written. This sense of technique carried over to English. (88)

Style is how one writes, in one sense, and, thus, we are blessed with style manuals. This etymology puts communication—in this case, writing on a tablet—at the core of style. It is interesting to note that Rybczynski's explanation also verges on a sense of *fashion*, which is distinguished below from style, in that what is written in wax is of necessity impermanent and always changeable.

The most venerable definitions of style tend to be the narrowest. The con-

"The best definition I can give of it, is, the peculiar manner in which a man expresses his conceptions, by means of language" (101–2). In this classical sense, style is, as Roderick P. Hart defined it, "the sum total of language habits distinguishing one message from another" (197). The focus just on language cannot, however, encompass the usages that would refer to a Pre-Raphaelite style of painting, to someone who always has great style, or to an employer who conducts an exit interview with grace and style.

Another limited view of style comes from the field of psychology. Some social scientists have studied style as what individuals predictably and systematically do in response to identifiable stimuli or as a consequence of stable cognitive conditions, that is, as behaviors that are largely understood as symptoms of personality traits. Gordon Allport's classic study of personality offers the rather broad claim that "style represents the most complex and complete form of expressive behavior. It concerns the whole of activity, not merely special skills or single regions of the body" (489). The promise of grand scope in that statement is not borne out in most scientific studies. Peggy E. Gallaher, a more recent social scientist, offers an equally far ranging reference to "*style*, which means the way something is done" or "expressive behavior," which she views largely as symptoms of personality traits. Her article identifies four dimensions of personal style: expressiveness, animation, expansiveness, and coordination. These four dimensions are expressed in particular, observable behavior. These psychological studies are valuable but have little to say about the connections between style and commodities, for instance, or broader political movements.

In everyday conversation, though, we use style more broadly than just as a term describing only language or personality dimensions. We refer to people who are stylish or have style, or we might refer to particular kinds of style such as Victorian, punk, or Goth. We refer to leadership styles or styles of architecture, hinting at wide networks of actions, objects, and experiences. This is the sense in which Stuart Ewen defines style as "a way that the human values, structures, and assumptions in a given society are aesthetically expressed and received" (3). When we link style to aesthetics as a way to express values, structures, and assumptions, then we have a rather broad umbrella term. Style in this sense refers to the ways in which actions, objects, events, gestures, and commodities, as well as the properties of language, are used to create aesthetically charged rhetorical outcomes in the self and others. It may be illustrated in Richard Majors and Janet Mancini Billson's description of a particular style, "cool pose," as incorporating "unique patterns of speech, walk, and demeanor" (2).

This wider sense of style is illustrated in Robert D. Hariman's fine study of political style, which looks at the way in which language, behavior patterns, gestures, social structures, and even clothing coalesce into distinct political styles. Hariman understands style as going beyond its restriction in the canon to rational discourse: "For the most part, the canon of style remains identified with cataloguing discursive forms in the artistic text alone rather than understanding the dynamics of our social experience or the relationship between rhetorical appeals and political decisions" (8). Like Hariman, I want to think of style as socially held sign systems composed of a wide range of signs beyond only language, systems that are used to accomplish rhetorical purposes across the cultural spectrum.

I want to think about style not only as a system of signs, as a kind of performance but also as the grounds of signifying upon which more and more of our social, cultural world is organized. Ewen expresses this perspective in arguing, "[S]tyle was definitely more than a question of fashions in clothing or in literary expression. It was part of an ether, a general sensibility, that touched on countless arenas of everyday life, yet was limited by none of them" (3). Michel Maffesoli likewise expresses a sense of style as transcendent, as forming the ground for social interaction: "In the strict meaning of the term, [style] becomes an all-encompassing form, a 'forming form' that gives birth to whole manners of being, to customs, representations, and the various fashions by which life in society is expressed" (5). If style is indeed the symbolic ether in which the social medium exists in late capitalism, then Ewen's commentary that "style today is a preoccupation of nearly all sectors of society" should not surprise us (3).

Style is not simply a matter of which shirt one puts on but is the transcendent ground in which the social is formed in late capitalism. When something is transcendent, it uses us as much as we use it. As I hope to show, the question of the extent to which style is intentional is tricky. Style is not so much something that one does as it is the grounds in terms of which something is done; or to put it bluntly, style performs us as much as we perform any given style. We may choose styles or styles may choose us. Judith Butler puts it succinctly:

> I think that style is a complicated terrain, and not one that we unilaterally choose or control with the purposes we consciously intend. . . . Certainly, one can practice styles, but the styles that become available to you are not entirely a matter of choice. (*Gender* xviii)

The constraints that people feel to perform or not perform certain styles speak of a particular look or style, but of a cultural concern with 'stylishness,' with 'aesthetics,' that is intrinsic to high tech" (5). Bakari Kitwana shows how hip-hop, which began as only music, fashion, or gesture, has grown into a whole cultural complex: "Certainly, the commercialization of rap music expanded the definition of hip-hop culture beyond the four elements (graffiti, break dancing, dj-ing, rap music) to include verbal language, body language, attitude, style, and fashion" (8). Anne-Lise Hauge-Nilsen and Margaret Galer Flyte describe the characteristics of good product design in largely stylistic terms, comprising as they do the whole environment of using an object: "[T]he most important attributes that contribute to pleasure in short-term product use are good performance, pleasing aesthetics, good feel/touch, control of the product, good quality, safety, good construction, good feedback entertainment and good usability" (268). Note how broadly aesthetic those descriptors are, how much they connect to the whole complex of living with and using an object. Finally, John Leland understands hip, certainly a kind of style, as a lifewide preoccupation, speaking of it as a transcendent rhythm beneath the flow of existence: "Living in rhythm—sonic, visual, intellectual, philosophical—is an essential promise of hip" (194). For all these scholars, style is a transcendent category organizing experience.

It is useful to distinguish between style itself as a concept, which is largely what I have been discussing so far, and the idea of particular styles, such as, Bauhaus, Gothic, Romantic, and so forth. These particular styles are unified sign systems with widely understood meanings and connotations. It is also useful to distinguish style from the idea of *fashion*. The idea of style as a language is explored in depth later, but here it would be useful to think of style as a language and fashion as the particular utterance of that language in the moment. It may not always be appropriate to utter a given language or a particular sentence, but the language remains as a reality, as a potential repertoire, even if not being uttered at the moment. In the same sense, a given style is a system of signs with particular meanings. *Fashion* refers to whether or not a particular style is in vogue at the moment. Rybczynski quotes Gabrielle Chanel expressing this distinction as "fashion passes, style remains" (xiii). "Hippie style" may or may not be currently fashionable, but it nevertheless remains a style that is available to be mined for its signs and meanings, and it may go in and out of fashion over the years. Rybczynski expresses precisely this distinction when he argues, "If style is the language of architecture, fashion represents the wide—and swirling—cultural currents that shape and direct that language" in any given historical moment (51). Virginia Postrel agrees in noting the inevitability of rapid change in what we call fashion: *Fashion* . . . applies not just to clothing and related products but to anything whose aesthetic form evolves continuously" (79). Malcolm

Barnard likewise employs this usage in distinguishing changeable fashion from "fixed dress," which does not change (61). Tribal or Vatican priestly clothing would be examples of such fixed dress. Jean Baudrillard refers to fixed dress in observing that "there is no such thing as fashion in a society of cast and rank, since one is assigned a place irrevocably, and so class mobility is non-existent" (*Simulations* 84).

A sense of style is defined as technique, as doing something. It is interesting that Barnard gives the etymology of fashion as what one does instead of what one wears, in the sense that one *fashions* a clay pot or a hat (8). This sense of what one does is, I think, going to be more compatible with our sense of fashion than it will be with our sense of style, for fashion is always the doing of something in the present moment, making use of the resources offered to one by different styles, which remain more permanent and ideal.

For style to function as a social medium, information about it must be widely shared. The mass media are the source of information on style, and that information is shared globally. People want to know about available styles and how they will be read by others, and we want to acquire knowledge of how to use the resources of style. The media tell us which fashions are currently in vogue. Paul A. Cantor stresses the importance of television in creating shared culture in general: "For good or ill, television seems to be providing students today with whatever common culture they possess" (ix), and an awareness of different styles and their meanings is a central part of that consumer culture. As Mike Featherstone says, "the concern with constructing an expressive lifestyle, to achieve some sense of satisfying order from the commodities and practices that surround the individual, generates a constant demand for information about lifestyles" (114). The information that is given in response to that demand is largely consistent and systematic; from today's different media, we tend not to get contradictory information about what style is and what it means. Diana Crane argues, for instance, that fashion photography marches to a beat set by youth culture: "Fashion photographers have synchronized their themes and images with those that circulate in youth cultures and that are disseminated by the media, particularly of rock music" (203). These youth cultures tend toward the global, with media consistently passing information on what is stylish back and forth among Tokyo, New York, and Berlin. David Theo Goldberg refers explicitly to the role of sports talk radio in creating shared styles

The media, in providing information about style, are providing information about the social world in which we live. Of course, this has been true for centuries, but today's electronic media have achieved a level of global reach and integration not previously seen. John Leland notes the importance of new technology and the media the technologies support for the development of "hip" youth cultures: "As a form of enlightenment, hip flourishes during periods of technological or economic change. . . . Youth cultures have organized around new machines and media" (61). Dick Hebdige argues that such information helps us to classify and order our worlds: "Now, the media play a crucial role in defining our experience for us. They provide us with the most available categories for classifying out the social world" (84–85). This means also that different communities learn from the media which styles are associated or disassociated them. Kitwana points out that Black culture, including style, is now disseminated by the media in contrast to earlier practices: "Despite slight local variations, the passing on of Black culture to the succeeding generation remained orderly and consistent from one Black community to the next. Today the influence of these traditional purveyors of Black culture have largely diminished in the face of powerful and pervasive technological advances and corporate growth" (7). Replacing local cultural authority, "now media and entertainment such as pop music, film, and fashion are among the major forces transmitting culture to this generation for Black Americans" (7). This replacement of local, "indigenous" authority with mediated authorities may not always be a good thing, although it certainly seems inevitable. Some media authorities may purvey undesirable values. For instance, Goldberg explores the idea of "commodity racism," which "manifests in consumer spectacles: advertising, expositions, museum exhibitions. It could be added that today commodity racism finds its principal expression in and through the hyperconsumptive spectacle of sports," surely a major source of information, correct or not, about the styles connected to different ethnicities (39).

David Slayden and Rita Kirk Whillock argue that this process of the media replacing local authority on style and culture is occurring across many cultural communities: "[C]ultural conventions have been replaced by production codes wherein points of cultural reference emanate from the produced realm of film and television, rather than from a shared experience of the everyday physical world" (ix–x). It could be said that this realm of the media is the experience shared in common by people around the globe. It is not an exclusive web of information—anyone with the right technology may access it. Information about style does not conform to any sense of exclusive "high culture" in which information is limited to maintain class privilege. The ability of mass media to create a globally shared space of information is precisely what allows style to become such a web of connection. "Popular films, novels, and TV . . . are frequently dismissed by highbrow critics for . . . conforming to generic patterns and their conditions of mass production," John Fiske notes. "Yet these qualities . . . are, in the realm of the popular, precisely those which enable the text to be taken up and used in the culture of the people" ("Popular" 218). The significance of all these observations is that despite vast cultural differences, the cultural authority that was once located at a mother's knee is now found on a screen. Although significant cultural differences remain, people now share to a great extent the same mediated experience, and it is from that experience that we learn about the centrality of style in our lives.

If mass media create an environment of signs that keep us informed as to what style is, what it means, and how it can be used, then we need to think more about style as a set of signs. The next section explores the idea that style is constructed of signs and images. This will lead one to a consideration of whether style is therefore dangerous or unimportant (although, clearly, it cannot be both).

## Style and Signs

One of the most widely recurring claims made about style is that it deals with signs but not their referents, with image but not substance. "The primacy of style over substance has become the normative consciousness," Ewen argues (2). One may have a French Provincial–style living room without having any real connection to France. One may wear cowboy hats, yet be, as they say in Texas, all hat and no cattle. The idea is expressed in many ways. Some argue that style is all "surface," others see it as the "skin" of real experiences, but however it is phrased, style is often accused of being inconsequential. Applying these observations to fashion, Barnard says, "In many everyday figures of speech, fashion, clothing, and textiles are associated with triviality and deceit" (2). The point is illustrated in Michel de Certeau's image of the "man about town": "Beneath the man about town's clothes—behind the mask—is *nothing*" (184). Jack Babuscio argues that the kind of style called *camp* is not only all surface but also makes all social roles superficial, locating them on the surface of experience: "Camp, by focusing on the outward appearances of role, implies that roles, and in particular, sex roles, are superficial—a matter of style" (24). On a related theme, Peter Ackroyd points to transvestism as a playing with surfaces that is transgressive precisely because it turns its back on substance. In the Victorian context, "the male transvestite would seem offensive on every level. His cross dressing is entirely useless and essential . . . . . . . . . . . . . . . . . . . . . . . . . . . . . . . . . . . . . . rather than of moral duty" (60).

George Ritzer articulates a widely used metaphor of the surface in reference to style: "What becomes important in spectacular society is the desirable surface of images and signs" (183). A preoccupation with surfaces is an engrossment in style, for Ewen explains, "The ability to stylize anything . . . encourages a comprehension of the world that focus on its easily manipulated surfaces, while other meanings vanish to all but the critical eyes" (262). Ewen argues that late capitalism depends on surfaces, for in the market "all manners of human expression and creativity are mined for their surfaces: their *look*, their *touch*, their *sound*, their *scent*. This booty is then attached to the logic of the marketplace: mass produced and merchandised" (52). Hebdige connects a focus on surfaces to aesthetic pleasure, which is key to the centrality of style: "We gain aesthetic pleasure from the surface experience of the intensities of the flow of images: we do not seek coherent lasting meaning" (127). Baudrillard uses a high-tech surface metaphor of the screen, reminding us that we learn of surfaces from the media: "Today the scene and the mirror have given way to a screen and a network. There is no longer any transcendence or depth, but only the immanent surface of operations unfolding, the smooth and functional surface of communication" (*Ecstasy* 25). As one example of a style that mines surfaces, Frank Mort offers gay style, beginning in the United Kingdom in the 1980s: "It was the surfaces of the body, linked to particular styles or looks, which began to be privileged as sites of sexuality, rather than an exclusive focus on one dominant sexual act" (179). In other words, what it meant to *be* gay was being collapsed into what it meant to *look* gay.

Such persistent references to style as surface express the idea that style is composed of signs that retain some meaning from original referents but are no longer closely connected to them. These signs are widely described as *floating signs* (or floating signifiers), as in Featherstone's claim that "the autonomy of the signifier, through, for example, the manipulation of signs in the media and advertising, means that signs are able to float free from objects and are available for use in a multiplicity of associative relations" (15). The sign that is a cowboy hat, for instance, need not be "anchored" to any real cowboy, nor would one nowadays assume that someone wearing a cowboy hat has that occupation. The concept of floating signs is quite widespread and is useful but cannot be absolutely true, for signs never float completely. For a cowboy hat to have any meaning at all—for it to retain the meanings of rugged, rural individualism that allow it to work within certain systems of style—it has to retain some tether of meaning, however long and stretched, to the original cowboys who first wore them.

Ewen refers to style in a surface language of skin, arguing that "whatever the 'skin,' or its vernacular origin, its meaning is most often compromised or lost once it enters the style market. . . . Style is something to be *used up*. Part of its significance is that it will lose significance" by being torn from that original context (52). Leon E. Wynter similarly uses the skin metaphor in claiming, "American industry has produced a lifelike artificial skin of commercial culture that's supple yet strong enough to cover us all" (10).

Style seems to require the appropriation of signs from contexts that originally gave them meaning. The ability to shift signs and their meanings from one context to another is of the essence in style. Hebdige relates that stylists were (and still are) called "*bricoleurs* when they appropriated another range of commodities by placing them in a symbolic environment which served to erase or subvert their original straight meanings" (104). Stylists in the fashion industry are described by Crane as removing signs from originating contexts: "These image makers scavenge a wide range of sources, from the history of film, television, and the arts to street cultures, gay subcultures, and pornography" (202). This is what happens when a designer today updates the Jackie or Twiggy look, with no need for today's cultural context to match that of the Sixties.

The idea of the signs that make up style as merely skin, surface, or floating stands in contrast to the idea of the kind of style that is enforced by *sumptuary laws* (Barnard 62, 78; Crane 3; Ewen and Ewen 85–87). A sumptuary law dictates a close link between sign and reality; the sign is anchored rather than floating. It usually applies to dress or clothing, which must accurately signal an occupation or station in life. Barnard points out that in feudal systems, clothing styles were assigned to different classes by law, both signaling and reproducing class (108–9). Even today, we have actual sumptuary laws when we do not want certain signs to float, when we want the surface or skin of a style to reflect a reality: One cannot without serious penalty impersonate a law officer or a physician, for example, for we want to *count* on signs of those occupations as signaling the real thing.

An understanding of style as mere surface points toward an understanding of the essential connection between style and rhetoric. If to persuade you about cowboy-ish matters I must actually be a cowboy, then my task is difficult, and my chances are poor. That is the situation in which rhetoric must be about, be connected to, a material reality. But if the surface/skin/screen spaces of style are what people respond to, then we enter a world where rhetoric rules, for surfaces are so easily manipulated. I can take on the skin of a cowboy, if that is what persuades, by adopting certain styles. Baudrillard puts it, "Surface and appearance, that is the space of seduction" (*Ecstasy* 62). Ewen notes the centrality of surface and image in the market, "Style, more and more, has become the official idiom of the marketplace. In advertising, packaging, product design, and corporate *identity*, the power of provocative surfaces speaks to the eye's mind overshadowing matters of quality or substance" (22), a situation in which "the preeminence of hard goods has given way to that of abstract value, nonmateriality, and the ephemeral" (157). Bill Green likewise notes the importance of the surface for the market: "Design, defined as human/product interaction in its broadest sense, is the most significant product differentiator, moving ahead of technological sophistication and even, in our affluent societies, of price" (1–2). Green reports that "the modernist credo that 'form-follows-function' is a very shaky concept" as form, or style, comes to dominate the market independently of function (2).

As it skins surfaces and removes them from real contexts for its own purposes, style ranges widely across times and places. It is allusive, constantly employing images and references from contexts other than the one in which it may currently appear. Matias Viegener argues that *camp* is a style that is particularly allusive: "Its primary mechanism is the insertion of an old, tired image into a new context, recycling history's waste, which is usually a product of an earlier mode of production that has lost its power to produce viable cultural meaning" (250). This allusiveness is a phenomenon that Postrel calls "costume echoes," attributing the term to Desmond Morris, and she observes, "Costume echoes apply to all sorts of surfaces, not just personal appearance" (100). The landscape of style today is thus one of constant churning of different styles that come and go in fashion, a dazzling array of references to past eras and icons. Featherstone identifies "the constant recycling of artistic and historical themes in the aestheticized commodity world. . . . the capacity of the ever-changing urban landscape to summon up associations, resemblances and memories" (74). Ewen notes that to remain in public memory, newly emergent goods and symbols must likewise invoke memories of earlier images: "Product designs, packages, or corporate symbols . . . must be able to be impressed on the *memory*; they must endure in the minds of prospective consumers. . . . Even newly designed goods must, in some way, evoke prior goods and memories" (246). We may refer to styles of this period or that, of one school or another. But the fact of the matter is that during any given period and in any given place, especially during late capitalism, many systems of style are being invoked, with no overall coherence although any given style may be internally coherent. Bauhaus is a coherent style that nevertheless emerged in a fragmented period in which many other styles were also current. Rybczynski says, "Most historical periods are marked by stylistic confusion; it is stylistic consensus that is unusual" (79).

In sum, a number of scholars have observed that style is made of surface, skin, or screen, and the observation is often a complaint. If style is "mere" surface, it would seem that it ought not be taken seriously. But consider a complementary claim, which is that style *is* substance. If we live in a culture that is increasingly one of sign and image, then a style made of sign and image may be as "real" as it gets, as real as anybody wants or needs for it to be. That is precisely our world, for as Ritzer argues, "Spectacular society is premised on a shift from production of goods to social reproduction. . . . The spectacle . . . reproduces itself through the production of signs and images" (185–86). If our culture buys and sells signs, images, and meanings more than it does hardware—if we are a culture engrossed in *The West Wing* more than in actual politics—if more people vote for the American Idol than for nearly every political candidate who has ever run—then we live in a world where signs are becoming a reality for people.

In short, in many ways, the opposition of style and substance is collapsing. Substance and style increasingly merge. It is tricky to critique a collapsed binary without seeming to replicate it. Ideally, one would find a third, synthetic term that represents a new unity. That won't do here, as *style* is a term in vigorous usage.

A number of authors seem to replicate the style-substance dichotomy even as they envision the ascendance of style, and I also may seem to do so. This is for several reasons. First, not everyone sees the matter in the same way, although we may usefully share ideas. Second, we live in a time of cultural change, and even if one side of a binary collapses into the other, it takes time to do so, time for language to catch up. Third, one may utter the collapsed half of a binary conditionally by way of invoking what is no longer there, as when one speaks of dodo birds in the Caribbean or literary studies in English departments. Fourth and finally, one may retain both terms of a binary to transfer the rhetorical force of one term to another. I, and I think many of this book's sources, intend to transfer the rhetorical *gravitas* of substance over to style by declaring that style is substance or substantial. In that way, my argument is meant to claim *rhetorical* status for *substance* and *ontological* status for *style*.

The distinction between style and substance reinscribes the old Platonic distinction between appearance and reality, sign and referent that has come to be regarded as problematic. This Platonic dualism may be seen clearly in *Gorgias*, where clearly stylistic practices, such as, cosmetics and cooking, are opposed to substantive disciplines, such as, gymnastics and medicine. These oppositions are likewise between mere signs of the good and the good itself. In a sense, the style-substance distinction for Plato is also one between signs and substance. Against that dualism is now a world in which style rules and with it the collapse of substance into signs/styles.

An important angle from which to approach a collapse of substance into style is to problematize the opposition between substance (or reality) and signs. Numerous thinkers have given reason to believe in the primacy of signs, to think, as Jacques Lacan put it, that for human experience, "it is the world of words that creates the world of things" (65). The Lacanian scholar Jon Stratton echoes this sentiment, "In the context of the fetishisation of appearance an object is determined by what it appears to be" (78) or the image determines the social reality.

One of the more spectacular, in several senses, of these thinkers recently is Baudrillard: "We no longer exist as playwrights or actors but as terminals of multiple networks" and as such, primarily as signs and representations (*Ecstasy* 16). This creates today's situation of "obscenity" in which "everything becomes immediately transparent, visible, exposed in the raw and inexorable light of information and communication," in other words, everything becomes first and foremost a sign (*Ecstasy* 21–22). When everything is a sign, everyone is in "ecstasy," which "is all functions abolished into one dimension, the dimension of communication" (*Ecstasy* 23). Baudrillard bemoans this state of affairs.

These recent theorists echo earlier work by I. A. Richards, who explains at length the ways in which signs organize the world so that what we are conscious of is always already full of signification, and by Kenneth Burke, who, in works such as "What Are the Signs of What," states that language pulls the world together in ways that serve different interests (*Language*, 359–79). Both theorists argue that perceived reality is always already structured by sign systems. One need not be a solipsist or believe in magic to argue that signs constitute the substance of human reality.

Because these other authors have made extensive philosophical and psychological arguments as to why signs undergird experience, this work focuses instead on culturally based arguments as to why the surface may be substance, why dismissing style as mere skin ignores the increasing centrality of skin and image in late capitalism, and why it makes less and less sense to think of style as opposed to substance. I think one could make the argument that style has always been important precisely because it is surface, and surface has always been an important dimension of experience. Mirja Kälviäinen expresses that idea: "Style deals in surface impressions, yet it forms a corridor between the world of things and human consciousness" (83–84). Sarah Buie makes the same argument about aesthetics considered as surface and that aesthetic appearances are about much more than appearances: "Aesthetics, of course, is not actually about the surface appearance of things, but about how the true nature of an undertaking, or an object, or an intention, is embodied and expressed in form. It is the direct, visceral way we understand what something means, what it is" (28). Postrel likewise places surface at the center of our lives: "When we declare that mere surface cannot possibly have legitimate value, we deny human experience and ignore human behavior" (xi). Or in the words of Oscar Wilde, quoted by Rybczynski, "In matters of importance, style is everything" (xiv). One may wring hands over this if one wants to, but it is first important to see that it is so. Maffesoli confronts what is a new cultural reality head-on: "The languishing civilization of an economic and utilitarian modernity is being succeeded by a new culture in which the sense of the superfluous, the concern for the useless, and the search for the qualitative all take on paramount importance" (12).

The market certainly values a world of signs, the surface, and the skin. If that is what people will pay for, then in a society undergirded by capitalism, what one might have called mere surface is perforce important. Postrel opines, "Surface itself has genuine value, for which consumers willingly pay extra" (67). Leland calls attention to the use of language in marketing, which is nothing but the manipulation of signs to create value in the market: "This is the essence of modern business, to create value through language. In the information economy, the play of language *is* value: if you buy a pair of jeans or a Hummer, what you're really buying is a story about yourself" (170).

Beyond the market, style has functioned as substance for different social groups. Mort argues that for gays, style comes to be a kind of sexual reality on its own terms.

> Jeans, haircuts, shoes and boots were not simply used to signify homosexuality, or to indicate sexual preference, as they had done [in earlier eras]. These forms of representation were now assembled as part of a visual culture which revolved around the objects and artefacts of consumer style. . . . [I]t was the commodities themselves and their symbolic arrangement which evoked sexual meanings. (178–79)

And Stuart Hall makes a similar observation for people of the African diaspora: "[W]ithin the black repertoire, *style*—which mainstream cultural critics often believe to be the mere husk, the wrapping, the sugar coating on the pill—has become *itself* the subject of what is going on" ("What Is" 289).

A useful way to understand how the surface that is style can be of more substance than is substance is to consider the difference between *use value* and *exchange value*. Any object or action examined might have use value: it does something or can be used to do something. A knife can be used to peel an apple; a wedding ritual can be used to create a marriage. Any object or action examined might also have exchange value: you can get something in exchange for the action or object, or you must give something in exchange to get it. Exchange value is a little trickier to understand. Money clearly has exchange value, because you can exchange it to get goods and services in return. Money also has use value but not a lot of it. However, you can use a dime as an impromptu screwdriver or a folded dollar bill under an uneven table leg. Objects that enter a market as commodities have the exchange value that is their price. Where exchange value really becomes interesting is when an object or action may be used, displayed, or performed to "get back" something of cultural or symbolic value in exchange.

An ordinary pair of sneakers purchased cheaply at Wal-Mart has use value. It will keep your feet off the road. A pair of brand-name sneakers endorsed and worn by a popular athlete may have exactly the same use value as the cheap sneakers, but because of the brand and the endorsement, it has acquired exchange value. When you wear the popular sneakers, what will you get in exchange for doing so? You will get popularity, inclusion, status, and so forth. Any old bed sheet will cover your nakedness, but if you go on a job interview, you should dress more formally, and the clothing you wear can be "exchanged" for a job offer, for the attribution to you by others of a professional image, and so forth.

Exchange value is nothing but style, signs, and surface over substance, but it is a major, if not the major, factor in commodification, consumer purchases, the economy itself. A store can charge several times what a competitor might charge for bargain-basement sneakers if the right icon is sitting on the more-expensive shoes. Exchange value forms a kind of economy of its own. If I wear cool sneakers, I can exchange the wearing of them for an attribution of coolness to me by others (even if I am a professor; work with me on this). And if I become cool, others can pick up that coolness by hanging out with me. I can start new trends and fads that will pick up coolness from my coolness; all this from the circulating of the exchange value of a really cool pair of sneakers. Featherstone says, "The cultural realm thus has its own logic and currency as well as rate of conversion into economic capital" (89). Given these considerations, it makes less sense to refer to style, skins, and surfaces as if they were not substantial. Exchange value helps us to see the substance of style.

A number of scholars have explored the distinction between use value and exchange value. It has not always been understood in the same way. Andrew Milner notes, "Marx subscribed to a 'labour theory of value,' in which the relative value of commodities was held to be determined by the amount of labour-power necessary to produce them" (19), a way of determining value that is now impossible to maintain with the massive intervention of technology in the production process but also with value coming from branding and style in ways that Marx could not have envisioned. In contrast today, as Zygmunt Bauman points out, "What endows things with value is not the sweat needed to produce them (as Marx would say), or the self-renunciation necessary to obtain them (as George Simmel suggested), but a *desire seeking satisfaction*" (*Community* 130). Fiske agrees in pointing out that the use-value of efficiency is not what constitutes "culture, which is concerned with meanings, pleasures, and identities rather than efficiency" (*Understanding* 1). Culture is instead based on structures of exchange value. This is discussed in greater detail later, but consider that use value can fuel only so much consumption. Once you have one pair of shoes to keep your feet off the road, you really don't need another one. Need has been satisfied—what else might drive you to the mall? We may say that substance in the form of use value vanishes entirely when we buy a twentieth pair of shoes that will add nothing to our practical abilities but is the latest, coolest fashion. Consider that the desire to consume that can be fueled by exchange value is potentially endless, as we can always be led to desire more coolness, more acceptance, and so forth. We may all be hard pressed to remember the last thing we bought only for its use value. Even much of our food is stylized—we buy exchange value in the form of the right *brand* or attractive *packaging*. One might say that use value has collapsed into exchange value as substance has collapsed into style.

Stratton explains the use value–exchange value distinction in one way by saying that "use-value is intrinsic to the commodity. Exchange-value, on the other hand, is determined by a commodity's relation to other commodities" (33). The use value of any given pair of sneakers comes from the qualities of the sneakers themselves, whereas their exchange value in terms of "purchasing coolness" comes from the brand stamped on them that that other pair over there does not have. Barnard expresses the use value–exchange value distinction as *material* and *cultural* functions, respectively (49). Fiske uses the same terminology in claiming that commodities serve two functions, "the material and the cultural" (*Understanding* 11). Ritzer likewise contrasts material with nonmaterial consumption and says we are increasingly moving toward the latter: "A seemingly fully nonmaterial process of consumption is beginning to replace its fully material (or, nearly so) forerunner" (144). Featherstone agrees, bringing us back around to a use-value distinction, in saying that "consumption, then, must not be understood as the consumption of use-values, a material utility, but primarily as the consumption of signs" (85), which *as* signs anchor exchange value.

Denis A. Coelho and Sven Dahlman call attention to the exchange-value concepts of comfort and pleasure, "both concepts that are receiving growing attention as a possible means of adding value to products" (321). One could think that comfort and pleasure would constitute use value, but Coelho and Dahlman are referring to the concept of comfort and pleasure. These are concepts that may be attached, through branding, for instance, to nearly any product as part of its image—its exchange value—regardless of how dull, cheerless, and painful the product is in actual use. Comfort and pleasure are values that would surely be parts of exchange value because one can use a screwdriver, for instance, regardless of its comfort and pleasure if use is the only consideration. One final example of the use-exchange difference comes from Andrew Ross: "Camp . . . is the re-creation of surplus value from forgotten forms of labor" (67). That surplus value is exchange value, created by the process of taking clothing, jewelry, and other items that barely retain use value and recharging them with a value that can be exchanged in social economies that "take that currency" of campiness (which, of course, not every social economy does).

Examples of the centrality of exchange value help us to understand how the signs and surfaces of style are considered their own kind of "substance," to be of major value. Rutsky argues that increasingly today, technology is viewed in terms of style rather than function.

> Unlike modern technology, high tech can no longer be defined *solely* in terms of its instrumentality or function—as simply a tool or a means to an end. In high tech, rather, technology becomes much more a matter of representation, of aesthetics, of style. (4)

He describes that style as something in "excess" of use value, which is nevertheless valued highly.

> Technological reproduction and montage are, in fact, the result of this attempt to rationalize representation. Rationalized forms, however, always contain an excess that cannot simply be reduced to functional forms and rational needs. This excess is, in other words, not a matter of function but of visual representation or copy; that is, the relation between the form of a product and its function is more or less arbitrary, allegorical; it is based on a technological simulation of functionality. And it is this simulacral technology that will determine the form of the mass-produced object, or rather, its style. (100)

Simulation is discussed shortly, but the thing to stress about this passage is the "excess" value that comes from the meaning that gives products value beyond mere use value.

The "look" of technology comes to serve an exchange value, Rutsky states, although he does not use the latter term.

> [M]odernist aesthetics is very often based on "the myth of functional form." Taking technology and mass production as models for art and artistic production does not, after all, make modernist art inherently more functional. . . . "functional forms" were rarely particularly technological or functional; they merely "looked" technological, functional. (11)

And, thus, functional forms had value not from use but from exchange, their ability to fit into social systems of business, science, and engineering. That the high-tech look is exchange value is proven by its ability to be stripped from an original technical context altogether and be used in connection with other commodities purely as exchange value. Clothing, accessories, and home decoration may have a high-tech look (and, thus, exchange value) with no technological function whatsoever. "'High-tech style' has been defined," Rutsky says, "by its 'imitation' of functionalism, or more precisely, by its imitation of the functional style of factories, warehouses, and industrial design generally" (107).

Signs, surfaces, and skins are central to style. Aesthetics and images play a role in the significance of style and contribute to a culture that is increasingly simulational at the same time that it is increasingly engrossed with style.

### Signs, Aesthetics, Images, and Simulation

Late-capitalist societies are more and more preoccupied with style. A major contributor to that engrossment is the pervasive aestheticization of everyday life. By aesthetics, I mean the sensory qualities of an experience. Aesthetics are also a mode of appreciating those qualities and can mean a systematic mode of appreciation, as when one refers to one who has no aesthetic sense or to a Southwestern aesthetic. Paul Willis suggests that aesthetics may be located in the active responses of audiences: "The aesthetic effect is not in the text or artifact. It is part of the sensuous/emotive/cognitive creativities of human receivers" (247). Aesthetic does not necessarily mean beauty so much as that dimension of experience that is connected to sensory appreciation and form. "Aesthetics is the way we communicate through the senses," Postrel explains. "Aesthetics conjures meaning in a subliminal, associational way" (6). Style, of course, is the manipulation of meanings connected to the aesthetic dimension of public presentation. Clearly, when we engage style in the sense discussed here, we engage aesthetics.

We live in an age of the aestheticization of everyday life. It is difficult to turn on the television without finding a make-over show advising the viewer on how to redecorate one's home, car, or face. To aestheticize is to strategize. One does not decorate, choose clothing, or select a style of grooming at random (even if a scan of most university professors would seem to suggest that people do). The aestheticized life is a life lived in purpose, even if many of those purposes are acquired and held below the level of conscious awareness. An aestheticized life is not one lived spontaneously but is governed by impulses to stylize, by an awareness of signs and images in the smallest detail of life, to be constantly attuned to appearance. So when we are surrounded by media sources telling us to Botox our faces and pimp our rides, we are being called to stylize our lives with a sense of purpose.

Just as style is a central part of life, so is aesthetics fundamentally a human mainstay. Postrel argues that aesthetics is a basic need for humans, not something added on after food and shelter (43–47, 74–75). If so and if aesthetics is intimately connected to style, then the manipulation of style in life is likewise a central human need. Kees Overbeeke, Tom Djadjadiningrat, Caroline Hummels, and Stephan Wensveen observe that people continually "act through the expectation of beauty of interaction" throughout life (11). The fundamental need for aesthetics is another way to understand how skins and surfaces may actually be substantial.

We live in an age in which the smallest and most mundane parts of everyday living are reworked into aesthetic experiences. It is a process similar to Ellis Cashmore's description of culture as found in "tiny seeds of experience" (166). It is an impulse that fuels and is fueled by an engrossment with style. Vivian notes the connection: "The current epoch appears to be informed, at least in its nascent stages, by an unprecedented investment in the *aesthetic*. . . . At such a historical moment, the category of *style* offers renewed explanatory force" (228). Featherstone writes extensively of the aestheticization of everyday life, referring to "artistic subcultures" that "efface the boundary between art and everyday life," so as to further "the project of turning life into a work of art" (66), attributing this aestheticization to the same "rapid flow of signs and images which saturate the fabric of everyday life" that constitutes style (67).

The aestheticization of everyday life, like strategic stylization, may happen more often or intensely in some circumstances than in others. Aestheticization is more likely to occur throughout everyday life in urban settings (70), Featherstone argues, attributing this to the decentered postmodern conditions more likely to be found in cities: "This celebration of the aesthetic potential of mass culture and the aestheticized perceptions of the people who stroll through the urban spaces of the large cities has been taken up by commentators who emphasize the transgressive and playful potential of postmodernism" (24). Featherstone seems to imply that aesthetics makes categories fluid and accommodates multiple identities and perspectives. The aesthetic (and style) that is hip flowers in urban settings, according to Leland: "Hip's signature voice—its jaunty talk and floating layers of meaning—comes together in dense, mixed neighborhoods" (45). Ken-Ichi Sasaki argues, interestingly, that "the most important factor in the aesthetics of the city is not visuality but tactility," by which he means the embodied experience of moving around in city spaces (36). De Certeau also emphasizes the embodied creativity that comes from walking in the city. The importance of teens, especially urban youth, as a demographic group to marketers may explain the centrality of their aesthetic in the popular imagination, for, as Marcel Danesi says, "Teen aesthetics are now the aesthetics of all" (14).

Aestheticization is also closely tied to commodification, a concept explored later in this volume, for the aestheticization of everyday life today is so often carried out through the purchase of goods and services. As noted earlier, witness the countless make-over shows on television that advise viewers to go buy something if they want to put their lives, dwellings, cars, and so forth into presentable form. As Featherstone argues, "The aestheticization of reality foregrounds the importance of style, which is also encouraged by the modernist market dynamic with its constant search for new fashions, new styles, new sensations and experiences" (86).

Beauty and sensory excitation reach at some point of value beyond basic survival. Thus, an aesthetic orientation is also an orientation toward exchange value, consumption of products is much more easily fueled by a lust for exchange value and for aesthetic pleasure than it is by use value. Not only is aestheticization carried out through strategic choice of commodities but commodification now depends on aesthetics, which is another way of saying that exchange value now dominates use value in market decisions. "Manufacturers can no longer distinguish themselves with price and performance, as traditionally defined," Postrel states. "In a crowded marketplace, aesthetics is often the only way to make a product stand out" (2).

Kälviäinen links everyday aestheticization to commodities: "[I]n the current aestheticization of everyday life, product taste is a significant factor incorporating embodied aesthetic experience, identity building, and social display" (77). Buie agrees: "The contemporary marketplace in America gives aesthetic form to the forces at work in the market principle and mass production" (27). Stratton offers Oscar Wilde as a founder of the contemporary society of spectacle, as one who constructed himself as spectacle through the strategic use of aesthetic commodities in his everyday life.

> This catalogue of precious consumables through which Wilde constructed his life as a visible work of art has, itself, a fetishistic quality. Each item adds to the image being constructed to produce a total image which is necessarily more impressive than the person who is putting the image together. In other words, Wilde is constructing himself as a spectacle. (183)

As part of using aesthetics to sell products, appealing contexts may be created, as Overbeeke and colleagues claim, "The designer needs to create a context for experience, rather than just a product . . . in which [the consumer] may enjoy a film, dinner, cleaning, playing, working. . . . Aesthetics of interaction is his goal" (10). An example of that creation of context might be the Cabela's sporting goods stores, which sometimes create panoramic scenes of game animals in faux-natural settings in order to sell hunting and camping gear. Rutsky observes the centrality of aesthetics to the marketing of high-tech goods: "In high tech . . . not merely the design but the very function of technology comes to be defined in stylistic or aesthetic terms—as state-of-the-art" (108). High tech itself comes to be an aesthetic descriptor attached to a wide range of products, according to Rutsky: "'High tech' . . . does not refer to any particular notion of technological style, but to a much broader sense of 'cutting-edge' aesthetics, of stylishness" (109).

The centrality of aesthetics in the everyday life could not be possible were it not for the centrality of images in everyday lives. These considerations will lead to examination of the close connection between style and simulation, but on the way there, note Featherstone's comment pulling these various threads together: "The overproduction of signs and reproduction of images and simulations leads to a loss of stable meaning, and an aestheticization of reality" (15). With this in mind, consider ways in which style and aestheticization depend upon the image and how the image is central to culture today.

Although style is not embodied entirely in the visual, it depends upon (and it forces) a privileging of the visual and of images in a culture. As Mort notes, "The practice of style privileged a visual perspective on culture" (28). Observing the centrality of the image, Baudrillard argues that "the solicitation of and voraciousness for images is increasing at an excessive rate. *Images have become our true sex object, the object of our desire.* The obscenity of our culture resides in the confusion of desire and its equivalent materialized in the image" (*Ecstasy* 35). The result, for Baudrillard, is "the promiscuity and the ubiquity of images, this viral contamination of things by images, which are the fatal characteristics of our culture" (*Ecstasy* 35–36). We need not share his pessimistic assessment to note the centrality of image in his vision of culture.

The psychoanalyst Lacan and his followers have developed a rationale for why images should be central (although it may not be adequate to explain why there has been an *increase* in preoccupation with the image). The "mirror stage" of the child's development in which the child discovers that he or she is represented in images and understands that he or she is more or less equated with images has a powerful effect, Lacan says: "We have only to understand the mirror stage *as an identification,* in the full sense that analysis gives to the term: namely, the transformation that takes place in the subject when he assumes an image" (1–3). The subject becomes "fictional" in Lacan's terms (2), with lifelong effect: "The *mirror stage* is a drama whose internal thrust is precipitated from insufficiency to anticipation—and which manufactures for the subject, caught up in the lure of spatial identification, the succession of phantasies that extends from a fragmented body-image to a form of its totality" (4). Other people become a kind of image for us and a kind of desired object: "[M]an's desire finds its meaning in the desire of the other, not so much because the other holds the key to the object desired, as because the first object of desire is to be recognized by the other" (Lacan 58).

Whether one accepts the Lacanian argument or not, it is clear our culture is engrossed in the image. Like Baudrillard, Ross sees this as an affliction: "The great illness of our age brought about by the increasing accessibility and acceleration of facts, is the replacement of *knowledge* by *information*" (82), which is brought about through images: "Knowledge deals in forms; information, in superficies and images. The ultimate unit of information is the image" (83). Not everyone takes such a negative view of images. One need not share their values to accept their descriptions of cultural conditions. For the moment, only note their centrality as well as Hebdige's observation that in spectacular subcultures, the visual is obviously "fabricated," meant to be noticed, and central to the culture's understanding of itself (100–101). The same might be said of all culture.

There is a close connection between the image and commodification, although the latter concept is developed later in this volume. Stuart Ewen and Elizabeth Ewen describe the connection between images and the market, "Mass imagery . . . creates for us a memorable language, a system of belief, an ongoing channel to inculcate and effect common perceptions explaining to us what it means to be a part of a 'modern world.' It is a world defined by the retail (individualized) consumption of goods and services" (24). Sean Nixon agrees: "Economic activity—including manufacturing processes—are more design and research and development intensive, and more concerned with the production and deployment of knowledge, images, and aesthetic symbols" than ever before in history (18). Guy Debord in "The Commodity as Spectacle" describes late-capitalist cultures' fascination with commodities as grounded in the image: "This is the principle of commodity fetishism, the domination of society by 'intangibles as well as tangible things,' which reaches its absolute fulfillment in the spectacle, where the tangible world is replaced by a selection of images" (110). An example of the connection between the market and images is given by Leland's explanation of "how hip works, attaching stories to one thing and not another—usually in accord with unseen needs of the economy. In the pantheon of hip characters, the blues singer was one of the first images concocted *as image* in the service of mass production" (36). Another example of the close connection between images and commodities is that of the dandy, whose "work" depended upon purchasing and displaying the right clothes, a sort of walking spectacular image. "The dandy," Stratton observes, "began its career describing the man who displayed himself to be gazed upon" (131).

A world of images is inherently unstable, as Ewen says, "the uninterrupted spectacle of cultural flux" (247). One cannot easily change a real tiger for a real mouse, but changing a picture of a tiger for a mouse is easy. In the same way, an aestheticized, stylized world based in images is likely to be inherently unstable. Or, such a world is also inherently malleable and, thus, rhetorical to its core, for what can be changed through the manipulation of signs, and images must be maintained through the manipulation of signs and images.

Some connections can be drawn among the unstable, decentered situation widely called *postmodern* and the themes of style, signs, aesthetics, and images. Featherstone pulls together many of these themes around the idea of postmodernism: "If we examine definitions of postmodernism we find an emphasis upon the effacement of the boundary between art and everyday life, the collapse of the distinction between high art and mass/popular culture, a general stylistic promiscuity and playful mixing of codes" (65). Rosalyn Deutsche makes the same connections among images, the aesthetic, and the postmodern:

> Postmodern life is characterized by the erasure of history and the loss of social memory. Social life includes multiple streams of contesting momentary images, which detach from particular locales, join the company of other images. Images, in appearing to capture history, become the great levelers, the informational counterpart of money, replacing material distinctions with their own "depthless" (that is, ahistorical) logic. (201)

Deutsche's comment about the homology between images and money is interesting and is echoed by Bauman's reminding us that "modern capitalism, as Marx and Engels memorably put it, 'melted all solids'" (*Community* 30). The triumph of late capitalism together with aesthetics in postmodern conditions is thus not a coincidence, involving as it does the dissolution of barriers and distinctions.

Postrel offers a widely held view that "aesthetics offers pleasure, and it signals meaning. It allows personal expression and social communication. It does not provide consensus, coherence, or truth" (10). But I think she is partially mistaken. Aesthetics is not a good ground for consensus, coherence, or truth in a modernist sense, if by that one means truth based on language and expositional argument. Truth is a concept that largely makes sense on a terrain of representational language, and so in that regard, she may be correct—Barnard, for instance, argues that meanings in fashion and style are rarely consistent (8–10)—but aesthetics nevertheless can ground a sense of fitness, decorum, and the appropriate in the place of representative truth. Beyond question, aesthetics can certainly offer a ground for consensus and coherence, as when one complains that somebody's clothing style does not hang together (coherence) or make sense, and one's friends agree (consensually) with that judgment. Political candidates are closely scrutinized to see whether their projected styles, or aesthetics, are coherent and attractive enough to generate an electoral consensus. What aesthetics does not do is insist on permanence or on application beyond particular examples or on universal consensus. The consensus and coherence achieved aesthetically are as changeable as style and as the postmodern world.

All around are flux and flow, and this postmodern situation is a fertile breeding ground for preoccupations with style and aesthetics. Postrel describes flux, or change, as aesthetically pleasurable: "Fashion exists because novelty is itself an aesthetic pleasure" (80). Ewen describes this situation, "Style today is an incongruous cacophony of images, strewn across the social landscape. Style may be borrowed from any source and turn up in a place where it is least expected" (14). Postrel agrees, "One mark of this new age of aesthetics, as opposed to earlier eras notable for their design creativity, is the coexistence of many different styles" (9) rather than the invention of a new, dominant style. Crane elaborates on Postrel's comment by using the nineteenth century as an example: "Nineteenth-century fashion consisted of a well-defined standard of appearance that was widely adopted. Contemporary fashion is more ambiguous and multifaceted, in keeping with the highly fragmented nature of contemporary postindustrial societies" (6). Of subcultural styles, such as, punks and mods, Hebdige observes, "The subcultural *bricoleur* . . . typically juxtaposes two apparently incompatible realities" (106). These aesthetic styles reveled in transgressing boundaries and creating coherences out of chaos. Leland makes the same point about hip: "As an aesthetic of the hybrid, hip embraces differences and loves experiment" (51). Aesthetics is a mode of perception and cognition that is comfortable with flux, flow, and multiplicity, and, thus, it is a perfect medium for style.

We are all bricoleurs. Nigel Coates argues that the city especially is a site of making a stylistic way in the midst of decenteredness and flux: "Duplicitous by nature, the city is something you can never know or understand completely, can never want to predict. Like us, the city constantly wrestles for control and the loss of it, always wanting something new to happen while wanting security to preside" (222). Malcolm Miles, Tim Hall, and Iain Borden agree in noting the diverse polysemy of the urban: "It is diversity itself—of publics and modes of settlement—which characterizes life in cities today" (3).

One kind of postmodern incoherence is described by Fiske as "the contradictions that are so typical of popular culture, where what is to be resisted is necessarily present in the resistance to it" (*Understanding* 4). An aesthetic grounding may facilitate a situation in which both resistance and the resisted exist together. That contradiction may violate the canons of traditional argument but coexists happily in, for instance, the purchase of a mass-produced pair of jeans that enriches a corporation but that become the canvas on which wearers might assemble rips, tears, and provocative signs or buttons that challenge corporate senses of decorum. S. Craig Watkins makes a similar observation of contradictions: "White consumers drive the production and consumption of rap music," much of which celebrates non-White racial sensibilities (93).

The intertwined issues of gender and sexual identity provide a good terrain for illustrating the convergence of style, images, and aesthetics in postmodern flux and decenteredness. Danesi notes, "The boom in unisex stores such as the Gap, Banana Republic, and Abercrombie & Fitch also made it obvious that differences in body image between males and females were becoming blurrier" (39). Alexander Doty puts "queerness" at our cultural center—it "is shared by all sorts of people in varying degrees of consistency and intensity" (2) and is, hence, "already part of culture's erotic center" (3). Queerness may be the epitome of the convergence described here, being played out largely in aesthetics and in a postmodern transgressing of boundaries. Ackroyd links postmodern flux to one type of queerness: "There has been a wide range of female impersonators in the United States, their popularity perhaps an emblem of an extraordinarily fluid and sexually ambiguous society" (112). He clarifies why this particular practice joins art with postmodern instability: "[I]n a performance where the sexual identity of the performer is not securely rooted, all other social and aesthetic images take on a curiously hallucinatory quality. That is why transvestism has become a persuasive presence in rock cultures, as an emblem of joyful disorder" (120).

Another concept that captures the links among postmodern instability and decenteredness, style, images, and the aesthetic is one that we have used already but now need to examine more carefully—the idea of *performance*. Judith Butler, the reigning monarch of performance, explains that performance is a lifelong project more than an occasional enactment, for "performativity is not a singular act, but a repetition and a ritual, which achieves its effects through its naturalization in the context of a body, understood, in part, as a culturally sustained temporal duration" (*Gender* xv). The style that is "cool ness," for example, is best understood as a physical performance, according to Danesi: "Coolness may vary in detail form situation to situation, from clique to clique, and from teen generation to teen generation, but it retains a common essence that can be called simply bodily aplomb" (44). A life of style is a performed life. Slayden and Whillock say that all discourse today is performative and hence stylized: "[W]e would argue that discourse, as such, has been subsumed by ritualistic and stylistic performances" (ix).

To say that anything is performative is to make claims concerning the centrality of style and aesthetics in that object, to assert that it might be performed one way today and another way tomorrow and, thus, *be* different things. So when Lesa Lockford claims "ideology is . . . performative," she is making a strong claim about what ideology is and what it means to have one, a claim that moves ideology onto a ground of aesthetic and stylistic enactment (9). Or when Miles, Hall, and Borden declare, "A city is, then, a set of practices. It is the place where things happen and people act," they are arguing that performance, rather than components, such as, class, steel, or concrete, is the very substance of the city (1).

Butler, of course, has famously insisted that we think of "gender . . . as a *corporeal style*, an 'act,' as it were, which is both intentional and performative" ("Performative" 272–73) and, of course, if gender is what it is as performed here and now, it will be what it will be as performed differently tomorrow or in another place. Lockford sees as performative the enactment of gender stereotypes that occur all around us every day.

> Insofar as cultural norms for femininity govern women's bodies, they are performative. Acceptable forms of feminine gesture, motility, deportment, adornment, physical embodiment, and activities are dictated by cultural norms. Indeed, so pervasive and specific are the cultural dictates controlling the acts that constitute women's gender performances that a cultural stereotype for feminine qualities is easily recognizable. (6)

Style may even preempt biology. Ackroyd notes that the performance of femininity by male actors in Japanese kabuki is sometimes taken as a model for biological women: "The careful make-up, the stylized gestures and the falsetto voice are designed to reproduce the essence of femininity, with such success that women themselves watch the performances of the *onnagata* in order to learn how to act and react" (95).

The performance of gender is stylistically linked to the performance of sexual identity, and the practice where this can often be seen is camp, which may depend upon exaggerated manipulation of the performance of gender stereotypes. Leland calls camp the "unruly nephew" of hip style and notes the performative quality of both in saying that they require "an audience" (8). It is telling that Stratton speaks of the "production" of a sexual identity in his discussion of Oscar Wilde's achievement:

> The [nineteenth-century] idea of the man of the world as a removed, critical commentator was subsequently to be reworked in the homo-

sexual aesthetic of camp. Central to this development was . . . the trial of Oscar Wilde. Here, there was a confluence of the ideas of the dandy, effeminacy, sensibility, and the aesthete with the production of the species of the homosexual. (132)

David Bergman lists four features "basic to camp: irony, aestheticism, theatricality, and humor" (20). Camp emphasizes its deliberate nature by overplaying style. Bergman describes camp as "a style (whether of objects or of the way objects are perceived is debated) that favors 'exaggeration,' 'artifice,' and 'extremity'" (4–5). Bergman gives as an example "'The Liberace Effect,' that is, to be so exaggerated an example of what you in fact are that people think you couldn't possibly be it" (14). Camp makes so obvious the performative nature of both gender and sexual identity that it may be read as highlighting the performative nature of being in general. Babuscio notes, "Camp emphasizes style as a means of self-projection, a conveyor of meaning, and an expression of emotional tone. Style is a form of consciousness; it is never 'natural,' always acquired" (23). This constitutes an argument for the "floatiness" of style's signs, for if style is performance, then it is not "supposed to be" referential or about some preexisting reality any more than is a performance of *Macbeth*.

If a world of style is a world of performance, another key concept needs consideration, and that is simulation. This phenomenon is described in greater detail in my earlier work *The World* than is possible here. In sum, a simulation is an experience composed of signs that do not represent reality. The "holodeck" experience of many science-fiction films is a classic example of a simulation, for none of the images one sees are real. Two characteristics are key to simulation. First, it is a closed world in which one acts without reference to anything external. Of course, Baudrillard in *Simulations* has famously argued that our world today is so entirely composed only of signs that there is no longer any real to which signs can refer—the map has replaced the territory (2)—"the real is no longer possible" (38). Not everyone agrees with so extreme a position, but the lesson to take from Baudrillard is the increasing centrality of simulation in global culture. Second, a simulation is infinitely replicable—it is a world of endless copies. Baudrillard makes the point by defining simulation's opposite, reality, in terms of reproducibility: "The very definition of the real becomes: *that of which it is possible to give an equivalent reproduction*" (*Simulations* 146). A clear example would be the video game, a world of signs that have no clear representations but also a world that is endlessly repeatable with a press of the reset button. Theodor W. Adorno and Max Horkheimer, writing in an age long before today's cinematic special effects, complained, "Real life is becoming indistinguishable from the movies" (95), a claim that is the central thesis of Neal Gabler's *Life: The Movie* and certainly descriptive of a simulational world if true.

A world of stylized performance is a world of simulation, and vice versa; the cultural conditions leading to one foster the other. Stratton makes the link explicit in connecting simulation to spectacle: "The experience of the logic of simulation is an effect of living in an increasingly spectacularised world. This new, hyper-real experience is staged when we are within the spectacle" (59). Slayden and Whillock assert the links among performance, images, and simulation: "So much of our performance and image-oriented culture depends on simulated experiences far removed from physical reality. Our images of ourselves are distorted, disembodied, with control elusive and often imagined" (227).

Simulation may be experienced any time one is immersed in signs without primary concern for their references. The more "lost" we can become, the more simulational the experience. Film, video games, and so forth were offered as examples above of common experiences that can become simulational. Ritzer explains that restaurants may be simulational, referring to "'Disneyesque' simulacra like the Atlanta restaurant Pittypat's Porch" (49). Both currency and credit are simulations, Ritzer argues, because they are signs referring to no tangible real good, such as, gold (101). Of course, one can argue that gold's value is largely simulational and based on conventional exchange value. Watkins argues that for White youth, the experience of hip-hop can be a kind of simulation: "Hip hop was their fantasy island, a place to travel largely through the pleasures of consumption—rather than actual contact into a foreign world—where they could live out some of their wildest desires" and let us recall how important hip-hop *style* is for those same youths (97). Fredric Jameson makes a somewhat different argument for the simulational nature of pop music, arguing that it has no meaningful origin or founding song but only endless repetition, a key characteristic of simulation: "[W]e never hear any of those singles produced in these genres 'for the first time'; instead, we live in a constant exposure to them in all kinds of different situations . . . [due to] the structural absence, or repetitive volatization, of the 'primary texts'" (123).

Baudrillard refers to the "seduction" of simulation and connects it to a world of floating signs without real reference: "Seduction only comes through empty, illegible, insoluble, arbitrary, fortuitous signs, which glide by lightly, modifying the index of the refraction of space" (*Ecstasy* 59). Recall that signs cannot float absolutely and still be signs; they retain some kind of long tether to the contexts that once gave them meaning. Nevertheless, taking the point to extremes, Baudrillard argues, "[T]he age of simulation thus begins with a liquidation of all referentials—worse: by their artificial resurrection in systems of signs[,] . . . a question of substituting signs of the real for the real itself" (*Simulations* 4). Others have made the connection as well, if not to such an extreme, between floating signs—essential to preoccupation with style—and simulation. Ewen notes the early development of photography that allowed signs of real things to float away from that reality and how photography thus undergirded an increasingly unreal culture: "Technically reproduced surfaces were beginning to vie with lived experience in the structuring of meaning. The image offered a representation of reality more compelling than reality itself, and—perhaps—even threw the very definition of *reality* into question" (25). Stratton argues that the trajectory of technical development of photography has contributed to better and better representations of what is not really "there": "The history of the development of these technologies may be understood as a striving for 'better' representation, which, in effect, means a concern with the image quite different from any interest in the thing represented," (59) and, thus, "rather than being concerned with increasingly faithful representations of 'reality,' [modern visual technologies] can be better understood as forming a trajectory towards greater simulation" (60). As technology becomes able to create self-contained worlds on the screen, we move away from expecting images to be representational.

In *The World*, I argued that terms, such as, *simulation* and *reality*, are not tenable as distinct entities, whereas in the current volume, I may seem to be writing in contradiction. Instead, I argue that simulation and reality are sets of attributes that are found in more or less proportions within different conceptions of style and whatever is not style. Simulation is the spirit of style, even if perfectly simulational experiences are never found.

One last key concept is needed to add to the mix of factors contributing to a world preoccupied with style. Walter Benjamin's germinal article "The Work of Art in an Age of Mechanical Reproduction" contrasts the "aura" or individual tradition and history attached to an original work of art with the degradation of individuality that comes with reproduction. The original work of art has an "authenticity" that is lost when it is mass-produced. Writing in the 1930s, Benjamin was seeing the first waves of mechanically reproduced images, such as, film, that by our time have overwhelmed the culture. But mechanical reproduction was, of course, a reality long before his time. Benjamin's contribution lies not in noticing mechanical reproduction but in calling our attention to the difference it makes in our lives and in his insightful explication of the dimensions of art as well as reproduction.

Of course, mass reproduction is also key to commodification, for that is why one reproduces endless copies—to sell them. As Raiford Guins and Omayra Zaragoza Cruz note, "Mass-produced commodities have been regarded as inauthentic, formulaic, simplistic, and banal" (5). It is reproduction, not just entering the market, that destroys the authenticity of the original work of art. One could argue, as does Baudrillard, that late capitalism is founded on the possibility of mass-scale reproduction: "We know that now it is on the level of reproduction (fashion, media, publicity, information and communication networks) . . . that the global process of capital is founded" (*Simulations* 99). Original works of art may be sold, but they are not made for entering the global marketplace, which depends on millions of copies being made; for that, one must make a poster. Such originals have that unique aura of which Benjamin writes. As John Seabrook observes, "From Wordsworth to Rage Against the Machine, art created for idealistic reasons, in apparent disregard for the marketplace, was judged superior to art made to sell" (68). The original work of art has a history or tradition attached to it; when it is copied, as Stratton notes, "commodities are experienced as having no history" (71). Copies have no history (the argument goes) because, Rutsky explains, "[T]he reproduction, alteration, and reassembly of elements removed from their previous contexts becomes an end in itself. Stripped of both aura and instrumentality, these elements become 'purely' stylistic or 'aesthetic'—empty signifiers that can be recombined in virtually any way" (106). Building on Benjamin's argument, Rutsky says that it is technological reproduction that allows the possibility of floating signs in the first place: "Technological reproducibility . . . produces a proliferation of images and data that have been broken free of any set meaning or context" (7–8).

The distinction between the original work of art and the mass-produced copy may be found in many parallels today. Buie contrasts the small, traditional market on the human scale (the street market, the corner shop) with the large, mass-produced big-box store.

A sense of scale and place has been lost, the products are homogenized, and there is almost no personal transaction in their purchase. . . . In contrast, traditional markets vividly express our genuine erotic interdependence. Aesthetically, that translates into direct physical experiences: centralized spaces on a human scale, a walking scale, that create intimacy, contact, interaction, responsiveness. (28)

Seabrook expresses another parallel to the original and the copy in contrasting the "small grid" of local culture with the "big grid" of large corporations. The former comprises "artists who were 'independent' and art that was 'authentic,'" clearly a parallel with Benjamin's original work of art (100).

The distinction between high-tech and low-tech style is actually keyed to mass reproduction, according to Rutsky, who argues that "the techno-logic of high tech is based precisely on an aesthetic-cultural logic, which is also to say, on the logic of technological reproducibility. In high tech, technology comes to be defined in terms 'of reproduction rather than production'" (104). In this way, high tech becomes an aesthetic style based on mass reproduction, for "the process or logic of technological reproducibility itself comes increasingly to be seen as 'aesthetic,' as a matter of style" (Rutsky 107). Baudrillard uses "object" in the sense of Benjamin's "original" and "commodity" as "reproduction" in arguing that the commodity "is abstract, formal, and light in comparison with the weight, opacity, and substance of the object. The commodity is legible, as opposed to the object, which never quite reveals its secret" (*Ecstasy* 22–23); Benjamin also describes the original work of art as keeping its distance and not revealing everything about itself, in contrast to the reproduction, which may be completely understood.

Today, the cultural world and critically the world of style depend on mass-produced and reproduced copies for which there are no originals. Most of us have very few original works of art, especially compared to the rows of copies that fill our shelves and closets and walls. Notice the close connection between Benjamin's concern with reproduction and my earlier definition of simulation, which featured copying; Benjamin is likewise describing the social and aesthetic conditions that have led to a culture increasingly taken with simulation. People stylize and aestheticize their worlds today precisely because of the universal availability of mass-produced, identical copies of goods that are the means by which we stylize. We must know what it will mean to wear a certain pair of jeans or shoes in public. We must be able to predict how people will react to our driving a pickup truck as opposed to a two-seat convertible. We know these things because jeans, shoes, trucks, and convertibles are mass-produced, and what they mean is substantially, if not completely, shared by most people we will encounter. It is not true, as Baudrillard claims, that "it is the duplication of the sign which destroys its meaning" (*Simulations* 136), for duplication changes meaning but does not destroy it. Original meanings of the sign may be altered, but reproduction and commodification would not be possible were signs truly stripped of meaning. Were we surrounded by a world of original, one-of-a-kind goods, our ability to stylize with rhetorical effect would be much reduced because our ability to predict the meanings of the components of style would be reduced. Likewise, we replicate incessantly the gestures, movements, and expressions that we find in texts of popular culture so as to manage impressions and facilitate communication using style. In doing so, we use styles that nearly everyone knows, shares, and follows; true eccentrics are hard to find any longer.

Benjamin calls attention to a paradox in this cycle of endless repetition and reproduction, for the original work of art has an "authenticity" that is lost in reproduction. Yet, authenticity is a preoccupation with many. Postrel describes authenticity in terms of "formal harmony, balance, or delight.... a connection to time or place . . . self-expression" rather than mass production (114–15). We feel that sense of authenticity when we experience the original work of art from which posters are made: this is *it*, this is the real deal. Our culture is shot through with a longing for authenticity precisely because it is so engrossed in images, floating signs, simulations, and style. There is thus a cultural longing for authenticity, for the real, that is expressed in numerous texts and advertisements.

In popular music, such as, rock and roll or hip-hop, we see strong rhetorical appeals to authenticity despite that nearly all the music one can obtain today is mass-produced and widely marketed. Wynter notes, "Culturally, the most significant connection between the rock-and-roll and hip-hop revolutions is the swift, surprising ascendance of 'the real' . . . as the paramount measure of cultural relevance" (78), and he argues that "the real" is often defined today as what is African American (79–83). Why that may be true is an issue worth a book in itself. Watkins agrees: "[H]ip hop's claim to fame is the claim of authenticity in its undaunted portrayals of ghetto reality" (2). Of course, once the authentic experience of the streets (which is a kind of original) gets caught up in the mechanics of reproduction and the market, the original authenticity comes into question. As Seabrook puts it, "independence sells, and the price it sells for is the end of independence" (108–9), Hence, the desperate attempts by successful hip-hop artists to maintain their street credibility in the media.

Ritzer tracks the tensions between the copy against the reproduction in marketing generally through his thesis of McDonaldization. McDonaldization is the very soul of reproduction, the process of ensuring that identical products reach consumers with maximum efficiency. That logic of mass reproduction may be countered, Ritzer argues, by marketing that disguises reproductions as one of a kind: "Another potential threat to McDonaldization lies in the area of customization, or what has been called 'sneakerization.' . . . That is, instead of one or a few styles of sneakers or trainers, we now have hundreds of different styles produced for various niches in the market" (54). Donald A. Norman makes the same point: "Numerous manufacturers have tried to overcome the sameness of their product offerings by allowing customers to 'customize' them" (*Emotional* 219). An example of that general strategy is the sweatshirts widely available in stores, such as, Old Navy, that sport logos and slogans of fictitious bars, marinas, and other vacation spots, brand-new shirts printed so as to appear old and faded as if they really were purchased in some derelict bar in the Florida Keys five years ago. Such products, in fact new mass reproductions, are attempts to simulate an aura, a tradition, a history of authenticity that was never there. It is an attempt to speed up the process by which, through time and use, manufactured copies "acquire stories" as Norman claims (*Emotional* 221). Similarly, Crane notes that "designer clothes are generally sold in stores whose interior decoration is deliberately created to convey an image of high culture, not unlike an art gallery" to emphasize the status of the clothing as one of a kind "art" whether it is mass-produced or not (163). In this way, as Jameson observes, the culture industry strives "to produce something which resists and breaks through the force of gravity and repletion as a universal feature of commodity equivalence" (121). And after all, every mass-produced commodity begins a journey in the direction of becoming an original work of art the moment it is purchased and begins accumulating history. Eventually, even the shiniest new shoes become the treasured old loafers that you wore back when. Grandmother's hallowed turkey platter is barnacled with history and aura but was once one of thousands on a store shelf.

However, in terms of celebrity, Ewen argues, aura and authenticity are actually gained through mass reproduction: "If great art loses its aura in the marketplace of mass impression, the individual life of the celebrity achieves an aura through mass reproductions" (93). It might be more accurate to say that the aura attaches to the "original" celebrity, not to his or her reproductions, but it is an interesting observation anyway.

Style is a cultural preoccupation with signs and images, grounded in aesthetics. Such a preoccupation flourishes under conditions usually described as postmodern, conditions of decenteredness, flux, polysemy, flow, and so forth. A world engrossed with style is a world of performance and simulation, and because simulational, it is a world described by Benjamin as one of infinite reproduction. The last major concept to consider is *systematicity*. A style is a system of signs, even if they are floating and simulational, and as a system, it functions as does a language.

## The Systematicity of Style

Ewen refers to style specifically in linguistic terms, as "the most constantly available lexicon from which many of us draw the visual grammar of our lives" (20). While acknowledging the importance of the visual, remember that style may be apprehended through all the senses: the taste of Old Milwaukee beer versus that of Cristal champagne, the feel of leather versus vinyl, and so forth. Barnard regards fashion as a kind of language: "[F]ashion, dress and adornment are . . . some of the signifying practices of everyday life . . . which go to make up culture as a general signifying system" (38). Danesi is explicit in considering the style element of fashion as like a language: "Clothing is the material means through which body image becomes body language" (45). Postrel likewise speaks of style as a system for thought and expression: "We use form to communicate, and we infer meaning from familiar aesthetic elements" (94), and here she means form in the sense of the regularities and patterns that are styles. Mary Douglas and Baron Isherwood describe consumer goods as if they were a language, for "goods in their assemblage present a set of meanings more or less coherent, more or less intentional. They are read by those who know the code and scan them for information" (ix), and just like words, "[A]ll material possessions carry social meanings" (38). Douglas and Isherwood take pains to distinguish the use of consumer goods as mere messages from goods as the system from which messages are formed, in other words, a kind of language that is, of course, central to style: "[C]onsumption goods are most definitely not mere messages; they constitute the very system itself. . . . The meaning is in the relations between all the goods" (49). Goods are, in other words, a sort of language.

To argue that style is like a language in its systematicity is not to deny that style may be composed of floating signs in a postmodern situation of flux. As noted earlier, no signs truly float completely. I have Mexican rustic furniture in some rooms of my home, and those signs have surely floated from their original context, but they retain enough meanings from that context to function in how I stylize my home. It is precisely from remaining in a system of other signs, even if they are all in flux, that the elements of style keep their meaning even if the meaning is slippery.

An important dimension of language is ritual, the highly conventional use of language to perform important social or spiritual tasks. Style likewise has strong ritual properties and in that way is like a language. Douglas and Isherwood argue, "Goods . . . are ritual adjuncts; consumption is a ritual process whose primary function is to make sense of the inchoate flux of events," in this case, through style (43). Bill Green agrees in calling our attention to "ritual and the way in which products may contribute to one of the most basic of human pleasures. Ritual is deeply embedded in the human condition" (4). Ritual is, of course, the regularized structure of everyday life, not a Sabbath-only kind of performance, and it is carried out through stylized goods. One may think of the kinds of clothes one buys, bespeaking group affiliation as well as differentiation, as moves in political struggle. Think of how much of the current "culture wars" are waged in terms of which forms of entertainment one buys or opposes. The use of style in ritual to create a terrain of political struggle is evident also from a different angle in Nikolas Rose's comment that "devices of 'meaning production'—grids of visualization, vocabularies, norms and systems of judgement—*produce* experience; they are not themselves *produced by* experience" (130). Rose's argument parallels the view often expressed that holds that language creates rather than merely reflects experience.

One characteristic of a language is that people do not have complete control over what the constitutive elements of the language mean, and so it is with style. As noted before, one cannot wear or do whatever one likes and declare to the world that the garment or action mean what the individual says they mean. I have spoken before of the ways in which people are constrained by style, and that constraint works in much the same way that language works. For instance, Lockford looks at the example of large women in this society that values being thin and applauds their attempts to perform their weight with assertion and freedom. But she offers this caveat: "While there may be some large women who experience their self-performance as a defiance of cultural standards and who experience this defiance as both empowering and subversive, it is arguable whether or not they can truly escape cultural meanings" (28–29). None of us can escape the cultural meanings of language nor of style, which functions like a language.

Of course, language is not the only system of meaning even if it may be our clearest example. Ewen also equates style with another such system, money: "In so many arenas of life, style has become the *legal tender*" (22). Currency is, of course, the very ground of capitalism, the system from which it springs. It is a language used worldwide, with different currencies easily translated from one to another. Everyone knows how money works. Similarly, Ewen and Ewen describe knowledge of clothing as a kind of cultural lingua franca extending globally: "Clothes consciousness and the attention to fashion constitute near-universal elements within American culture; their lure and mystique are worldwide" (133).

One important element of style can be the kind of music one prefers, especially because styles of music are often connected to other elements of style, such as, fashion, decoration, grooming, and movement. Wynter describes disco in this systematic way, treating it in economic terms: "[D]isco wasn't just records—it was the first global information economy" (91). People all over the world knew what the clothing and moves of disco meant and how to use them socially. A number of observers have noted the systematic nature of hip-hop style. Watkins also uses the trope of economy: "[H]ip hop, dating back to its humble beginnings in the seventies, had always spawned its own economy," (57–58) with *economy* here understood as a system for exchanging both goods and meanings. Danesi argues that "what probably makes hip-hop lifestyles attractive to some youths is, paradoxically, its highly organized structure" (83). As a style, hip-hop is inclusive of many elements that cohere systematically, for, as Watkins observes, "All the things that traditionally matter to young people—style, music, fashion, and a sense of generational purpose—have come under the spell of hip hop" (148). Finally, Tricia Rose speaks of hip-hop in the linguistic terms of writing or *inscription*: "Life on the margins of postindustrial urban America is inscribed in hip hop style, sound, lyrics, and thematics" (401). To so inscribe, hip-hop style would need to work systematically like a language, and it does.

The point has been brought up already, but an important element of any system is that it can be used for communicative purposes. That is especially true for style, which is not only a system of signs and meanings but also a means for communication. Remember that communication is hardly unidirectional; we both generate meaningful signs and also read the signs of others. Norman is, of course, speaking of a major element of style: "Design is really an act of communication" (*Design* x). Barnard declares, "Fashion and clothing are means of communication" (27), but he does qualify this claim in some interesting ways and describes two models of stylistic meaning, the process and the semiotic models (30–32). The *process model* is communicative in a conventional sense: one picks elements of style that communicate a reality about the self, how one is in fact. The stronger semiotic/structural model, on the other hand, holds that who or what one is develops as a result of the style one displays. In the first instance, one is cool and chooses certain styles to express that. In the second model, one is cool because one displays certain styles. It is interesting to consider how far that second model can go in explaining social realities. Is there a sense in which one is gay, of a certain class, or of a certain race *because* of one's style? Questions such as this occupy the rest of this study.

When we think about style as a system, it is also important to think about how style works as a system to bind together its component elements. If we see a man wearing worn cowboy boots, faded jeans, a faded shirt, a red bandana knotted around his neck, and a top hat, it is clear which element of that assemblage of items does not fit. Or remove the top hat and replace it with a cowboy hat, then have the man go skipping and hopping down the street. Now the element of style that is movement does not fit a unity that would otherwise obtain among the signs that the man displays. To have a sense of style or of different styles is to have a sense of a unity among signs peculiar to each particular style.

This unity is not trivial; it has powerful consequences for social and political experience. The African American youngster who is "accused" of "talking White" by her classmates has displayed signs connected to her speech or vocabulary that, rightly or wrongly, do not match a unity of style expected by her accusers. When presidential candidate Michael Dukakis rode around in a tank, a helmet perched oddly on his head, a wooden expression on his face, during the 1988 presidential election, the ridicule he drew by that action had a lot to do with his performance that seemed out of place in the presidential style he was trying to put together. The unity between President

George W. Bush's fractured English and the other elements of a homespun, Texan style that he displays is taken note of by both his friends and foes, and either celebrated or derided because it fits within a unity of style that people love or hate.

What is the unity that holds styles together, at least in terms of expectations (as we know, the unexpected element of style in an otherwise consistent tableau sometimes succeeds just as it often fails to draw approval)? One can, of course, "violate" that unity, but think of the social and psychological pulls on people not to do so. Think of that persistent inner voice telling our cowboy, as he considers donning the top hat, "Better not, pardner." There is nothing to prevent you, Dear Reader, from sporting a tiara as you next go out to work, but I have a feeling that few or none of you will because a tiara fits into very few style systems these days. Kälviäinen refers to the sense of what fits or belongs in aesthetic constellations: "Something might be aesthetically pleasing for a consumer in the pure distanced sense but does not appeal to their taste because it does not fit their orientation and life-model" (78). What pulls together that sense of orientation? What sort of form is that life-model? What is the source of the unity that works as the gravity pulling the elements of particular styles together?

Here, following Dick Hebdige, it is a *homology*, or a formal similarity, among the components of a style that creates the unity that holds a style together. The idea of homology, developed in my earlier work *Rhetorical*, can be summed up as, a homology is a formal pattern or structure shared by members of a set. The human mind responds powerfully to such form; Norman observes, "Much of thought results from a kind of pattern matching system" (*Design* 117) and that "subconscious thought matches patterns" (*Design* 125). This is especially true in a simulational society, for simulations are governed by models, forms, and patterns; as Baudrillard claims, "Only affiliation to the model makes sense, and nothing flows any longer according to its end, but proceeds from the model" (*Simulations* 101). Form is key to becoming who we are. Lacan speaks in homological terms of the continuity in the subject and how it is established: "The unconscious is that part of the concrete discourse, in so far as it is transindividual, that is not at the disposal of the subject in re-establishing the continuity of his conscious discourse" (49).

Because people respond powerfully to form and pattern, the coherence suggested by a style's components can be powerfully motivating. Hebdige argues, for instance, that the pattern of repeated appropriation and reversal of respectable or mundane objects and actions, such as, trash liners or safety pins, is what makes a unity of "punk" style. Hebdige is explicit in referring to "style as homology," and he claims that "the internal structure of any particular subculture is characterized by an extreme orderliness: each part is organically related to other parts and it is through the fit between them that the subculture member makes sense of the world," and that is what he calls style (113). After having examined the phenomenon of camp several times, from it I might conclude that if there are "gay" styles, they are coherent styles around a pattern of exaggeration and irony. This idea of homology as the unity holding styles together is explored further in this book.

A number of scholars have looked at the idea of style as a unity holding together sets of signs, actions, images, and objects. Ewen and Ewen make this observation.

> These are some of the facts of our lives: disparate moments, discon-
> nected, dissociated. . . . Viewed together, however, as an ensemble, an
> integrated panorama of social life, human activity, hope and despair,
> images and information, another tale unfolds. They reveal a pattern of
> life, the structures of perception. (xxi–xxii)

Different cultures and eras may have different engines of patterning, but a culture preoccupied with style and aestheticization will organize its life's patterns and its perceptions around forms given by style. Maffesoli is explicit in claiming that "style can be understood as the 'principle of unity,' that which unites deep down, the diversity of things" (9). Rutsky explicitly links style and homology in this way:

> And certainly, the marketing emphasis on product styling (as opposed
> to form) is based on the recognition that utility is accessory to a con-
> sumption whose basis is the homology between the commodity form
> and the form of the sign; for it is the style of the product that, through its
> reproduction or simulation of certain values (e.g., functionality, technol-
> ogy), makes them liable to exchange and consumption. (100–101)

Kälviäinen speaks of the context into which products enter that, if it feels right for the product, is in some sort of homologically consistent pattern.

> The context for the product use encompasses the environment, the
> location, place and region, the objective social situation and recognized
> routines and ritual of the whole use experience, where the product
> belongs. Furthermore, the new product serves as a component of the
> whole ensemble of products in this environment. (79)

Her reference to the ensemble is quite a homological way of thinking, for what unites different and diverse products within a context but homology? She gives a specific example of such a homology among disparate products: "A Rolex watch, a Brooks Brothers suit, New Balance running shoes, a Sony Walkman, and a BMW automobile bear no relation to each other via function or form, but many consumers might nonetheless group them as a symbolic whole associated with a certain role" or, we might say, a certain style (81).

Vivian describes styles homologically as a kind of aesthetic vibration unifying disparate elements, and discusses their role in creating unities among their parts.

> The style of an epoch, therefore, brings its various social, economic, political, and institutional elements not into objective or consensual harmony, but into some sort of characteristic configuration suffused by a cultural aesthetic. . . . The style of an epoch thus encompasses a unity engendered by (sometimes profound) disunity. Or, instead of unity, however qualified, one might refer to style as the cultural expression of an aesthetic vibration: this vibration may be harmonious or violently discordant, it may produce cohesion or dispersion, but collective style invokes a meaningful resonance among disparate, even "contradictory," social interests. (229–30)

Several scholars have described particular kinds of homologies obtaining among certain elements of style and among elements of style and personal or social experience. The concern for homology as unifying is widespread in music studies, for as Simon Frith observes, "What's been at issue is homology, some sort of structural relationship between material and musical forms" (108). Film is often an example of homology at work. Graeme Turner points out, "Now, popular film is rarely presented to its public as a single product or commodity. Often, it is a kind of composite commodity" (6). So there is a sort of homology linking together all of the products (films, soundtrack albums, action figures, and so forth) that make up the latest Batman film, although the unity here is also at the level of content because they all have to do with the Batman. But films may participate in and may even help to create homologies of style cutting across disparate content. Seabrook points out that George Lucas planned the *Star Wars* series by studying the mythologies of many cultures (144) and that the films bring together in a coherent package "quotations" from many different texts and cultures (146). The films thus create a kind of style that makes sense by joining together far-flung elements. Ewen and Ewen describe the role that early cinema played for new immigrants, for it created a unity incorporating the experiences of young immigrant women: "the history of these transitional female archetypes parallels the social and sexual struggles of the immigrants' daughters. If they were torn between fresh notions of sexuality and constricting family structures, the vamp and the gamine . . . seemed to point the way to new definitions of femininity" (68).

Peter N. Stearns suggests interesting formal patterns that function homologically to ground emotional styles in Victorian and contemporary societies.

Comparing patterns of Victorian expression of emotion and current repression of it in the name of being "cool," Stearns argues that "this approach seeks to determine larger consistencies in emotional norms that relate specific emotional standards to a broader style" (5), with style working homologically to achieve that larger consistency. He notes, "It is obvious that larger emotional cultures like the Victorian style result in part from the accumulation of smaller changes that relate to more specific parts of the emotional spectrum," suggesting a unity across many different enactments of style (61). He goes on to offer a discussion of how emotional styles structure other broad areas of culture, which is certainly a homological way of thinking (70–76).

Hariman's study of political style suggests homologies uniting different ways of leading. Similarly, Paul du Gay suggests a homology of style unifying ways in which bureaucracies work: "While the concrete ways in which . . . government rationality has been operationalized have varied quite considerably, the forms of action they make possible for different institutions and person—schools, general practitioners, housing estates, prisons and so forth—do share a general consistency and style" (155). This remarkable claim suggests a homology of style unifying everything a government institution touches.

Several authors speak homologically about style and space. De Certeau sees rhetorical tropes as a kind of homological unity among different ways of appropriating public spaces, especially in the city, for

> the "tropes" catalogued by rhetoric furnish models and hypotheses for the analysis of ways of appropriating places. Two postulates seem to me to underlie the validity of this application: 1) it is assumed that practices of space also correspond to manipulations of the basic elements of a constructed order; 2) it is assumed that they are, like the tropes in rhetoric, deviations relative to a sort of "literal meaning" defined by the urbanistic system. (100)

And he cites synecdoche and asyndeton as two such tropes that are widely evident (101). Buie sees another organization of space, the market, as a stylistic expression of values beyond its borders, for "the traditional marketplace is a true expression in form of life's vitality" (28). Of course, her emphasis on form is homological, suggesting a stylistic pattern of vitality including these markets and other forms of vital experience as well. Siegfried Kracauer speaks of aesthetic dimensions as unifying different kinds of spaces and, thus, claims that hotel lobbies are stylistically homologous with a "house of God" (146).

A number of scholars have identified homological structures connected to fashion. Crane notes that "student consumers used fashion discourses to render fragmentary, disparate styles coherent and to construct meaningful self-identities using clothing," suggesting homologies creating coherence across both dress and personal identity (209). She argues that fashion is shaped not only by "cultural trends" but also by whole networks of organizations and forces that are nevertheless unified within particular styles (15). Rybczynski identifies several homologies uniting fashion and home décor. He argues that "a strong connection exists between the way that we decorate our homes and the way that we dress ourselves" (21), for "since homes and clothes are timeworn ways in which to convey status, there is a conformity in the types of materials and symbols used to convey social standing" (24). Note that the homology uniting dress and decoration also includes a sense of what fits one's social status. In an example that should resonate with teachers in ancient universities, he complains that modern-dressed students in Gothic buildings "just don't fit in. They should be wearing boaters and blazers, tweeds and flannels" (35). His example raises the question of what is the unity of style making boaters consistent with gargoyles (I refer here to architecture and not faculty).

Style is seen as a unifying center pulling together actions and objects defining sexual identity and gender. Babuscio describes a gay sensibility in terms that resonate both with style but also with unifying a widespread net of actions and experiences through homology: "I define the gay sensibility as a creative energy reflecting a consciousness that is different from the mainstream; a heightened awareness of certain human complications of feeling that spring from the fact of social oppression" (19). One manifestation of such a gay style and sensibility is camp, which Esther Newton describes in homological terms: "Camp is not a thing. Most broadly it signifies a *relationship between* things, people, and activities or qualities, and homosexuality" (46). Pamela Robertson thinks in homological ways about camp as a style connected to gender as well as sexual identity, arguing that "camp as a structural activity has an affinity with feminist discussions of gender construction, performance, and enactment and . . . we can examine a form of camp as a feminist practice" (156–57). Ackroyd points to the homological function of transvestism as expressing the form of boundary crossing in general in James Fenimore Cooper's novel *The Spy*: "The book concerns itself with disguise and masquerade, and with the confusion implicit in divided loyalties. In such a context, transvestism becomes a potent symbol for ambiguity" (141). Doty suggests homological relations, although he does not use the word, when he points to stylistic ways in which class and sex may stand in for each other in texts, such as Laverne and Shirley (54), and when he discusses what he claims is a widespread mythos in American literature of an erotic bond between White- and dark-skinned men, where race and sexual identity may stand in for one another in terms of how they are stylistically expressed (74).

We are now equipped with a way of understanding style as an aesthetic unity of behavior and expression, relying largely on images, stemming from and fueling postmodern, simulational cultural contexts. Ready to consider more specifically how style works to structure our lived experiences for us, the next chapter turns to ways in which style organizes experience, culture, perceptions, and commodification, and through this organizing function takes center stage in life under late capitalism. The chapter shows how capital's need for hyperconsumption is consistent with style's centrality through commodification.

# 2

# The Social and Commercial Structuring of Style

Stylists are not interesting for what they write or for what they
do but for something that they are.
— Quentin Crisp, *How to Have a Life-Style*, 94

If we learned anything in chapter 1, it is that style is a complex concept
signaling a variety of components, such as, aesthetics, images, simulation, and so forth. So the claim in this chapter that style is at the center of
how society and commerce are organized today means to reference that
complex of elements rather than any simple notion of how one dresses or
walks down the street. This chapter has two concerns: first, ways that style
structures social organization broadly conceived and, second, ways in which
style and consumption are vitally interdependent in today's global economy.
The central theme in this chapter is structure and organization. Style is
categorical. As a system of signs, style undergirds how we structure experience and perception—hence, how we structure our thoroughly capitalized
global society.

## Style Organizes Experience, Culture, Perceptions

Let me tell you about two recent shopping trips I had. I am in the Big Brothers
program. I am White, my two Little Brothers are African American. About
six months ago, they wanted to go shopping for some shirts so off we went
to the mall. We passed one store full of shirts, which I pointed out to them.
They took one look, rendered a decisive "no," and kept walking. This happened again and yet again. Finally, in pity, they took me aside and explained
that every store we had passed sold White-guy shirts. They were looking for
Black-guy shirts. Taking me to the second-story railing, they pointed out
White guys and Black guys going below and the differences in the shirts
they wore. It was a revelation to see the short, tight-fitting, White-guy shirts

and the voluminous, long, Black-guy shirts, as if for the first time. It was a difference I had simply never noticed.

Recently, my then-twenty-three-year-old daughter came to visit me, and we went to the mall. It was a repeat of the trip with my Little Brothers in some ways. We passed one clothing store after another. "Want to go in?" I asked. No, I was told, this store was for young teenagers—that store was for older women—this one for older teenagers—she even identified one store that she swore catered to middle-aged lesbians with short hair. I had passed these stores all my life with no notion of what a world of social specificity and identity they comprised. This is what style does for us—it organizes our social world. It gives us places to be and to shop, and it gives us places where we don't belong. Style affirms who we think we are and expresses who we want to be. Much of how style does all that is through commodities, for much of the social organization in the world outside the mall nevertheless began right there with a choice of which shirts to buy and where to buy them.

The first issue to develop here is that style organizes the social. Beginning fundamentally, style does so because it is a speculative instrument, like a language, that creates systems of categories for social perception. Style organizes the social through aesthetic perceptions and categories, such as, clothing, the look and feel of the urban environment, geographic associations, race, and culture. In making and organizing those categories aesthetically, style creates tensions between social allegiance and individuality, tensions likely to increase under conditions of postmodern complexity. The social organization of style is never value free. Style's aesthetic organizes such value-laden dimensions of the social as gender and sexual identity, class, time, and space.

Scholars have noted the centrality of signs and images, the building blocks of style, in social organization. In today's large, even global societies, mediated signs may be the only basis for organization because it is through mediation rather than physical contact that so much socialization takes place. John Hartley makes this point in stressing the centrality of narrative in that process: "In modern, complex, fragmented societies, no one can hope to know the other members of their community directly. The only *real* contact with others is, paradoxically, *symbolic*, and rendered in the form of stories, both factual and fictional, in the electronic and print media" (*Politics* 207). I can expand the point by saying that signs and images are increasingly our only point of contact with our social units, and such is the stuff of style.

Style, because it works like a language, creates categories for thinking and making judgments. Style is a speculative instrument. It is therefore a system for organizing our perceptions and actions in addition to being a system for communication. Michel de Certeau argues that "style and use both have to do with a 'way of operating' (of speaking, walking, etc.) but style involves a peculiar processing of the symbolic, while use refers to elements of a code. They intersect to form a style of use, a way of being and a way of operating" (100). Style helps to organize and process the symbolic nature of the world around us. As Mary Douglas and Baron Isherwood say of goods, a key element of style, "commodities are good for thinking; [they are] a nonverbal medium for the human creative faculty" (41). They can do this because "goods are used for marking in the sense of classifying categories" that help us to organize our thinking (50). Malcolm Barnard gives the example that "it is because one knows the code regarding open and closed collars that one understands whether smartness or casualness is signified" (82)—clothing in this case helps to organize our judgments about social situations. When Barnard argues, "Modesty is a result of wearing clothes rather than a reason for wearing them," he is pointing out the fundamental, organizing capacity of that element of style (56).

George Ritzer adopts Pierre Bourdieu's concept of field to talk about the ways in which the contexts of style are speculative instruments for actors and interactions.

> [T]here is great differentiation in consumption settings. We can use Pierre Bourdieu's concept of "field" to help us think about these diverse settings. The field is a network of relations among the objective positions within it. Positions may be occupied by either agents or institutions and they are constrained by the structure of the field. There are many semi-autonomous fields within the social world. (61)

It is useful to think of style as an element of those fields. Disco style is another way of referring to the many elements of disco, such as, objects, actors, behaviors, and so forth, that cohere in certain settings. To understand a given experience as "disco" is then likewise a way of thinking about experience, of organizing it, around parameters given by styles. Simon Frith points to the organizing function of hip-hop: "Hip-hop, in other words, with its cut-ups, its scratches, breaks and samples, is best understood as producing not new texts but new ways of performing texts, new ways of performing *the making of meaning*," which is, of course, how we organize and understand that part of experience (115).

Style as a speculative instrument has become an important basis for organizing the social in late capitalism, the terrain on which social groupings are arranged and judgments made. Michel Maffesoli sees just such a grand structuring role for style in asserting, "Style, as a force of aggregation, would be the property of culture in its founding inception. It is what at a determined moment assumes the synthesis of values and thereby imposes a recognizable order and form" on the social (11).

Scholars of language have long argued that people become who they are called to be in texts. The concept is well developed in Antonio Gramsci's or Louis Althusser's theories of how texts "interpellate" people to adopt certain subject positions. Jacques Lacan articulates a similar stance: "What I seek in speech is the response of the other. . . . In order to find him, I call him by a name that he must assume or refuse in order to reply to me" (86). Style, which I have argued is a kind of language, functions in the same way, calling people to become certain subjects and to organize themselves in certain ways. Glenn C. Geiser-Getz says, "The self and the other are increasingly defined by the images of film and television, by the choices of consumers in a world of commodities, and by ritualized performances" (248), all recognizable as elements of style. Increasingly, who we are in relationship to others is both constituted by and represented in the styles we perform. As Marcel Danesi puts it, albeit unenthusiastically, "In our image-obsessed culture, having the right 'look' has, in fact, become a widespread narcissistic fixation—a fixation that, as our 14-year-old informant astutely intimated, now largely shapes social relations among adolescents" (37). While it may be easy for parents to see the centrality of style in their children's social worlds, the same is true for all of us.

The engine of style's influence in organizing culture is not by way of explicit propositions but by modeling, performing, and aestheticizing. John Leland refers to the influence of what has traditionally been called hipster style in that way: "As an *influence*, hip moves in concentric ripples—from hipsters to sympathizers to wannabes to the broader public. . . . Mostly this influence travels as behavior or style rather than as an articulated principle" (288–89). David Slayden and Rita Kirk Whillock also note that the way in which style influences the public is by way of performance more than exposition, for "the rise of the image and the decline of the word have been accompanied by a reconstitution of actuated selves and communities into image-oriented performances, products, and presentations" (ix), and, of course, style traffics largely in image.

Style orders people in social organization through aesthetics. Some scholars argue that there may be universality in aesthetic reactions, such as, Donald A. Norman: "The principles underlying visceral design are wired in, consistent across people and cultures" (67). That is not to say that every culture orders itself the same way, but that every culture organizes around transcendent principles such as harmony, contrast, repetition, and so forth. Virginia Postrel agrees in claiming that there are biologically based "aesthetic universals," such as, symmetry and proportion (32), but she qualifies her claim by saying that "aesthetics is neither a natural absolute nor a complex social construct" (33). She stresses the "personal and cultural" constraints on meaning that mediate universal reactions (6–7). It is by employing those personal and cultural dimensions of aesthetics that we organize the social.

Frith also argues for the centrality of aesthetics in social organizations: "Social groups . . . only get to know themselves *as groups* (as a particular organization of individual and social interests, of sameness and difference) through cultural activity, *through* aesthetic judgments" (111). He mentions both sameness and difference as organizing principles, and one must note the importance of being aware of styles that are not one's own, that may even offend the aesthetics of one's own group, for as Andrew Ross reminds us, "'Taste' is only possible through exclusion and depreciation" (69). We know who we are and who *they* are because of the different aesthetics that mark our styles.

A sense of self, the social, and community constructed on the calculated aesthetics of style might seem unworkable given Zygmunt Bauman's observation, "'Community' means shared understanding of the 'natural' and 'tacit' kind, [thus] it won't survive the moment in which understanding turns self-conscious" (*Community* 11), yet he argues that today, community must be consciously constructed and is thus in danger (*Community* 13–14). Intentionality, mindfulness of image and aesthetic, might seem to be a prerequisite for style. But style is peculiarly constructed where it comes to conscious intentions. In the discussion of the aestheticization of everyday life, I stressed the idea that aestheticization must be strategic rather than random. Art is structured. Yet, intentionality, the kind of self-consciousness of which Bauman speaks, is sometimes tied to expositional language, to the voice in one's head that could articulate a plan or speak a desire to do this or that. Style depends upon conscious intention sometimes but not always. Aestheticization is the kind of strategy upon which style depends, but it may be out of a range of articulation. When one makes judgments based on style and aesthetics, one does so consciously yet not always articulately. One *knows* that this walk goes with this outfit even if one cannot say why. For that reason, I believe that style can be the basis of constructing communities and subjects, even changeable ones beyond any moment of conscious creation.

Clothing is an aesthetic element of style that organizes the social. It does so by alluding to class, status, gender, occupations, and other categories of human organization. Diana Crane argues, "One of the most visible markers of social status and gender and therefore useful in maintaining or subverting symbolic boundaries, clothing is an indication of how people in different eras have perceived their positions in social structures and negotiated status boundaries" (1). Barnard claims, in a tradition inherited from Thomas Carlyle and Oscar Wilde, among others, that clothes make society possible (50): "Fashion and clothing . . . may be the most significant ways in which social relations between people are constructed, experienced and understood" (9). Barnard claims, for example, that clothing both signals and reproduces the idea for social mobility as well as social class (111). Barnard insists that clothing does not only reflect a social organization that already exists in some sense but also rather constitutes that organization: "Clothing or uniform, then, are not to be understood as reflections, or epiphenomena, of already existing class relations but as the ways in which those class relations are constituted" (112). Peter Ackroyd observes that "dress has always been worn for the purposes of protection and ornamentation, but it is generally now adopted in order to project the wearer's appropriate place in the social and moral order of the community" (34). Of course, one way that clothing organizes the social is through garments deemed proper for males and females. In that sense, as Ackroyd notes, "The transvestite also breaks down those barriers of 'society' and of class which are themselves based upon social and economic stereotypes" (64) when he or she violates the gender code that is spoken through clothing.

The urban environment is another terrain on which style organizes society. We read the myriad messages given by others' appearances and behaviors, and through observation of the complex unities of style that are presented, we place others and ourselves in relationship to them. This is especially true of the city, as an otherwise incomprehensible mélange of social groups gives urgency to the need to mark and organize categories. As Mike Featherstone observes, "Although the crowd with its rapid flow of bodies may be a place of unspoken encounters, the process of de-coding and delight in reading other people's appearances goes on apace" (76). Stuart Ewen refers to the importance of style for social organization in the rapidly changing cities of the early twentieth century, in which waves of new immigrants created a need for social organization, which was largely based on style: "In such a broad milieu of strangers, style was a dramatic necessity. One was repeatedly made aware of self as other, of one's commodity status within a vast social marketplace, and style provided its uses with a powerful medium of encounter and exchange" (76).

Geographical organization of the social generally, beyond cities, depends on style, for there are aesthetic style markers of locale as well as nationality. Peter N. Stearns examines the component of style that is physical expression of emotion: "We will see that the South, for example, retained traces of earlier distinctions concerning jealousy and grief, preserving a greater interest in intensity" (186). The kinds of emotional display that are part of one's style mark geography, and here we may think of the stereotypically reserved New Englander or the cool-hunting Californian as well as Stearns's Southerner.

Racial and cultural groupings are aesthetically marked by certain styles that then come to be stereotypical expectations for that group, even if many members of a given set do not display such markers. What is important is the ways in which stylistic expectations, or stereotypes if you prefer, contribute to the organization of social judgments and categories. The gesture, phrase, or foodstuff comes to *mean* the group and thus to organize society in its categories. As Stearns observes, "The stereotyped roles for actors of Mediterranean origin as steamy lovers or for African Americans as exuberant, emotionally spontaneous athletes and musicians contributed to the rise of these groups in the world of emotional symbolism" (282). In her book *Where We Stand: Class Matters*, bell hooks gives a sensitive study of the different ways in which class, gender, and race interact in social organization, and much of her analysis is based on the different style markers of those categories and how such markers are used in organization. Richard Majors and Janet Mancini Billson's extensive study of "cool pose," especially among African American males, also makes the point about style and social organization: "Being cool, or adopting a cool pose as we call it, is a strategy that many black males use in making sense of their everyday lives" (xi). Although "people of all racial ethnic, class, and gender groups use cool behaviors to some extent," Majors and Billson argue that it is especially a style marker that has become culturally attached to Black males (xii), and, of course, it depends on a wide range of markers based on movement, gesture, speech, clothing, and so forth. Danesi explains that "playing it cool meant not being carried away in any direction, even one that in moderate proportions could be approved" (141). Although cool pose has become a style marker for African American males, Majors and Billson point out that it is only one of many styles that may work to define that group: "Cool pose is a strategy *available* for use in the black community but is only one of many coping strategies developed within the American context" (xii). They stress the importance of style through performance for the African American community in general: "For many blacks, life is a relentless performance for the mainstream audience and often for each other" (4). In marking out that social group, cool may especially function, as Stearns describes it, as "an emotional mantle, sheltering the whole personality from embarrassing excess" (1).

It is worth taking note of Leon E. Wynter's argument to the contrary in terms of style markers of race: although, in the past, styles were sharply divided by race (1–2), now "everyone—young and old, working and upper middle class, college and high school graduates—wears the same sneakers, baseball caps, jeans, boots, and designer names" (4). He is referring, of course, to the aesthetic marking of race through style. While there is certainly a dissolving of boundaries separating racial or cultural groups in terms of style, two points must be made. First, that people wear clothing "across" racial lines does not mean that the clothing does not demarcate those lines nevertheless.

The racial meanings attached to certain styles may be the very reason why some would dress "across" racial lines. At this writing, the FUBU brand of clothing still means "for us by us," the "us" being African Americans, even if people of all races are wearing that clothing. And, second, despite crossover and overlap, there remain patterns in which people of one ethnicity would rarely display a style of another ethnicity because of the social pressures generated by style. To test the point with a personal experiment, any reader of European origin should don complete African dress, such as, dashikis, colorful cloth, head wraps, or any reader of African origin should dress in traditional Japanese kimonos or similar robes and see what sort of reactions are generated both by others in public and by that little voice inside of one saying, "It's not your style."

An interesting article in the *New York Times Magazine* answers the question, "Who's a nerd, anyway?" by answering, "Someone very, very white, for one thing." The article, by Benjamin Nugent, reviews some research done on performance of the social "nerd" role. In each case, markers specifically of style are associated with racial identification, thus bespeaking a culturewide system of signs of style that are racially specific.

As people organize themselves socially, an unavoidable tension exists between the individual and the group. We want to belong, to affiliate with others. We also want to feel special, unique, and important, to stand out from the group. These two desires are issues of social organization, and they clash. Bauman points out, "Missing community means missing security; gaining community, if it happens, would soon mean missing freedom" (*Community* 4). Yet, the clash is largely unavoidable, and the tension between the social and individual is usually a reality for people. That clash is expressed in and worked out through style. Postrel expressed the clash in terms of aesthetics, a major component of style: "Aesthetic identity is both personal and social, an expression both of who we are and with whom we want, or expect, to be grouped" (102). Indeed, we see in style that the tension between those two poles is necessary for a fulfilled life, for most people. Barnard puts it this way:

> People appear to need to be both social and individual at the same time, and fashion and clothing are ways in which this complex set of desires or demands may be negotiated. . . . [F]ashionable clothing is used in western capitalist societies to affirm both membership of various social and cultural groups and individual, personal identity. (12)

Ewen identifies the same tension and connects it specifically to style: "Style is a realm of being 'exceptional' within the constraints of conformity" (108). We want distinctive jeans—but we want jeans, a commodity easily recognizable as what "everyone" wears. If we adopt styles that are too individual, we risk exclusion and ostracism. "The tendency for consumer culture to differentiate," Featherstone notes, "to encourage the play of difference, must be tempered by the observation that differences must be socially recognized and legitimated: total otherness like total individuality is in danger of being unrecognizable" (87).

The tension between social affiliation and individuality is inherent in capitalist production. The first chapter described the phenomenon of "sneakerization," in which mass production that becomes truly complex can make mass copies of many variations of a product, thus mimicking uniqueness. Stuart Ewen and Elizabeth Ewen note, "[I]f fashion gave more and more people access to a language of individual expression, its mass production tended toward the opposite: mass expression" (161), yet one could not have the "raw material" for individual expression without the mass production that enrolls one in a group identified with those who use that kind of commodity. Products that offer both social affiliation and individual uniqueness are what will generally do best in the market.

Style may be categorical, but it is not neutral. Social organization is never value free. Style organizes the social and does so by also expressing values and judgments about people and groups. This expression of values is of the essence for style, for as Ewen argues, "style is a way that the human values, structures, and assumptions in a given society are aesthetically expressed and received" (3). As examples of especially "value-laden aesthetics," Postrel offers punk and goth, which are clearly identifiable also as styles (18). Frith states that popular music "embodies" social values (117). In another example, Witold Rybczynski agrees that style of architecture expresses the values evoked by certain time periods: "The best buildings . . . are precisely of their time. That is part of the pleasure of looking at buildings from the past. They reflect old values and bygone virtues and vices" (47). We see a Jetsons love of technology and the future in early Sixties architecture, a preference for cool simplicity in Swedish Modern design.

The values expressed by style have rhetorical effect as well, as in Ewen's claim that "good citizenship is the prime object of good city planning" (206), clearly the use of style to urge particular values upon the public. Ewen means that the "good citizen" will be one who behaves commercially in commercial districts, privately in residential districts. Try selling hotdogs out in front of your suburban home or tucking in for the night down in the financial-district streets on a ventilation grate and see how you are judged.

Style is value laden because it is rhetorical and rhetorical because it conveys values. As Postrel notes concerning a major component of style, "aesthetics is both a major tool of rhetoric and a significant source of economic value" (181–82). Put rhetoric and values together, and you have *struggle*. Values of empowered interests and their opponents may be expressed in style, and this marking of conflict is also a kind of social organization. To dress up for your court date or to dress down in defiance of authority is an act of rhetorical struggle on a terrain of style. Young female professors are advised to dress up in the classroom to struggle against patriarchal opposition they may find in their students. The gestures and objects of style carry social values that both reinscribe and contest hegemonic ideology; as Dick Hebdige notes, "commodities are indeed open to a double inflection: to 'illegitimate' as well as 'legitimate' uses" (18). Here especially we see the rhetorical impact of style.

Style can be a way of asserting value judgments out of the articulate or conscious awareness of others when to do so explicitly may be rhetorically or politically inappropriate. Lacan points to the allusive quality of language in saying that "the function of language is not to inform but to evoke" (86). So it is with the language that is style, and an evocation can be made without explicit claims. Whole texts of argument may be compressed into the use of upper-class accents and gestures in reply to working-class accents and gestures without raising the issue of class. John Seabrook discusses ways in which distinctions between high and low culture, with their attendant style, are covert ways of expressing value judgments concerning class: "No one wanted to talk about social class—it's in poor taste even among the rich—so people used High-Low distinctions instead" (46). People "use" those distinctions in how they dress, decorate, groom themselves, and so forth—people use *style* marked as high or low as well to organize class. Of course, ideology lives out of conscious awareness, and so the often-subliminal work of style indicates its ideological import.

An interesting and important way in which style expresses values in the categorical organizing of the social is its management of gender and sexual identity. Ewen makes the fascinating argument that in capitalist societies, widely shared values for preferred female-body styles reflect the society's ideas of wealth and material worth (176–84). He argues that when capitalist societies most value material possessions—the real, fleshy stuff of gold and jewels, richly decorated houses, and elaborate dress—women's preferred body styles become fleshy and heavy (see late Renaissance painting, for instance, such as, the art of Peter Paul Rubens). But when one lives as we do in an age in which intangibles are more valued (the rich still want lots of stuff, it is true, but what really counts as their wealth is stocks, bonds, and other intangible things—offer a rich person an overstuffed sofa or a tasty stock option these days, and there's no question which one he'll pick), preferred female-body styles likewise become intangible, and the waif-thin style comes to the fore.

Men's preferred body styles, Ewen argues, express social values concerning the nature of work and production. Men's work today is fragmented, and few see the whole product of whatever they work on. Today, Ewen argues, images of male perfection show parts and pieces of the body hyperdeveloped in isolation from any connection to an overall healthy whole. Advertisements and photos in men's magazines show isolated, individual body parts in close-up, gleaming and oiled like machines of production (189–93). Ewen sums up these two male and female patterns: "If the idealized conception of the female body has provided a locus for the articulation of modern structures of value, the 'masculine physique' has been the tablet on which modern conditions of work, and of work discipline have been inscribed" (188). I would also observe that as "proper" men's work becomes less and less the use of hard, steel machines, men's bodies in the media (outside of muscle magazines) become less chiseled and become massive, rounder, smoother, and more feminized with longer hair and bee-stung lips (check out the ads in *GQ* magazine, for instance).

Other scholars have also noted the ways in which style and its component commodities express values related to gender and sexual identity. Frank Mort argues that debates about changing roles of masculinity in the United Kingdom often are expressed in commercial terms of consumption patterns, especially in advertising cultures (17–18). Through products, he says, "consumer culture involved an elaborate series of negotiations between homosocial and heterosocial accounts of the male self" (71). Sean Nixon agrees, arguing that the personal values and practices of professionals in those advertising cultures affect how the whole culture works (5), and that many of them share a value of a "self-conscious style of masculinity." As a result,

> the industry has been central to the dissemination of new popular representations of masculinity shaped through the repertories of style and individual consumption from the mid-1980s through to the present. These advertising representations have been key to the consolidation of a new set of masculine identities shaped through the world of commercially produced goods and services. (6)

Postrel identifies another stylistic standard for the expression of masculine body image: "For two generations after Hitler, well-muscled Nordic men looked like villains, not Adonises" (90).

Style is also a way of marking class and expressing values related to class positions. How we groom, carry, and clothe our bodies reflects class values, for as Featherstone claims, "the body is the materialization of class taste: class taste is *embodied*" (90). Ewen and Ewen observe that the mass production of clothes beginning in the nineteenth century allowed fashion to be a more mobile sign of class than it had been before and allowed people to dress "beyond their station" or class (116–17). One's tone of voice and choice of vocabulary, issues of style, may also express values of class. For instance, David Theo Goldberg argues that "talk radio is marked by class," a marker that can only be carried stylistically through voice given the medium (31).

An interesting pair of ways in which style organizes the social is through marking time and space. It does so in value-laden ways. Certain styles are deemed as appropriate for specific times and spaces by every society. Such expectations may be violated, but the violations always make sense in relationship to the widely agreed-upon meanings of time and space assigned to specific style markers. Clothing can mark time and space together. Barnard makes a distinction between fixed costume and fashionable costume, claiming that the former is a marker of specific spaces and locales, while the latter adapts to particular times (13–14). An example of fixed costume in this sense would be the robes and insignia of state that the Queen must wear in particular locales of ceremony, while fashionable costume would be the new Easter outfit, the back-to-school clothing.

A number of scholars focus on the ways in which style organizes social *time*. Douglas and Isherwood remind us that goods are used for marking off periods of time, life cycles, and seasons, and the goods that are used stylistically surely do that—think of fashions that are appropriate for certain holidays or times of year or home decorations such as Kwanzaa candles or Fourth of July flags (43–44). Douglas and Isherwood state that for goods there is an "inverse correlation between use frequency and rank or quality" (86), and thus the authors point out the connection between the esteem of goods and their frequency of use as a marker of time: "The cultural aspect of necessities is revealed as their service in low-esteem, high-frequency events, while luxuries tend to serve essentially for low-frequency events that are highly esteemed" (83). The style with which one sets the table every day is high frequency, marked as different from the style with which one sets the table only at Passover. Goods mark cycles in social life, for they "reveal their usefulness in the total scheme of periodicities in which they serve. . . . .The consumer, instead of being regarded as the owner of certain goods, should be seen as operating a pattern of periodicities in consumption behavior" (Douglas and Isherwood 89). If goods have such an effect, clearly they organize social time. John Hartley's very interesting paper likewise explores periodicities, examining the frequency cycles of public writing, a concept that includes architecture, and he notes the ways in which fast or slow frequencies are organized in societies by elements that could often be considered stylistic ("Frequencies").

Hip style "organizes time," Leland says, and "hip produces a continuous present tense, cut loose from past and future" (273). He claims that hip powerfully and compellingly organizes the social through that present tense: "The emancipation of the present tense, which now informs every new product or advertisement, is a deceptively radical force. It undermines the authority of work, school, church and family, which all demand that we subordinate the present to the future" (42). Leland specifically identifies style as the means by which hip maintains a constant present tense that paradoxically reminds people of the end of time, or death.

> Hip's continuous present tense serves as a reminder that time runs out.
> . . . Hip conveys this memento mori through style. The joyous fatalism
> of the blues, the slapstick violence of pulp, the self-invention of outlaws
> and confidence men, the homicidal swagger of gangsta rap, the goofball
> nihilism of punk—all are most compelling, and funniest, when they
> are rubbing elbows with death. (277)

Leland says that the city especially is organized by hip style in the present time frame: "The shift to the city involved a shift in tense. If farmers dwelt on the past and future, living between last season's seeds and next season's harvest, city life existed in the present" (47). Leland also argues that against the modern valuing of work time, "Hip flips this script, defining leisure time as productive, and working hours as time down the drain. . . . The more useless hip is—the further from the machinations of work—the more productive, because it colonizes more time" (274). Of course, he refers to the *appearance* of uselessness in style, rather than the actuality. Hip artists and musicians may be working desperately hard but must not *appear* to give a rip. His point resonates with an analysis later in this chapter of the ways in which style flips production and consumption, regarding consumption as a kind of production.

Ewen offers support for the idea that style organizes social time when he argues that style "offers other visions of change, drawn from an endless repository of images" (16). Style allows a sense of constant change, of perpetual turnover, as different styles come and go as manifested in fashion: "Style is a visible reference point by which we have come to understand life *in progress*. . . . A sense of rootedness or permanency is elusive in the world of style" (23). Styles themselves are stable, but they allow the churning of fashion. A society aware of many styles will then become a society organized around quick cycles of time.

Scholars also note the ways in which style marks certain *spaces*, organizing the social geographically. Leland has much to say about the ways that hip organizes time. Hip also marks space, for hip specifically denotes American space, being "the signature American style, the face the New World invented to shake off the Old" (13). Leland argues that hip style is particular adept at organizing the social by marking certain urban spaces: "We often think of hip as marking geographic space. Every city has a hip neighborhood" (272). One can tell one is in such a space by the styles of people, buildings, and the streets. Our memories of cities are marked by specific styles. New Orleans and Salt Lake City do things differently, and their streets look different. Aldo Rossi argues that "the city itself is the collective memory of its people, and like memory it is associated with objects and places. The city is the *locus* of the collective memory" (172). Collective memory of places is, of course, central to the idea of style, with an understanding that some styles are French Provincial, some are Southwestern, just as some styles evoke Jacqueline Kennedy, and some allude to Janet Reno. The city's memory of itself is thus embodied in styles that carve out different districts and neighborhoods or distinguish itself entirely from other towns. Tricia Rose states that hip hop, which, of course, is a major style in popular culture today, organizes the urban space internally: "Hip hop replicates and reimagines the experiences of urban life and symbolically appropriates urban space through sampling, attitude, dance, style and sound effects" (402). Certain spaces in the city are marked with class and cultural inflections when they become places for the expression of hip-hop style.

Some style is transgressive of established spatial arrangements, such as, graffiti in public spaces. Graffiti contests the spatial organization of the city by the powerful. Les Back, Michael Keith, and John Solomos note, "Graffiti is always an intrusion, and in this sense it is premeditatedly—but purpose-fully—*out of place*. So, understanding urban writing is ultimately about ap-preciating the symbolism of the surface on which it is inscribed" (70). The new kind of space that graffiti creates is, they claim, not subject to hegemonic control: "Graffiti writing itself constitutes a kind of unruly alternative public sphere in which political argument and verbal debate are substituted with a kind of nondiscursive battle between opposing groups armed with spray cans and marker pens" (94). Being nondiscursive, the battle is fought on aesthetic grounds of blank versus tagged surfaces and thus on a terrain of style. Style is a place where power (erasure of graffiti) and resistance (reinscription) join in their dance of power.

This chapter's first major point, just explored, is that the social is organized categorically in large part through style. Style maintains the tension between the individual and the social expresses social values, and organizes time and space. Now the chapter turns to a theme that has been of necessity present all along in this book but now deserves fuller development, and that is the idea that style and consumption are integrally linked.

## Style and Consumption

The first chapter looked at ways in which style used a wide range of actions and objects in the world to form systems of signs like languages. This section engages more directly the idea that commodities, marketed goods, are signs with complex dimensions of meanings shared by communities that are both publics and markets. Style operates within a market system, and in late capitalism, that is a system of meaning shared globally. A preoccupation with commodities and their production is, as Andrew Milner reminds us, a peculiar characteristic of capital, for "capitalism alone of all hitherto existing modes of production is essentially a system of commodity production . . . for the market" (19).

Style's use of commodities is closely connected to its value-laden organization of the social. Capital creates systems of meaning for commodities that hold together both markets and societies. A number of scholars observe that markets and cultures are becoming the same thing—style is a major instrument of both commodification and culture. In using commodities to organize the social, style relies on stereotypes linking products to social categories. Different patterns of consumption in style are treated as markers of social groups. Groups, such as, classes, use the values expressed by commodities to communicate to themselves and to the world. The connection of social organization to commodities through style is fueled by the creation of desire; this section references some theories of desire that explain how it is maintained in capitalism. The urban environment is a particularly fruitful site for the creation of desire for commodities. The hyperconsumption of style entails waste, which is a hallmark of style. In late capitalism, social and personal orientations shift from production to consumption as a result of the maintenance of desire. A desire for commodities is linked to style through the cultural ascendancy of simulation.

There is a connection between the values inherent in style's social categorizing and style's centrality in capitalism. R. L. Rutsky argues that the emergence of style in the capitalist mode of commodities congeals values in the form of particular objects.

> In capitalist consumption, then, style does not simply represent certain preexisting values. Values, in any case, are always already represented; they can only be known through specific forms. Style, rather, simulates or technologically reproduces those value forms, turning them into "objects" of exchange whose significance depends on their context. (101)

Others have likewise noted the process by which style translates values into commodities to be purchased. Ewen states, "Colliding world views are translated into style, images to be purchased" and, it might be added, struggled over rhetorically through style (15). Whereas, as noted earlier, the social is categorically organized through style, much of that style is *purchased*.

Mirja Kälviäinen points to the systematic meanings embedded in commodities: "Consumers' constructions of meaning in product use rely on their capacity for symbolic thought and coding, which in turn is determined by the individual's cultural capital" (80). Her focus on cultural capital is interesting, moving culture as it does onto a terrain of capital. This is precisely what happens in late capitalism and especially in style: the culture from which one gets an understanding of what goods mean is increasingly coextensive with the market. The terrain of socializing, public spaces, and sites of pilgrimage are increasingly the market. Kälviäinen applies this analysis to style: "Products are used for interpreting the symbolism of collective dreams displayed in life-styles. We use products to carry meaning through these systems governed by rules and context" (84), except, I would argue, that our collective dreams *are* our life-styles.

Products are inseparable from style because they are bound to systems of meaning holding cultures/markets together. Mort argues that precisely this process intensified in the 1980s, when "overwhelmingly, style was identified with the consumer marketplace. Commodities were the principal medium of cultural exchange" (24)—note Mort's move from *style* to *commodities* in the market to the core of *culture*. Ewen and Ewen make the point even more bluntly: "Consumption is a social relationship, the dominant relationship in our society" (51). Iderpal Grewal remarkably locates cultural identity at the intersection of style and consumption: "To be Indian or Pakistani or Bangladeshi in the United States means shopping at particular stores, be they Pakistani or Indian, wearing and buying sabwar-kameez and saris, and living in relation to an ethnic style" (181). The style is, of course, composed of precisely those commodities. Cultural meaning is thus embodied in style-marked commodities. Barnard notes the cultural source of meaning for products, such as, fashion: "In the same way as a binliner, for example, is not an item of dress until someone wears it, so a garment is not an item of fashion until someone uses it to indicate their actual or ideal place in a social structure" (19). Similarly, Ewen and Ewen state that immigrants and migrants, especially to cities, have historically used clothing products to manage their image and appearance and to make claims of belonging in new circumstances (140). Note the ways in which social organization, style, and products come together in these observations. Ritzer opines that the merger of markets and societies is the inevitable result of the sort of preoccupation with image and sign that are typical of spectacle: "The end result of these techniques of the spectacular economy—manufacture of pseudo-needs, marketing of fully equipped blocks of time, mass pseudo-festivals, and distribution factories—is the domination of social life by commodities"

(187). Ewen even argues that the merger of culture and the market can occur retroactively through the restructuring of history: "As style becomes a
rendition of social history, it silently and ineluctably transforms that history
from a process of human conflicts and motivations, an engagement between
social interests and forces, into a market mechanism, a *fashion show*" (248).
We come to understand history through the organizing medium of styles
that mark eras, events, and locales.

The idea of branding demonstrates the integral link, Seabrook suggests,
between commodity and culture, for "the brand is . . . the catalyst, the fila-
ment of platinum that makes culture and marketing combine" (163). A clear
example would be brands, such as, G-Unit or Ecko, that have come to mark
hip-hop cultures. A brand is a unified perception of how a product works
within a culture to solidify notions of value and community. Seabrook offers the example of the Star Wars complex of products, surely a brand if
ever there was one, noting "the marketing and the movie have become the
same thing" (152), and in doing so, the complex of the Star Wars brand has
become embedded in culture as well. Nixon observes that recent trends in
advertising are to build long-term meanings of a product "through its style,
look and feel" (40), which is, of course, what branding does, and these long-
term meanings inevitably embed products and their uses within cultural
contexts and systems of value.

Supporting the idea that cultures and markets are becoming the same
thing, Stearns posits an interesting idea that the expectation for people to
enact "cool" styles of performance today has gone hand in hand with foster-
ing attachments to commodities: "The new emotional culture deliberately
fostered surrogate attachment to objects as a means of preventing emotional
intensity among people" (274). Such a shift of attachment is not, obviously,
complete, but it points to a trade-off and in the cultural axiology to increasing
equivalence between cultures and markets as the latter grows at the expense
of the former as a site of emotional attachment. We would expect, then, that
ways of interacting with and through products would increase as the size of
markets increase, and Postrel suggests that this has happened, arguing that
aesthetic and stylistic diversity has increased enormously in recent years as
the size of connected markets has increased to global dimensions (47–48).

Seabrook's idea of "nobrow" is another argument for how culture and
markets are merging through style and commodities in that the old cultural
distinctions of high, middle, and low culture and taste are dissolving into
standards set by the market, not traditional social distinctions (12).

> For more than a century, this was how status had worked in America.
> You made some money in one commercial enterprise or another, and

then to solidify your social position and to distinguish yourself from
others, you cultivated a distaste for the cheap amusements and common spectacles that made up the mass culture. (17–18)

In place of such an arrangement, now culture has become a "megastore"
divided into "Identity—Subculture—Mainstream Culture" (66). One may
understand "mainstream" as precisely the global system of style that I am
describing here. Note that this development dissolves primarily cultural
distinctions and judgments into the medium of the market.

Another argument for the merging of culture and the market is the extent
to which the public treats or wants to treat products as if they had personalities, thus making a commodity social. Jan Noyes and Richard Littledale
comment, "To a certain degree we already anthropomorphize and attribute
emotions to inanimate objects" (57) and, we might add, especially to commodities. Indeed, we are constantly encouraged to do so by advertisements,
for we are more likely to buy products that are good, attractive friends to
us. "Assigning personalities to products and the general idea that products
have personalities are meaningful approaches for designers," says Patrick
W. Jordan, pointing to a study indicating that these attributions are not
simply projections of the designer's own personality, for "there was no evidence that designers preferred products that matched their own perceived
personalities" (42). Norman's *Emotional Design* focuses largely on the need
for design to meet emotional needs, some of which is expressed in anthro-
pomorphizing products.

When style makes use of significant products, it is the speaking in the
language of commodities. De Certeau states that "'popular culture,' as well as
a whole literature called 'popular.' . . . present themselves as 'arts of making'
this or that, i.e., as combinatory or utilizing modes of consumption" (xv), and
the making of styles is precisely how that process occurs. Styles are made
out of commodities in social usage and placement, that is to say, much of
what the commodities *mean* has to do with social organization. Consider
how products with meanings of luxury are linked to specific communities.
Patrick Reinmoeller says that "luxury is pleasure with products that emerges
from communities" (128); note that it is the pleasure and sense of luxury, not
primarily the product, that is generated by communities. If no community
cared about champagne, it would become just another wine. Cognac was
sliding in popularity over a period of decades until the hip-hop community
came to care about it, which boosted sales.

Styles make use of stereotypes, or abstractions and generalizations if you
prefer, and Kälviäinen explains that products can often ground those stereotypes, being connected as they are to role expectations: "As people have

a tendency to possess different products that are of the same style, stylistic expression and interpretation makes stereotyped collections of products for certain roles possible" (84). Depending on your experience, you could probably identify the sets of objects that stereotypically compose the styles of Grand Ole Opry stars, of television evangelists, or of arts-and-crafts-show hosts. Kälviäinen says that as a result of that process of stereotyping, "possessions play a profound role in differentiation from others, comparison with others and integration into social groups" (81). Stereotypical meanings attaching to commodities allow those commodities to make up the styles of particular groups; therefore, the meanings of commodities come to have implications for specific social groups as well. Although different clothing styles may mark different groups (such as, male or female), Crane argues that an interest in fashion per se is marked, being seen as feminine or "effeminate" (179). Some commodities practically define youth cultures; Jon Stratton notes, "Youth cultures in Britain have become segmented style groupings within a wider spectrum of consumption-oriented youth styles" (180). Likewise, bell hooks says, "Today's youth culture is centered around consumption" (*Where* 81). Note the popularity of the mall as a destination of preference for the young in which to socialize.

We use stereotypes to organize and classify ourselves and others, and we do the same with commodities. The examples in the preface to this book are some clear instances of the centrality of stereotypes in style. Douglas and Isherwood argue that "consumption uses goods to make firm and visible a particular set of judgments in the fluid processes of classifying persons and events" (45). Think of the unspoken dress code at a place of business as the embodiment of what the people there value, how they see themselves and others. Featherstone agrees: "The tendency is for social groups to seek to classify and order their social circumstances and use cultural goods as means of demarcation, as communications which establish boundaries between some people and build bridges with others" (63). A product system that is constantly used to mark out social groups is that connected to hip-hop, for example, which is also firmly embedded in the market, for, as Wynter comments, "Hip-hop is preternaturally commercial" (197). Think of beverages (cognac, Cristal champagne), clothing, and headgear among those products.

If style stereotypically marks out certain groups, it can also offer the symbolic hope of unity among groups specifically through purchasing the same commodities. As an old parody song goes,

> I see by your outfit that you are a cowboy.
> I see by your outfit that you're a cowboy, too.
> We see by our outfits that we are both cowboys,
> if you had an outfit you could be a cowboy, too.

"Advertising . . . constructs a fictive United States where everyone has access to everything," bell hooks correctly observes (*Where* 80). How often that advertising shows happy and diverse communities frolicking around a communal product. We can find common ground by adopting similar styles, we are told, and surely here we see some of the appeal of hip-hop across cultural lines. Suburban Whites can mask their estrangement from African Americans by drinking what Ludacris drinks. As hooks wryly says, "Martin Luther King's vision of a beloved community gets translated into a multicultural multiethnic shopping spree" (*Where* 82). The unity offered by capital then comes from the reduction of many groups into capital's own system of valuation, according to Fredric Jameson, who argues that "capitalism systematically dissolves the fabric of all cohesive social groups without exception, including its own ruling class, and thereby problematizes aesthetic production and linguistic invention which have their source in group life" (125). Ironically, it is this reduction of group identity to the signs of value that allows style to form social groups around commodities so strongly. I think that style tells us how capital can both sell us commodities based on stereotypes of difference and yet dissolve our differences. Because of style's dependence on floating signs, because of its aesthetic merger of sign and substance, style allows people to use commodities that *mean* a wide variety of social groups at the same time that it makes it easier for people to signal group meanings that are different from their own. For a White suburban teen to use commodities like hip-hop style that signals African American origins is possible because it is style, which both marks categories but allows the crossing of boundaries among them.

Whether marking groups as distinct or bridging differences, commodities ground the social judgments enabled by style. Commodities by definition bear exchange value, and that enables them to ground social judgments. As Kälviäinen puts it, "Taste functions as a translation from lifestyle preferences and orientation to products, so that certain consumer groups display products that correspond with their orientation or demonstrate, via exclusion, what does not correspond with it" (77–78). As she says, commodities mark and thus separate social groups. This means, of course, that styles that depend on commodities will be a ground of social judgment as well, being both judged and the basis on which we make judgments. As Wynter explains, "In an age dominated by media and information consumption, commercial values increasingly inform if not control our perspectives on social reality and relationships between people," and many of those commercial values are grounded in the visible evidence of the commodities one buys and displays (193). Ritzer even argues that today's patterns of hyperconsumption began in the morally charged Protestant work ethic: "The later Protestant Ethic led, albeit unintentionally, to the spirit of modern *consumerism*. . . . It was also individualistic and involved in illusions, day dreams, and fantasies; in other words, it was a world of enchantment" (117). Fantasy, of course, is key to engrossment with exchange value, which drives consumption today.

Different patterns of consumption draw social judgment, and these patterns are often seen in one's style. Ritzer follows Yiannis Gabriel and Tim Lang's typology of consumers in identifying choosers, communicators, explorers, identity seekers, and hedonists (62–64). Each type expresses different judgments embodied in patterns of consumption. Social expectations today are that acceptable life-styles will be grounded in life-styles of consumption. Those who do not consume in socially acceptable ways may come to be regarded as eccentric, flawed, or even, as Ritzer puts it, as a "dangerous consumer": "It is not only that flawed consumers do not consume enough, but when they do consume—and in a consumer society virtually everyone consumes—they consume the 'wrong things,' things that pose serious threats to those who are deeply involved in, or profit from, consumption" (233). You can tell such dangerous creatures by their style: they have few clothes, and none of them are fashionable, they live in studio apartments for decades on end when they can afford better, they take the bus instead of buying a car, and so forth.

Hebdige calls attention to the ways in which social groups use style and thus commodities to communicate their values, for "it is through the distinctive rituals of consumption, through style, that the subculture at once reveals its 'secret' identity and communicates its forbidden meanings" (103). Although Hebdige refers to punks and rastas, one can think of the ways in which commodities perform the same ritual, community-defining task for subcultures of lawyers (robes, woolsacks), medical personnel (scrubs, stethoscopes), and academics (everything either black or fusty and mouldywarp). John Fiske also points to the ideological and social freight of commodities, which reflect their social uses and origins: "Every commodity reproduces the ideology of the system that produced it: a commodity is ideology made material" (*Understanding* 14). *Produced* in this sense means *produced as a certain kind of commodity*, the term means its use after mere purchase, as when certain Orthodox Jewish men *produce* a specific style of black fedora as a subcultural marker with ritual implications after they buy them. Commodities must embody social values, for "to be made into popular culture, a commodity must also bear the interests of the people (*Understanding* 23). Wynter points to the en-racing and de-racing of commodities, arguing that a recent cultural change in the United States has been a move away from racially specific products, for "products that aspire to be seen as 'all-American' are almost compelled to depict a racially diverse image" (151). It is through commodities, Wynter argues, that values of inclusiveness are now expressed: "The transracial vision has acquired an aspirational value in the broad market not because it's politically correct but because it's how America wants to see itself: as a unified multiracial culture" (152).

Class is a social group that is, of course, a site of tremendous judgment and evaluation. Although one's class position may certainly include the amount of money one has and one's location in a system of production, hooks tells us that "class is much more than money" (*Where* 157). Milner takes a traditional stance: "The available sociological evidence clearly shows class position to be a primary determinant of cultural behavior, attitudes and life-style, irrespective of this general level of 'awareness' of class" (11–12). But because consumption is increasingly more important than production in defining oneself, Crane argues, people now have the freedom to construct identities outside of their economic status (10). Class may be part of the meaning of commodities that are displayed, and in this sense, one may transcend one's material circumstances for social purposes, as in the person of little means who nevertheless has one really nice outfit to wear out in public. One may have money but refuse to display such signs, and at least on the level of social style, one's class may then be of lower status. Not only are the signs of class floating but also the extent to which class is equated with, defined by, certain commodities is the extent to which class floats more than it used to. This creates a situation of class confusion at least, in which one may identify with a class to which one's resources would not assign one. As hooks puts it, "As individuals without class privilege come to believe that they can assume an equal standing with those who are rich and powerful by consuming the same objects, they ally themselves with the class interests of the rich and collude in their own exploitation" (*Where* 77). Featherstone says that at the other end of the class spectrum, "consumer culture" has "prestige economies" containing goods that mark users as set apart at the same time that it contains "symbolic goods" that feed anyone's fantasies and dreams (27). It is interesting that he defines prestige and status, usually attributes of class, not in terms of one's financial situation but in terms of commodities consumed and displayed.

We have already noted how one's pleasurable leisure activities, including the enjoyment of entertainment, are central to style. For most of us today, leisure is embodied in commodities, whether goods or services. Paul Willis argues that "the main cultural materials and resources used in the symbolic work of leisure are cultural commodities" (241), which anchors style and leisure in the market. He adds that "cultural commodities are catalyst, not product; a stage in, not the destination of cultural affairs" (242), in other words, they are building blocks of culture. When we enjoy ourselves, we do so using commodities, whether services, experiences, or material objects, that are fun, exciting, pleasurable—and also the stuff of which our cultures are built.

This observation concerning pleasure and leisure leads to a discussion of *desire*. When I discussed the distinction between exchange and use value in the first chapter, I noted that one's desire or need for use value is limited, whereas desire for exchange value, indeed, desire itself, is theoretically unlimited. In late capitalism, an industrial capacity that far outstrips the needs of most people under its aegis must induce hyperconsumption based on desire rather than need. It is worth noting again that commodities are sold to us on the basis of an induced, or artificial, desire.

I intend here no doctrinaire, lengthy, or dogmatic discussion of one theory of desire over another, although there are many available in the critical studies literature. I just want briefly to put desire together with style insofar as style is an intersection between culture and commodification. I want to place before us an awareness like Ross's comment that "defining this empire of consumption is *desire*," (84) and one may turn to his more-developed discussion of desire to get the goods on the term (84–85). Ross, for instance, points to pornography to remind us "that desire lives by the proliferation of images" (85), and we should remember that a world of images and signs is key to style as well. Bauman argues that social and administrative judgment in general is moving onto a terrain of the fulfillment of desire, for "temptation and seduction have come to replace normative regulation and obtrusive policing as the principal means of system construction and social integration" (*Community* 130–31).

Stratton relies on Lacan's theory of psychoanalysis to link desire to commodities, culture, and style. Lacan's theory is, of course, too extensive to develop here, but let us turn to Stratton's use of it for this purpose. Lacan's theory of desire, Stratton argues, is inherently social and cultural. This is because, in contrast to Freud who described the individual in the family, Lacan describes the individual in the modern state and the large societies that the state governs (3–4). If people fear a phallic inadequacy before the state, surely they might doubly entertain such anxiety in the face of the global corporations that have gained enormous power even since Lacan, and which base their power on selling us always-inadequate compensations for that anxiety. Of course, in the future, we will increasingly see mergers of state and corporation. Lacan and his interpreters are thus well situated for describing desire as it works in the world of corporate power and the public's engrossment in simulation and image that maintains that power. Desire itself is social in that it is essentially desire for social, personal connection, for Stratton explains that "what Lacan is claiming is that each individual's desire is, in fact, the desire to be desired by someone else" (6). Consumption is fueled, Stratton explains, by desires evoked in cultural fetishism, defined as "an effect of a feeling of inadequacy, of relative impotence, provoked by the experience of the power of the state" (15), to which power we might add corporations. Such a feeling may be harnessed as desire for commodities, that is, desire to consume, and Stratton argues that the gustatory metaphor of consumption is valid for describing desire in general, for "the model for consumption remains eating; the model for the desire to consume is hunger" (146). Note that hunger is always satisfied only temporarily—it always returns. And in a world of increasing obesity, the simulation of hunger (e.g., in advertisements calling the well-fed to feel famished) never goes away. So it is with desire for commodities. We are constantly hungry for social connection and security in today's societies, Lacan argues, and that desire to consume may be harnessed toward never-ending purchases of commodities.

John Storey points to Lacan's theory of "lack" as a way to explain how desire becomes centrally situated in the contemporary psyche.

> Through language we enter what Lacan calls the symbolic. This is the order of culture. It is here that we acquire our human subjectivity. Language allows us to communicate with others, but it also intensifies our experience of "lack." Our demands can now be articulated through language, but they cannot make good our experience of "lack"—they only intensify it. Our entry into language, and the symbolic, opens up a gap between our need for the original moment of plenitude and the promise and failure of language; it is in this gap that desire emerges. (94)

One way that Lacan himself expresses the impossibility of satisfying desire is this: "Let us say that in its fundamental use the phantasy is that by which the subject sustains himself at the level of his vanishing desire, vanishing in so far as the very satisfaction of demand hides his object from him" (272), and we might observe that "phantasy" in this case may encompass the allure of products, the meanings that commodities contribute to the performance of style. Stratton links lack to style explicitly: "The construction of the individual as lacking has become increasingly generalized. . . . In addition, there has been a shift to 'lifestyle' advertising in which advertising places products as elements in a more general, image-based lifestyle" (14). This psychological mechanism may especially drive women to consume, given their special relationship to lack, for as Stratton argues, "The internalization of their positioning as phallic substitutes, combined with their own sense of their 'lack' of the phallus, provokes in women a drive to consume" (17). That drive, of course, is artificial rather than natural, arising out of the circumstances of late-capitalist patriarchy, but it serves its purpose of driving desire that will lead to consumption.

Malcolm Miles, Tim Hall, and Iain Borden link desire to another special provenance of style, and that is the city: "Alongside the scenario of the urban war story is the excitement, anonymity and access to a world of personal affinity which the city enables—danger, but also desire" (4). Where but the city are we especially exposed to the twin towers of government and corporation with such intensity. I have noted that a particular terrain of style in the city is fashion, and Ewen and Ewen likewise connect fashion to a manipulation of desire: "The major accomplishment of the mass-fashion industry was its ability to plumb the wells of popular desire" (167). It is on that terrain, they argue, that style, desire, and commodification particularly come together: "The process by which social desire was translated into commodified forms was more present within the realm of fashion—on the surface of things—than anywhere else in the unfolding consumer society," (169) and, of course, their reference to surfaces signals style as well.

Desire is made central to style and its connection to social organization so as to fuel hyperconsumption. As previously noted, the industrial capacity of late capitalism requires constant consumption. Because desire is never fully satisfied, its constant arousal and placement at the heart of social organization mean that desire is evergreen. As Rutsky argues, "Consumption has become . . . a self-generating machine whose only 'function' is to reproduce an increasing surplus of its own technological style, its own simulacral technology—a surplus value whose only end is more consumption, more sales" (101). Note that Rutsky links a number of issues already discussed, tying hyperconsumption to style and its dependence on surplus (exchange) value as well as simulation. As a result, as Ritzer relates, consumers "are led to buy and spend more than they intend; they are led into hyperconsumption" (8). Ewen and Ewen describe the mindset of hyperconsumption as an ideology: "The creation of an industrial force and of markets necessitated an abolition of social memories that militated against consumption. A consumptionist ideology required a worldview in which people and nature were not merely separate, but at odds with one another" such that nature must be turned into products and consumed (36). Ritzer points to the recent expansion of easy credit as a force supporting the drive to hyperconsume: "The credit card, as well as the industry that stands behind it and aggressively pushes its growth and expansion, is not only important in itself, but also as a window on modern society" (71). He further explains that "the credit card industry plays a role by encouraging consumers to spend more money, in many cases far beyond their available cash, on the capitalists' goods and services" (76).

Inevitably, any society that overconsumes will waste. In late capitalism and its preoccupation with style, waste becomes an inevitability, if not a virtue. Bauman observes that overconsumption, waste, and excess have become expected in recent years: "Excess, that sworn enemy of the norm, has itself become the norm; perhaps the only norm there is" (*Community* 131). And bell hooks argues that overconsumption and its wastefulness afflicts all classes, for "tragically, the well-off and the poor are often united in capitalist culture by their shared obsession with consumption. Oftentimes the poor are more addicted to excess because they are the most vulnerable to all the powerful messages . . . which suggest that the only way out of class shame is conspicuous consumption" (*Where* 46).

If overconsumption is a value, indeed an economic necessity, it follows that waste will come to be valued as well. One might say that waste is present in any amount of the acquisition of exchange value, for arguably everything above a level of need, or of use value, is wasteful. Style embodies exchange value, so it is interesting to observe that a number of scholars have linked style to waste. Ewen makes the connection most directly: "It is in the representation and aestheticization of waste that the modern phenomenon of style plays its most ubiquitous and persistent role" (239). Ewen and Ewen, however, note that while wasteful consumption is valued, it is also represented as "sinful," especially in ways that denigrate women: "In the emanations of the mass culture, the suburban wife was also characterized as the bearer of the guilt of sin. While the culture encouraged her to buy and assemble a fashionable veneer, her commitments to the marketplace were simultaneously ridiculed as wasteful and frivolous" (176). Such condemnation could well fuel a never-satisfied desire to continue consuming in the hopes that more commodities can create social acceptance. The perception of consumption as sinful fades with every uptick of eBay's stock.

Ritzer refers to Thorsten Veblen's work to observe, "The element of waste is common to both conspicuous consumption and leisure" (209), and, of course, both those concepts are central to style (see also Barnard's discussion of Veblen, 114). Reinmoeller calls attention to luxury items, central to a certain kind of style and nearly all exchange value: "Luxury products are often criticized as wasteful products" (126). Ewen argues, "For most people living within consumer society, waste is seen as an inherent part of the processes by which they obtain replenishment and pleasure" (236), and we should note that replenishment and pleasure both go beyond use value. Ewen extends the argument to note that waste is inherent in the spectacular society generally, for "the principle of waste is not embedded in any particular image, but rather in the incessant spectacle that envelops the marketing of merchandise" (241–42). Because spectacle is central to style, then so is waste.

One obvious way in which style is wasteful is that as it emerges in fashion it churns, one style replacing another as fashion changes. This is the sense in which last season's sweaters are hopelessly outdated and must be replaced even though they are as useful as ever—and, of course, they will become fashionable again in five years. Ewen notes the obvious: "One of the main points of a style is that it will not remain current" (4) or fashionable, although it continues as a style. And Norman argues that much of the appeal of new fashions is precisely that they replace the old, that there is pleasure in the churning: "What is liked today may not be tomorrow. Indeed, the reason for the change is the very fact that something was once liked" (*Emotional* 58). Something cannot be "the latest thing" without something else being wasted as outdated. Indeed, Norman argues that such an attitude is key to the idea of sophistication: "If you design for the sophisticated, for the reflective level, your design can really become dated because this level is sensitive to cultural differences, trends in fashion, and continual fluctuation" (*Emotional* 67). Ewen and Ewen argue that broad cultural expectations for wasteful churning may also make ideas and images destined to fall out of fashion: "In a society where novelty and disposability make up the backbone of the market, images and ideas fall into disuse as soon as new ones enter the scene" (193). Ewen comments that this waste of images, once established as a cultural expectation, is how we come to understand history as well: "This is the quintessence of waste as history, history as style; a pulsating parade of provocative images, a collage of familiar fragments, an *attitude* of rebellion and liberation" (257). We come to understand the history of the Sixties, for instance, as a collage of bell-bottoms, combat gear, tie widths, eyeglass frames, music, incense, and so forth. Civil rights activists and southern racists alike become encoded as distinctive styles. A parallel process of churning may occur as we move from one social context to the next, in which changing from one style to another is required. It is wasteful but stylish that we need one outfit for work and another outfit for a night about town.

Another major consideration in the link between style and commodities is, as a number of scholars have suggested, that societies under late capitalism have experienced a significant change in people's personal and social orientation from *production* to *consumption*. People used to define themselves in terms of what they did, what they produced, and where they were in the structure of production. The process of production was understood to end as goods left the site of production and entered the market. People worked for GM, or they were homemakers, or they were plumbers, and those identities keyed to production grounded their senses of identity and affiliation. Today, a number of observers argue, people define themselves in terms of consumption. People will change jobs if not careers often, so sites of production become unreliable in grounding identity. We are increasingly what we buy or own; we are the entertainment models we purchase through attendance at films or by watching television. Clearly, linking social and personal identity to consumption is a way to greatly increase consumption, which is in the interests of the corporations. Such a linkage is also bound to destabilize the subject, for identity and affiliation can change with every trip to the mall. Consumption also becomes a kind of production as people creatively use commodities in everyday life.

Fiske puts the matter most clearly: "Every act of consumption is an act of cultural production, for consumption is always the production of meaning" (*Understanding* 35). We find meaning in how we consume, where older generations found it more in how they produced. Bauman notes the shift from production to consumption: "Out of the chrysalis of the capitalist society of producers there emerged (metaphorically speaking) the butterfly of the society of consumers" (*Community* 130). Another way to describe this shift is to speak of consumption as a kind of production, as the site of many people's "business" nowadays. De Certeau sees consumption in that way, not only as the act of buying but also as the whole process of using commodities.

> To a rationalized, expansionist and at the same time centralized, clamorous, and spectacular production corresponds *another* production, called "consumption." The latter is devious, it is dispersed, but it insinuates itself everywhere, silently and almost invisibly, because it does not manifest itself through its own products, but rather through its ways of *using the products.* (xii–xiii)

De Certeau imagines the process at work.

> The thousands of people who buy a health magazine, the customers in a supermarket, the practitioners of urban space, the consumers of newspaper stories and legends—what do they make of what they "absorb," receive, and pay for? . . . In reality, a rationalized, expansionist, centralized, spectacular and clamorous production is confronted by an entirely different kind of production, called "consumption." (31)

Consumption as a productive practice begins rather than ends with a purchase. When Willis argues, "There is a kind of cultural production all within consumption," he is agreeing with de Certeau in identifying the active, productive, and culturally relevant role taken by consumption (243).

Seeing the individual as primarily defined by his or her location in a system of production is, of course, a classical Marxist stance. Ritzer notes the decreasing importance of production in that Marxist sense: "Marx focused mainly on production. . . . However, in recent years, to the degree that production and consumption can be clearly separated, production has grown increasingly less important . . . whereas consumption has grown in importance" (109–10). *Importance* in this sense refers to how people see themselves and create meaning in life. Crane makes a similar argument, that consumption is more meaningful than work now for many: "Leisure activities tend to shape people's perceptions of themselves and are more meaningful than work for many people" (175). Stearns agrees: "The development of new emotional constraints, particularly the new barriers against intensity, helps account for crucial directions of twentieth-century leisure. . . . Leisure was life. . . . Its divergence from normal rules was precisely its emotional function" (272). And Willis agrees: "Whereas it may be said that work relations and the drive for efficiency now hinge upon the *suppression* of informal symbolic work in most workers, the logic of the cultural and leisure industries hinges on the opposite tendency: a form of *their enablement and release*" (242).

Ritzer also argues that the means of consumption are increasing in economic importance: "I distinguish the means of consumption from that which is consumed. Fast-food restaurants are different from the hamburgers we eat in them. The means of consumption will be seen as playing the same mediating role in consumption that the means of production play in Marx's theory of production" (110). He adds that just as the means of production in classic Marxist theory were meant to control workers, so the means of consumption are meant to control consumers (111–12).

Production can be a kind of code here for one's class. So Milner's discussion of class leads him to this observation concerning the shift from production to consumption: "For [Anthony] Giddens, as for [Max] Weber, class is an effect of the market, rather than of the mode of production" (86). If class is defined in terms of what one consumes and how one consumes it, clearly the concept must be understood in terms different from production. "Human consumption," Willis observes, "does not simply repeat the relations of production" (244). Ewen states that class traditionally was seen as one's relation to structures of production (62), but now, we live in "a consumer society, filled with mass-produced status symbols, in which judgment about a person is not based on what one *does* within a society, but rather upon what one *has*" (68). One may object to seeing class as determined by consumption for good reasons, not the least of which is that such a myth may be precisely what charms the poor to overspend in an attempt to transcend their class. But a shift from production to consumption also empowers lower classes, contrary to what may be the case regarding their position in production, in that creativity comes from the kind of production that is consumption, even if it entails financial cost. Yet, the productivity of consumption can be most meaningful and empowering when it employs cheap commodities, precisely the strategy of the inventive poor. "The productivity of consumption is detached from wealth or class," Fiske maintains. "Often the poor are the most productive consumers—unemployed youths produce themselves as street art in defiant displays of commodities (garments, makeup, hairstyles) whose creativity is not determined by the cost" (*Understanding* 35). The kind of empowerment that comes from productive consumption is, Ewen contends, that style replaces work and production as a source of freedom and fulfillment for many, and style is, of course, the creative manipulation of commodities once purchased. Expertise in style requires no college degree, prestigious address, nor trust fund for empowerment. This process of remaking commodities is a kind of production all of us engage in as we stylize our lives. As Norman notes, "Through these personal acts of design, we transform the otherwise anonymous, commonplace things and spaces of everyday life into our own things and places" (*Emotional* 224). The poor and dispossessed may be especially productive in this way, turning thrift stores and half-off sales into raw materials for inventive, even cutting-edge style.

Alexander Doty offers another example of productive consumption, in that queerness is productive from the point of view of the consumer of texts: "The queerness of most mass culture texts is less an essential, waiting-to-be discovered property than the result of acts of production or reception" (xi). Leland sees hip style as another example of inventional consumption in much the way Fiske describes consumption: "This is a constant of hip: it lies in the process of invention, not the products. For example, to dress hip means to play coherently with the language of fashion" (174), with commodities after they have been produced and purchased. Ewen and Ewen echo Fiske's inventional stance, talking about the creative things people do with commodities: "The acceptable arena of human initiative is circumscribed by the act of purchasing given the status of consumer or audience. Within the logic of consumer imagery, the source of creative power is the object world, invested with the subjective power of 'personality'" (49). Leland reflects Fiske's concept of coherent play through the metaphor of DJ culture, referencing what hip-hop DJs do through sampling, scratching, and other use of commodities, transforming them through manipulation: "DJ culture, which is about the manipulation of information, reflects the economy at the start of the new century" (319).

The shift from production to consumption may be seen in relationship to gender. Stratton talks about some longstanding patriarchal prejudices: "Women—who . . . have been constructed as the consumers to men's role as producers—have come to be portrayed as inveterate and indeed compulsive consumers" (236). But if consumption is coming to be seen as productive work, then women are poised to work as important and canny producers of culture through consumption. Leland also describes a shift away from production in gendered terms: "The economy of the late 20th century changed from a model that is traditionally masculine—building things—to a traditionally female one, which sells images" (258). If he does not mention consumption explicitly, note how closely linked to hyperconsumption is the proliferation of and engrossment with images, which alone can attach exchange value to products. Mort also talks about the shift from production to consumption in terms of men, arguing that they were freed by a new emphasis in the twentieth century on the need for creative work in assembling styles out of commodities, for "liberation was now given an entrepreneurial emphasis. Men who had long been hidebound by convention were being set free by the workings of the market" (83).

Let me link the ongoing desire for commodities to style through one last connection: simulation. The first chapter discussed the extent to which style is simulational, creating structures of meaning out of floating signs with tenuous links to material referents. The close link between style and commodities may be seen in the observations of scholars that consumption is often a kind of simulation, especially when it is for purposes of style. By that, they mean that it is an exercise in playing with signs, engaging with exchange value, sealed off from the practical use value that the commodities may represent. We consume so as to construct simulational worlds. Commodities make us soldiers (military-surplus shops), rice planters (Pier One chairs), or Asian (as in various restaurants), if we are not already.

Ritzer makes the link between simulation and commodification explicit: "If I had to choose only one term to catch the essence of the new means of consumption as well as their capacity to create enchanting spectacles, it would be *simulations*" (135). He describes the simulational nature of commodities as "enchantment," a process much to be desired by merchants attempting to fuel hyperconsumption.

> The idea of a phantasmagoria is crucial to understanding the new means of consumption as enchanted worlds. On the one hand, it implies a cornucopia of goods and services that offers the possibility of satisfying people's wildest fantasies. . . . On the other hand, phantasmagoria also implies a negative side of enchantment—a nightmare world filled with specters, ghosts and a profusion of things that seem simultaneously to be within one's grasp and impossible to obtain. (121)

Of course, by *phantasmagoria* he means simulation in the sense used here. Ritzer explains why capital needs to create simulations in the market: "In order to continue to attract, control, and exploit consumers, the cathedrals of consumption undergo a continual process of reenchantment" (126). This process is further linked to style because, as Ritzer explains, it requires the visual image, in which style excels: "The reenchantment of the cathedrals of consumption depends on their growing increasingly spectacular" (133).

Malls, the Internet, and stores must all enchant through creating productive worlds of visual images. Ritzer argues that the (highly visual) Internet gives new impetus to simulation and enchantment, for "these new dematerialized sites of consumption, especially those associated with the Internet, have a far greater potential to produce phantasmagoria or dream worlds than their more material predecessors" (148), perhaps because they are so visual and spectacular. And, yet, the simulations of spectacle must be constantly reinvented, for they inevitably lose their enchantment, as Ritzer notes: "The boredom intrinsic to spectatorship requires the continual re-enchantment of the new means of consumption" (193). Guy Debord also links the spectacle and commodities: "The spectacle is the moment when the commodity has attained the *total occupation* of social life" (111); recall that it is characteristic of simulations to fill one's world to the horizons, to be sealed off from any outside, which resonates with Debord's language of total occupation.

Examples of simulational consumption abound. To the extent that any restaurant one enters has a theme (Chinese, Southwestern, fine dining, and so forth), restaurants may be seen as simulational experiences. "Today's diner often looks for theater more than food," Ritzer observes. "Hence the growth of 'entertainment' chains like Hard Rock Café" (26). Pornography creates a particularly powerful (for many) simulation. Ritzer offers another example, of malls: "Entertainment is also central to the shopping mall. Malls are designed to be fantasy worlds" (28), evoking simulation again. Tourism is another example of simulational consumption. Bauman explains, "The tourists want to immerse themselves in a strange and bizarre element . . . on condition, though, that it will not stick to the skin and thus can be shaken off whenever they wish" ("From" 29), classically a condition of simulation. Bauman also references simulation's aesthetic dimension: "The tourist's world is fully and exclusively structured by *aesthetic* criteria" ("From" 30). Note that participating in all of these environments is central to people's life-styles and will be part of how they construct and present themselves to the world.

This chapter has shown the way in which style is central to social organization as well as commodification. Putting the two together, I would say that late-capitalist societies organize themselves largely around logics provided by style. It should not be surprising that if style is as central to life in such societies as shown so far, that style should also have major consequences in terms of the creation, distribution, and challenging of power structures. Power inevitably leads us to politics. The next chapter turns in a more focused way to the political consequences of style.

# 3

# The Political Consequences of Style

A stylist's ambition is initially to rule himself and then, charged
with this inner certitude, to rule the world or the country, or
at least the borough. As soon as we define the pleasures of
style in these terms, we see that politics is, if not the easiest,
certainly the most direct way of achieving satisfaction.
—Quentin Crisp, *How to Have a Life-Style*, 108

In 1822, the recently crowned King of Great Britain, George IV, visited Scotland, the first monarch to do so since 1641. Questions of Scottish political and social identity were in the balance. It had not been too many years since Prince Charles Stewart in 1745 led the last serious armed attempt to put a Scottish king on the throne of England or failing that to recover Scottish independence. Increasing economic and social ties were weakening the insularity of traditional Scottish society, however. Scots were weighing issues of who they were and what was their relationship to the British people to the south. George IV's own dynasty began not too many years before with the German George I, who spoke no English whatsoever. George IV had to be received in just the right way to juggle all these sensitive political balls successfully.

To solve the problem, that grand old man of Scotland, Sir Walter Scott, gave a party. Scott was "hugely popular," "a major international force"—and author of the romantic *Waverley*, "one of the most significant books of the nineteenth century" ("Writing"). Scott was in some ways as much a man of our time as his. He understood the power of style, surface, and floating signs. Scott is widely regarded as the inventor of the historical novel, spinning compelling tales of knights in armor and Gothic dungeons that neither his public nor he had ever seen. We might regard him as a preelectronic expert in the art of creating hugely successful simulations for the public. His party for the king was to be an exercise of that talent.

Scott gathered the heads of the "clans" of Scotland, a kind of social organization that had been fading in importance for some time as modernism crept north of the Tweed and the Clyde. Scott instructed these worthies to make kilts and matching regalia from the tartans or plaid cloths distinctive of each clan, and to wear them to the party for the King. The trouble was, Scott was told, many clans had no such thing as a tartan. Kilts, yes, but distinctive plaid designs designating their clans, no. Never you mind, said Scott, make something up. So the clan leaders did, dreaming up tartan patterns as if they had been hanging in the wardrobes of stone castles forever. As one historical source observes, "He practically re-invented Highland society and clan tartans (which had not previously existed in this form) for the visit" ("Famous"). Scott did so for the King as well, creating the "Royal Stewart" tartan design out of whole cloth, so to speak, a "false tartanry" that never existed before the party ("Famous"). At any rate, George was a Hanover, not a Stewart. Scott even put the unfortunate monarch into a set of "salmon-pink leggings" to go with this Highland simulational outfit ("Writing"). Although "heavily criticized" by some of his fellow Scots for this charade ("Writing"), Scott's exercise in sartorial rhetoric was an instant popular success. The peaty aroma of ancient age attached to the tartans at once. Scottish people were quick to take on the system of tartans as if it had been around for centuries. Not only did the invented link between clan and tartan become a reality from that moment on but also the political challenges of cementing ties between the north and the British monarch were successfully addressed through that ploy. To this day, Scots wear tartans for special events, British monarchs reinscribe the invented tradition by wearing tartans on appropriate occasions, and Scotland shows no signs of outright secession or Jacobite rebellion.

Consider some briefer examples. One instrument of the British colonization of New Zealand and the subjugation of its indigenous people, the Maori, was suppression of *Ta Moko*, the elaborate "tattoos" covering the face and body in their tribal traditions. British authorities were repelled by the designs, which were certainly not the sort of thing found back home in Pall Mall. Ta Moko was, however, a sign of Maori identity and culture and cherished by the Maori people. Each design told the story of the individual who wore it. To the British, it was a mark of resistance to their rule and to what they saw as the inexorable march of European civilization. Attempts to outlaw Ta Moko eventually failed, and it is now a site of the recovery of Maori identity as more and more people are adopting that practice (Hatfield and Steuer). Ta Moko in that sense is a strategic part of a Maori civil rights movement taking place on many fronts.

In 2004, French lawmakers launched an effort to ban all wearing of clothing or insignia with religious meaning in schools and other public places. Although the most immediate protests focused on the banning of Muslim head coverings for women, the BBC reported that the prohibition was actually much wider: "It will not just affect Muslim girls—large Christian crosses and Jewish skullcaps are also banned, as almost certainly are Sikh turbans" ("French Headscarf"). The controversy remains active at this writing.

In the campaign leading up to the presidential election of 2008, style loomed large. One journalist, Guy Trebay, reported concerns over whether a sweater worn by Senator John McCain was "gay": "Fashion insiders for their part shrugged off the look as more appropriate to the buffet line at an assisted living center than the pages of *Out*" (1). Trebay reports that David Letterman congratulated Senator Barack Obama on wearing "a very electable suit" (1). Tellingly, Trebay quotes a marketing executive: "Voters are looking for a new language and new thinking. . . . Obama helps bring in that new language visually by breaking the dress code of blue suit, starched shirt, and red ties" (2). Note the reference to a point made in the first chapter that style is a kind of language—in this case, a political language. Another journalist reports controversy arising over Senator Hillary Clinton's low-cleavage blouses and coral jackets (Wheaton). Columnist Ellen Goodman accused such journalists of "covering pulchritude instead of policy" yet wonders, "Does anyone remember what Hillary was talking about on CSpan2?" Style and not argument was the terrain of much of the political campaign.

These examples illustrate *recent* political struggles carried out on a battlefield of style: clothing, accessories, design, grooming, skin markings, and so forth. What I mean by political in these examples is contests over the distribution of a society's resources, both material (money, schools, military contracts) and representational (meanings, images, signs). Politics may have to do with elections or with cultural artifacts, but it usually entails struggle over resources. Such struggles run the gamut from the humorous to the deadly. Within two years of the French ban, Algerian Muslim youth were burning cars and dying at the hands of police bullets as they protested a variety of grievances, the head-scarf issue among them—and the Maori struggle continues in earnest.

The idea of style as a political battlefield is as fresh as this morning's paper. On the morning that I write this, my newspaper reports that a Dallas schoolboard member is urging the city council to enact a total ban on "sagging," or the wearing of baggy pants at or below the crotch level. Because many will read such a style as marking young males and African Americans—and because the photo accompanying the article shows three young African

American males, their pants at about mid-thigh—it is not hard to find a politics of control and containment in this proposal (Stengle).

The idea of style as a political battlefield is also ancient. Simon Schama describes the sixteenth-century Field of the Cloth of Gold, a courtly spectacle staged by Henry VIII of England and François I of France to intimidate the Holy Roman Emperor, Charles V (and perhaps each other). This struggle for domination of Europe through costume, dance, and pageantry rather than weapons was quite serious. "It came to war anyway," Schama says, "not with swords and lances but something much more deadly: style," as both kings engaged in weeks of "displays of outrageous ostentation" in northern France (243).

This chapter explores the ways in which style can be a site and an instrument of political action, influence, and struggle—extending issues on which we have already touched. To assert that there are political consequences of style is certainly not to deny that there are political consequences of other kinds of discourse and signification. Style is increasingly the site of political communication and action in the world.

## Can Style Be Political?

In what sense are texts of popular culture "political"? That question includes the issue of style as political, for style is continuous with and inseparable from popular culture. Before addressing it directly, consider why it has become an issue at all. One might pose that question because of recent complaints about the direction of politics, complaints precisely about the convergence of politics and popular culture. Rita Kirk Whillock complains specifically about an inability to distinguish audiences from publics today:

> [T]he mass media are responsible for our inability to distinguish audiences from politics. Audiences are demographic clusters that are significant only because of their market share or size, not because of the collective wisdom or their public voice. Publics, by contrast, are groups of people on whom success or failure of our institutions depends. (7)

Whillock's concerns are clear: politics is merging with entertainment. If that is true, then politics is clearly merging with style—if the trend continues, can politics remain politics? Whillock replies in the negative, for "public communication has become ritualized, a form of entertainment rather than a vehicle for exchange and debate" (13). A language of style, entertainment, and images is, she argues, "deadly to the art of politics" (25). Carol Becker explicitly agrees with these views, complaining, "America has . . . evolved a media apparatus of such proportion that it has come to obfuscate the truth and to mediate every experience we have in the public sphere, and often in the private as well, transforming politics, painful personal testimony, tragedy, and world events into entertainment" (108). The implication is that if something is entertainment, then it is not politics.

The result of replacing politics with entertainment, as these complaints have it, is a collapse of a public sphere of interaction and shared deliberation. Zygmunt Bauman complains, "Ours are times of disengagement. The panoptical model . . . is giving way to self-surveillance and self-monitoring by the dominated. . . . Instead of marching columns, swarms" (*Community* 127), and we might add that the complaint sees those swarms in the shopping malls and in front of screens. Any imperative to work jointly toward justice, Bauman claims, loses its power when pleasure becomes the dominant value, as it does in so much of popular culture and certainly in style (81). A disengaged, preoccupied public gives way to fascism, as people no longer wish to monitor and control the power of the state. "A host of modern commentators have also warned," Bradford Vivian argues, "that a politics reduced to aesthetic displays of power and appeals to popular sentiment represents a hallmark of fascism" (231).

The question of how texts of popular culture and of style are political is a complicated one and requires breaking up into different issues. One question one might ask is whether engagement with texts of popular culture, including the display of style with rhetorical appeal, is a kind of political action. By political action in this sense, I mean intentional action designed to bring about desired outcomes in public settings, usually with results that redistribute power and resources. Most people would likely agree that a vote is a form of political action. So is a protest march, writing a letter to one's representative, visiting a senator's office to lobby him or her, and so forth. These are forms of political action that both the public and political professionals undertake, and, clearly, they bid to redistribute power and resources.

One way to think about whether style and other engagements with texts of popular culture are political action in this sense is to consider that political action must always be understood in terms of what people want. Redistribution of power and resources is always defined on a terrain of what is important to people. Traditionally, political action has been engaged in to affect material changes in wealth and empowerment through such projects as ending slavery, improving the streets and schools, strengthening the military, and so forth. I have argued ("Counter-Statement") that in the late-capitalist welfare state that many people around the world enjoy, such material matters are *good enough* so that they are bracketed off from political action. Although conditions may not be ideal, most people in what is called the developed world are provided with adequate food, shelter, clothing, basic, if sometimes shaky, rights, and so forth. In such a state of affairs, what people care about is no longer focused on getting the city council to pick up the garbage because the garbage does get picked up often enough. What people come to care about is shifted to a terrain of popular culture, including the significant dimension of style. People care about how they are received, what kinds of performances they give, and what style signals are given off by others. It may not be a scandal that more people will vote for the winner of a television talent-search show than will vote for candidates for public office if the television show is what they care about, and the candidate for public office seems not to offer significant changes in a world that will do.

Of course, one may reasonably complain that the world is not good enough and that, therefore, popular culture cannot be a meaningful site of political action, indeed, it is a distraction. To this objection, I must place in opposition another sense of bracketing off, a sense of public agency. I contend that every age has conducted its political business on the floor of a power arrangement that is bracketed off from significant effects of any political action. That floor or platform of sedimented power is for a given era not exposed to political action. In such a situation, very few have any sort of agency to affect that frozen bedrock of power. Moments of political revolution may break that floor, crack the ice of power but only for a moment and rarely all the way down. The American Revolution, for example, saw momentous changes atop a bedrock of unchanging power structures, such as, economic arrangements in the colonies, including slavery. This sense of bracketing tells us that global late capitalism and the structures of state power that serve capital may well be impervious to any kind of political action at present. However, we should note that John Fiske holds out hope that the frozen floors beneath today's rhetoric can be undermined eventually through everyday tactics, such as, the manipulation of style: "Structural changes at the level of the system itself, in whatever domain—that of law, of politics, of industry, of the family—occur only after the system has been eroded and weakened by the tactics of everyday life" (*Understanding* 20).

Anticipating this argument, George Ritzer says that a consumer culture will never interrogate its commercial foundation (but I think this is likely): "While it is possible to see modern consumers as collectively suffering from false consciousness, it is difficult to see them achieving true consciousness and rising up against our commercial system [because] consumers do not have a class basis on which to build" (123). Note that Ritzer despairs of a *class* basis for politics—yet, one might envision other bases for politics. What political action is possible in Ritzer's view dances atop that corporate, global floor, and that would include the waltzes of style and the two-steps of popular culture. Bauman makes a similar argument, claiming that globalization entails "the separation of power from politics: power, as embodied in the worldwide circulation of capital and information, becomes extraterritorial, while the extant political institutions stay as before, local" (*Community* 97). In our world, capital is simply bigger than the state, and the latter has been understood to be the site of politics. That sort of political involvement is bound to be limited from the start. Jean Baudrillard puts it pessimistically: "The theatre of the social and of politics are progressively being reduced to a shapeless, multi-headed body. . . . With the disappearance of the public place, advertising invades everything" and with it, a fundamentally unmoved and unmovable structure of commerce (*Ecstasy* 19). Frank Mort talks about the bracketing off of commerce from politics and its more hopeful implications for gays and lesbians, for in the 1980s, increased "gay consumption was double-edged. If the growth of shopping and other services seemed to shift the community away from activism and politics, it also stimulated a self-confidence in urban, public space" (166), which is also a desirable political outcome for a previously marginalized group.

Another way to think about the question of style, popular culture, and politics is to ask whether engagement with texts of popular culture, including the display of style with rhetorical appeal, is a kind of discourse that influences political action. This is not quite my first question, which asked whether style and its brethren were political action. The present question focuses on the form, which is *discourse*, and the result of that discourse, which is to *influence* political action. Of course, it is difficult to make a clean break between the two questions. A protest march would seem to be a kind of political action in and of itself but may also be a kind of discourse designed to influence the political action of others, such as, legislators. If one has difficulty seeing style as a kind of political action, it may be clearer to see it as a kind of discourse designed to influence political action and, therefore, in a class with forms of political discourse that are more traditional, such as, campaign ads, speeches, and so forth. The wearing of business attire and the wearing of "urban cowboy" attire may both be the utterance of a kind of conservative language expressed in style, calling to others to adopt similar conservative styles.

Finally, I want to reference the widely observed distinction between *structural* and *functional* levels of political efficacy. The functional level of effect is personal, short term, and specific. If a text asks you to vote for Jones tomorrow and you do so, that is a functional effect. The structural level of effect is social, long term, and diffuse. Political messages, regardless of their functional effect, may create the structural outcome of engendering wide social faith in the integrity of the electoral process.

In many ways, the structural level is more important, but it is harder to trace. Because the structural is ideological, what happens there is most likely to be out of conscious awareness, so one cannot fruitfully just go and ask people about structural effects (as you can to some extent about the functional). Claims for structural political effects are based on theoretical assumptions that societies and their derivative subjects are textually shaped in the long term and that the potential for structural effects may be adumbrated from reading off of particular (but the more the better) texts. I endorse this view and reference many sources below that share such a theoretical stance.

I have proposed some ways of thinking about the question of popular culture and its relationship to politics and power rather than any definitive answers to those questions. Within those questions are located the slightly more focused matter of the *politics of style*. This chapter examines what several scholars have thought about the issue. Of course, following the indictments seen above of politics and popular culture, many claim that style cannot be political, including John Leland: "MTV and the rise of cool hunters proved that the counterculture of the 1960s had it wrong: that the personal was *not* the political, and that a stylistic license to ill . . . did not translate into political or economic change. All it translated into was iller styling" (304–5). Yet, within two pages of that indictment, Leland states that style creates greater racial and sexual acceptance: "If radical individualism created the modern consumer, it is also likely that the respect granted the radical consumer has facilitated other liberties, like gay acceptance and the multiracial embrace of hip-hop culture" (307). Clearly, the question of style and politics is complex and liable to contradictions.

Several scholars have argued that style has important political implications, that, as Stuart Ewen describes, "Style is also a significant element of power" (23). Ewen refers to the way style is used to affect the mechanisms of real power, as in the examples with which this current volume began. He cautions, however, against the illusory feeling of power that may come from positive emotional reactions to style that do not go beyond the immediate aesthetic rush: "In a world where a genuine sense of mastery is elusive, and feelings of impotency abound, the well-designed product can provide a symbolism of autonomous proficiency and power. Often this symbolism is nothing more than a gesture" (215). Ewen instead identifies "gestures" of style that do indeed have substantive political impact.

Robert D. Hariman studies political style specifically, yet his definition of his subject is broad enough to suggest political consequences of style in general: "[A] political style is *a coherent repertoire of rhetorical conventions depending on aesthetic reactions for political effect*" (4). Hariman's work shows that style is a major form of political communication and action. R. L. Rutsky claims, "There are direct political consequences of apparently immaterial and supposedly ahistorical phenomena like feeling, style, suggestion" (20), and he focuses on such forms of style as design and architecture as carrying political impact. Surveying recent political movements concerning race, gender, sexuality, and so forth, Virginia Postrel posits, "The great social and cultural shifts of the late twentieth century have also made aesthetics more important, more legitimate, and more varied, shaping the aesthetic age as surely as any technical or business innovation" (60; see also 83). It is the implied political impact in Postrel's statement of aesthetics and, hence, style on issues of race, gender, sexuality, and so forth that this chapter explores.

Dick Hebdige points to quite a few stylistic strategies of subcultures that aim to influence power but then cautions, "One should not expect the subcultural response to be either unfailingly correct about real relations under capitalism, or even necessarily in touch, in any immediate sense, with its material position in the capitalist system. Spectacular subcultures express what is by definition an imaginary set of relations" (81). Yet, the same could be said of the political efforts of any group conducted in the more traditional media of speech, letter, or article. How many have shot off a letter to the editor with a joyful but perhaps deluded sense that those in seats of power will now quiver in the face of such overwhelming logic. When we ask whether style is a kind of political communication and action, we do not ask whether it is always successful.

We must also be careful not to assume that style is only a political instrument when in the hands of individuals, of the people, or that it is (as Hebdige shows) always an instrument of rebellion and resistance. Style can certainly be an instrument of control by empowered interests, as in Adolf Hitler's use of architecture, pageantry, and costume to persuade the masses in Germany. Style can be an instrument of domination as well as resistance, as Stuart Hall argues, calling popular culture the site of "the double movement of containment and resistance" ("Notes" 64–65). This possibility for struggle using commodities and other instruments of style is in part what Lisa Lowe and David Lloyd mean: "Transnational capitalism, like colonial capitalism before it, continues to produce sites of contradiction and the dynamics of its own negation and critique" (139). For example, capital produces malls, which then become sites for uncommodified socializing or even anticommercial graffiti and shoplifting. Bauman argues that "the management of humans is being replaced by the management of things (with the humans expected to follow the things and adjust their own actions to their logic)"—of course, control over things these days means control over commodities, and that will intersect with the control of style in significant ways (*Community* 127–28). If Bauman is correct, manipulation of style will swing humans into its wake.

As an introduction to the use of style to affect power, one might note the ability of clothing to provoke change as well as to fend it off. Malcolm Barnard makes a distinction between *antifashion*, which is used to resist change, and *fashion*, which encourages it. Think about the ways in which staid and unfashionable style is an instrument of control held by the businesses that require certain styles in the office, and think about the destabilizing effect on any such business were its employees to begin showing up wearing such passing fashions as the garbage sacks of punk or the black eye-makeup of Goth style. Think of how one harbinger of cultural change in the 1960s was the fashionable excess of Carnaby Street and Twiggy. Change is of the essence in fashion.

This chapter examines some of the dimensions of style that connect to politics and power, in many cases revisiting issues raised before but now attended to with closer attention to their political implications. First explored are the connections among identity, politics, and style, then social and political struggle and style.

### Identity, Politics, and Style

Beginning by considering the meaning here of *identity*, how it works socially, and of what it is made, this section argues that identity is socially and symbolically constructed—that it is thus unstable and complex—and that identity is thus grounded in style. I revisit the idea of commodification to show how the market ensures the unstable constructedness of identity. Examples of the shifting construction of identity through stylized commodities are seen in new immigration, entertainment, clothing, ethnicity and race, and gender and sexuality.

Identity would seem to relate to the individual; it is the sum (and perhaps a shifting and unstable sum) of who we are, with whom we affiliate, and against whom we align. If identity is a "possession" of people, then it is not material like a nose or a car—although it may be embodied in the material—but it is a way we represent ourselves to ourselves and others. Identity is thus inherently symbolic and imaginary, for as Simon Frith says, "An identity is always already an ideal, what we would like to be, not what we are" (123). Identities are, Hall explains, "in the imaginary (as well as the symbolic) and therefore always partly constructed in fantasy" (Introduction 4). Thus, the sense of a unified consciousness that many of us have at the core of our reflections about ourselves is likewise constructed, for, Hall notes, "the unity, the internal homogeneity, which the term identity treats as foundational is not a natural, but a constructed form of closure" (Introduction 5).

Where do such ideas and images, the stuff of identity, come from? Many possibilities seem likely candidates, such as, the material experience of social groups, of economic conditions, and of the texts to which we are exposed. Key to all of them is the sense that identity is not created in isolation but emerges from the social, material, and symbolic contexts in which we live and from which we spring. "Identity . . . comes from the outside, not the inside," Frith says, "it is something we put or try on, not something we reveal or discover" (122). Or, as Hall puts it, "Identities are constructed through, not outside, difference" (Introduction 4), and difference only makes sense in a context of other identities and of signification.

If identity is created in the symbolic, social, and imaginary, then it is created through language and signs. John Storey states that language creates our sense of who we are: "Not only does the language we speak produce our subjectivity, we are subjects of its structural processes. . . . Our sense of self and our sense of otherness are both composed from the language we speak and the cultural repertoire we encounter in our everyday existence" (95). The idea that language is central to subjectivity and thus to identity is also, of course, the essence of Jacques Lacan's psychoanalytic theory: "The passion of the signifier now becomes a new dimension of the human condition in that it is not only man who speaks, but that in man and through man *it* speaks, that his nature is woven by effects in which is to be found the structure of language, of which he becomes the material" (284).

Students of critical studies will be familiar with the idea of subject positions, developed by Louis Althusser and by Antonio Gramsci. It is a concept that connects to identity. Texts call to or interpellate readers to adopt subject positions from which those texts may be read. Identity may be understood as the sum of the subject positions we have adopted, and identity is thus changeable as the subject positions that we take change. Identity thus stems from our long and repeated engagement with the language and signs of texts. Hall argues, "Identities are thus points of temporary attachment to the subject positions which discursive practices construct for us" (Introduction 6). Each person's body is thus the location of condensed subject positions, or, Hall continues, "the signifier of the condensation of subjectivities in the individual (Introduction 11).

If identity is created in language, then it is created rhetorically, for language is essentially rhetorical. Baudrillard argues for the total influence of persuasion in creating today's subject, which "becomes a pure screen, a pure absorption and resorption surface of the influence networks" (*Ecstasy* 27). We are constantly making claims as to who we are, described by Baudrillard as a process of "proving our existence" (*Ecstasy* 29). If this is true, then the identity of the individual derives not exclusively from any realistic or material source but also from the ongoing social influences of persuasion. Judith Butler takes this stance: "The 'coherence' and 'continuity' of 'the person' are not logical or analytic features of personhood, but rather, socially instituted and maintained norms of intelligibility"(*Gender* 23)—if instituted and maintained, then rhetorical.

Identity is therefore socially created. This social grounding is a necessary implication of grounding identity in language and signs in subject positions and rhetoric. Vivian claims that the self "acquires its nature and meaning within the heterogeneity, the 'ambience,' of a particular social milieu" (234). In a Bakhtinian mode, Vivian insists that the social comes first and generates individual identity: "The autonomous agent is no longer recognized as the constitutive atom of society; instead, the social and political relations that shape the contours of a community establish the assortment of social and political roles without which an individual would not exist" (235). When we say who we are, we say which social contexts we align with. Bauman states that in a time of shrinking real community, a sense of identity can substitute for actual connection: "'Identity,' today's talk of the town and the most commonly played game in town, owes the attention it attracts and the passions it begets to being a *surrogate of community*" (*Community* 15).

Identities under postmodern conditions are also likely to be unstable and in flux, regardless of their construction. Instability is an important part of why identity is political, for only if something can be struggled over and changed will politics and rhetoric connect to it. We have lost "the notion of an integral, originary and unified identity" (Hall, Introduction 1) in our postmodern world, at least among theorists. In its place, as Bauman claims, "the construction of identity is a neverending and forever incomplete process, and must remain such to deliver on its promise (or, more precisely to keep the promise of delivery credible). . . . Identity must stay flexible and always amenable to further experimentation and change" (*Community* 64). Bauman argues,

> If the *modern* 'problem of identity' was how to construct an identity and keep it solid and stable, the *postmodern* 'problem of identity' is primarily how to avoid fixation and keep the options open. In the case of identity, as in other cases, the catchword of modernity was creation; the catchword of postmodernity is recycling. ("From" 18)

The process of cycling identities is short, and thus identity is unstable over the long term, which Bauman describes: "In the life-game of the postmodern consumers the rules of the game keep changing in the course of playing. The sensible strategy is therefore to keep each game short. . . . The snag is no longer how to discover, invent, construct, assemble (even buy) an identity, but how to prevent it from sticking" so that it may change ("From" 24). Hall agrees that today, "identities are never unified and, in late modern times, increasingly fragmented and fracturing" (Introduction 4). Lacan argues, from his own perspective, for the ultimate decenteredness and instability of the subject as well:

Does the subject not become engaged in an ever-growing disposses-
sion of that being of his concerning which—by dint of sincere portraits
which leave its idea no less incoherent, of rectifications that do not
succeed in freeing its essence, of stays and defenses that do not prevent
his statue from tottering, of narcissistic embraces that become like a
puff of air in animating it—he ends up by recognizing that this being
has never been anything more than his construct in the imaginary and
that this construct disappoints all his certainties? (42)

Mike Featherstone also argues that identity today is unstable, and he links
it to the decentering of the subject: "One interesting aspect of the new urban
lifestyles and depthless stylistic eclecticism . . . is that it is linked to the notion
of a movement beyond individualism, to a de-centring of the subject" (101).
Featherstone implies that a preoccupation with style is itself decentering,
pulling the subject outward in alignment with different and conflicting signifying systems. It is in this vein that Fiske argues that subjectivities today are
nomadic: "The necessity of negotiating the problems of everyday life within
a complex, highly elaborated social structure has produced nomadic subjectivities who can move around the grid, realigning their social allegiances
into different formations of the people according to the necessities of the
moment" (*Understanding* 24).

Identity will seem especially unstable if one sees it as performed rather
than natural. David Slayden and Whillock say, "The conception and presentation of the self have become both increasingly fluid and imagistic, shaped
by the demands of the mediated environments in which such performances
take place" (ix). Of course, Butler famously argues that gender identity is
performative. Butler links the construction of identity explicitly to language
and other kinds of signification and claims that "identity is asserted through
a process of signification. . . . .the enabling conditions for an assertion of 'I'
are provided by the structure of signification, the rules that regulate the legitimate and illegitimate invocation of that pronoun" (*Gender* 183). Of course,
if gender identity can be performed, so might other elements of identity,
such as, class or race.

Some scholars have noted the peculiarly unstable nature of identity in
the United States. Here especially we see the fluidity and impermanence
of identity. This nation was founded on a myth of essential mobility, of the
possibility to make oneself into whatever one wanted, in contrast to the hidebound and class-haunted societies of Europe. As Leland observes, "From the
start, America offered the promise of reinvention: the erasure of past ties, the
chance to create a new identity. This remains the nation's principal fantasy"
(39). It was a myth, of course, undermined by a relentless and enduring rac-

ism that attempted to freeze identities along racial lines. But the myth of mobility endures in the consciousness of many Americans even now, about which Ewen says, "The notion that each individual has fair access to status and recognition and therefore can escape the anonymity and conditions of the common lot, has shaped the meaning and understanding of American *democracy*" (59). Note Ewen's linking of this myth of identity to the political process. Ewen also links the making of identity to style: "With the bourgeois market in style, however, images became—more and more—marks of individual, autonomous achievement" (29). Individual distinction, marked by signs of style, become central to American identity, for, Ewen maintains, "This highly individuated notion of personal distinction—marked by the compulsory consumption of images—stands at the heart of the 'American Dream'" (58).

So far, some arguments were reviewed for why identity is keyed to signs and language and is thus changeable and unstable; some hints were expressed about the connection between identity and style. This chapter now turns more explicitly to explore the links between identity and style, an important way to understanding how politics is played out in style.

Style is the major site on which claims of identity are made and contested today. Understanding this claim will help to understand how style is political. Observe the linkage of style, community, and identity in Ewen's claim: "Style is seen as a powerful mode of self-expression, a way in which people establish themselves in relation to others" (21). Note Ewen's emphasis not only on self-expression but also on the use of style to situation oneself in relationship to others, which begins to hint at political relationships. When Ewen argues that in industrial production, "personhood" is trampled, while in consumption individuality may be expressed, he is likewise linking style to relationship and politics by arguing that today identity springs from our location in a network of consumption more than production (60–61).

To see identity expressed in style, which is, of course, commodified, should not lead us to make the mistake that I think Andrew Milner does in seeing identity politics as merely an effect of capital:

> The new subcultures of difference were typically initiated by political movements of an often quasi-socialistic character, but sustained only by an effective monetary demand for commodifiable counter-cultural texts. It seems likely, then, that identity politics will eventually be better understood as an effect of, rather than an alternative to, post-modern late capitalism. (8)

It is, I believe, more complicated than that. Late capitalism is surely pleased that identity politics is often expressed in terms of which clothing or recorded music one buys—the commodifiable texts of which Milner speaks. And, surely, some of the subcultures of difference to which he refers do not go beyond posing in the latest outfits, just as many political movements throughout history prove to be squibs. But a nineteenth-century parallel of Milner's error would be to assume that the abolitionist movement was but an effect of traditional expositional speaking and writing, because it was carried out on that terrain. Real political work is done through the instrument of style, and it begins, as seen even in Milner's comment, with expressions of and struggles over identity.

Postrel neatly expresses the way in which style and its aesthetic preferences merge with identity: "*I like that* merges into *I'm like that.* Identity prevails" (101). The elements of style we favor come to be an expression of who we are, and those elements, of course, often products. Donald A. Norman expresses the link between commodities and identity: "The way we dress and behave, the material objects we possess, jewelry and watches, cars and homes, all are public expressions of our selves" (*Emotional* 53). Slayden and Whillock note that "much current research indicates that consumers view product purchases as social markers, as indicators of persona" (xii) or identity, specifically that "identities are consumer choices assumed and maintained or exchanged with today's styles and projected through ritualized performances" (226), grounding identity construction solidly in commodity choices. Mirja Kälviäinen agrees: "Acquiring and expressing identity through consumption has become a normal way of relating to products" (80).

Branding, the creation of strong product identities, allows the construction of personal and social identities from commodities, a point argued by Postrel (108). John Seabrook takes a similar stance in referring to "the mix of brands I invested my identity in" (60)—"in buying the shirt you're buying the label, which will become a part of your identity" (163), thus, "judgments about which brand of jeans to wear are more like judgments of identity than quality" (170). Seabrook argues that identity based on branded commodities results in community as well.

> Fanship, brandship, and relationships are all a part of what the statement "I like this" really means. Your judgment joins a pool of other judgments, a small relationship economy, one of millions that continually coalesce and dissolve and reform around culture products—movies, sneakers, jeans, pop songs. Your identity is your investment in these relationship economies. (170–71)

Leland agrees that branded products can create communities that anchor identities: "Where conventional advertising touts a product's quality or price, brands and logos operate like creeds, creating tribes in the same way that hip does" (293). A brand is a kind of identity for a group of products, and human identities can be built in part from those brands.

Earlier, the fluidity of identity was discussed. A number of scholars argue that identity is fluid precisely because it is constructed from commodified style. A commodified identity is a changeable one. Bauman gives a reason to understand this in pointing out that the objects used in identity construction today are increasingly disposable ones and are, thus, relatively speaking, more likely to be changed and changeable ("From Pilgrim to Tourist" 23). Featherstone notes our tendency to judge the status of others by the commodities that create their styles. But such judgment is unstable, for, Featherstone says, "In contemporary Western societies, the tendency is towards . . . an ever-changing flow of commodities, making the problem of reading the status or rank of the bearer of the commodities more complex" and thus, inevitably, making identity more unstable and fluid precisely because it is linked to those changing commodities (17). Frith argues that style creates identity, that "the issue is not how a particular piece of music or a performance reflects the people, but how it produces them, how it creates and constructs an experience—a musical experience, an aesthetic experience—that we can only make sense of by *taking on* both a subjective and a collective identity"; just because identity comes from such commodities, "identity is *mobile*, a process not a thing, a becoming not a being" (109). If it is true that, as Leon E. Wynter posits, "identity is rooted in cultures that can be freely traded in the marketplace, not imposed by race or ethnicity at birth," then identity is as fluid as the next trip to the mall, precisely because style is commodified (181). Note also Wynter's interesting statement that it is not merely commodities but whole "cultures" that are bought and sold at that mall to create identity. Diana Crane also explicitly links the instability of identities to the purchase of stylized commodities: "In postmodern cultures, consumption is conceptualized as a form of role-playing, as consumers seek to project conceptions of identity that are continually evolving" (11). New meanings are constantly being attributed to the goods with which we construct identities in a world of style, such as, fashion. Crane continues, "Fashion contributes to the redefinition of social identities by continually attributing new meanings to artifacts" (13).

I must complicate the claim that our styles are part of what we are, our identity, by returning to some themes considered at the very start of this book. For to say that our style expresses our identity implies an identity that exists first, and it also implies that the display of styles that announce identities are a matter of free choice. But some elements of style we control, and some seem to control us or are at least beyond our command. Lisa Walker brings us back to questions of gay and lesbian styles that were considered much earlier.

But are all aspects of signification equally adaptable? In the case of butch and femme sexual styles, clothing is one of the most commonly read indicators of identity. . . . While they may be as culturally de-fined as clothing—though this is not entirely obvious—other aspects of sexual style are not so easily modified. A deep voice or a high voice may not be modulated with ease. . . . If the subject does not have control over these apparently basic elements of self-representation, what does this suggest about identity? (10)

The extent to which style is something we consciously choose to display or not is complex—the question wouldn't matter were style not a major com-ponent of identity and therefore politics. Walker mentions elements of style that are hard to manipulate physically, such as, the register of the voice, but one must also think about elements of style that are hard to manipulate for social and symbolic reasons, such as, the displaying of risky signs that mark stigmatized groups.

One example of the construction of a fluid and changeable identity through style with political impact is given by Ewen, who describes the ways that new immigrants to the United States in the early twentieth century, especially new arrivals in the cities, managed issues of identity through consump-tion and thus style. Some clothing or home decoration styles bespoke their cultural affiliations with the Old Country and some with the new (71–72). In this way, style was explicitly a component of identity, for "style was also understood as a tool for constructing personhood. Style was a way of say-ing who one was, or who one wished to be. The emerging market in stylized goods provided consumers with a vast palette of symbolic meanings, to be selected and juxtaposed in the assembling of a public self" (79). Those im-migrants discovered a lesson repeated often throughout history that "the quickest route to reinvention in a new land is through fashion" (Leland 46). Such observations are relevant again as new generations of immigrants ar-rive in the United States. I am privileged to know a family who arrived in Milwaukee fresh from the civil war in what was Zaire. The children, then ages thirteen, ten, and five, were palpably from a non-American culture in terms of language, dress, gesture, in short, style. But within two months of going to urban public schools and watching American television, every one of the children was replicating hip-hop videos in everyday life, at least in terms of public style. They were using style markers to ask for acceptance from their new American friends.

A very broad site of the construction of identity in commodified style is through popular entertainment generally. Bauman links aesthetics, com-munity, and style: "The need for aesthetic community generated by identity concerns is the favourite grazing ground of the entertainment industry"

(66). We might specifically think of music, in which a sense of who we are is built up by a sense of the music with which we identify. Frith argues that "the experience of pop music is an experience of identity: in responding to a song, we are drawn, haphazardly, into emotional alliances with the performers and with the performers' other fans" (121).

Noted already are some ways in which clothing styles create identity. As Crane argues, "Clothing, as one of the most visible forms of consumption, performs a major role in the social construction of identity" (1). She also points out the tension between styles that enable the construction of identity and styles that constrain that construction.

> Clothes as artifacts "create" behavior through their capacity to impose social identities and empower people to assert latent social identities. On the one hand, styles of clothing can be a straitjacket, constraining (literally) a person's movements and manner.... Alternatively, clothing can be viewed as a vast reservoir of meaning that can be manipulated or reconstructed so as to enhance a person's sense of agency. (2)

Style creates cultural, ethnic, and racial identities all around the world. That is to say, styles inevitably come to mark specific ethnicities. In the United States, we can see this clearly, especially in the contrast between White and African American identities and styles. This, of course, is the main point of the work of Richard Majors and Janet Mancini Billson: "Cool is critical to the black male's emerging identity as he develops a distinctive style. This style is highly individualized and is expressed through variations in walk, talk, choice of clothes (threads), and natural or processed hair ('do')" (4). Note the equation of identity with style in their argument. "By acting calm, emotionless, fearless, aloof, and tough, the African-American male strives to offset an externally imposed 'zero' image" (5), and we see here indications of the political importance of an identity based on style. In sum, they argue, "the black male's cultural signature is his cool" style (30). Ellis Cashmore argues that White identity is often constructed as a mirror image of Black styles: "Black people have served as a kind of mirror to whites, but not one that gives a true image: more like a warped, polished surface that provides a distorted representation. Much of Whites' self image has been constructed as a response to what they believe blacks are not" (164). Note the emphasis on the social and political basis of identity, which is constructed as over and against another group's style.

A variation on the theme of styles that mark race is the commodification of styles that do so. In an era in which it is increasingly, at least in the market, "cool to be Black," one need look no further than hip-hop for an example of the marketability of certain ethnicities. Bakari Kitwana describes this process.

Beginning in the late 1980s and continuing well into the 1990s, media and entertainment corporations rediscovered Blackness as a commodity. This marketability was signaled by the heightened commercialization of rap music as well as the mainstream visibility of Black fashion, models, entertainers, and athletes. (123)

Kitwana reminds us that in the film *Boyz N the Hood*, Laurence Fishburne's character was named Furious Styles (124). Wynter extends Kitwana's argument by reminding us that "Blackness" may be a commodity even when no actual Blacks are involved. Referring to blackface minstrelsy, Wynter says, "A century later we see a similarly unabashed putting on of unmistakably African-American tropes by nonblack performers, especially in the required usage of today's version of 'Negro dialect' and the de rigueur 'ghetto style' costuming and posing of teen pop stars" (45). Because Whites are actually the main market for such poseurs, we are reminded that the construction of identity through style is done through floating signs and is relatively free and changeable.

Wynter goes on to argue, against my claims here, that "commercial culture automatically strips the politics of race and ethnicity from nonwhite icons and culture. Even gangsta rappers aren't politically black in a sense that anyone over thirty-five would recognize" (267). Several responses come to mind, not the least of which is that politics itself may be changing in ways that many over thirty-five would not recognize. That gangsta rap is commercialized only points to the argument made at the start of this chapter that an empowered, dominant late capitalism is the frozen bedrock upon which politics now dances, so if Wynter is looking for gangsta rap or any other cultural form to do political damage to that bedrock, he will be disappointed. And, finally, even commercialized cultural forms, seen clearly in gangsta rap, do their political work very clearly in *constructing identity specifically*. Gangsta rap is a repertoire of styles that allow people to make claims about their identity, and it could not do so were those styles not charged with political meaning.

Tricia Rose takes a position aligned with mine in arguing that hip-hop is an instrument of power management and thus politics through creation of identity, for "style can be used as a gesture of refusal, or as a form of oblique challenge to structures of domination. Hip hop artists use style as a form of identity formations. . . . Clothing and consumption rituals testify to the power of consumption as a means of cultural expression" (409). Kitwana argues that there may be negative consequences for the construction of identity through hip-hop styles, for "the rebellious 'don't-give-a-fuck' self-portrait of many young Blacks in popular culture (primarily in rap music lyrics, videos, and film) has been consumed as definitive and authentic" by Whites and other non-Blacks (42). Hip-hop need not be African, of course, to be a marker of Black identity. Nor need it be consumed largely by diasporan Africans to be a sign of Black identity, which means that those not of African heritage are always both a little suspect but also a little connected in their consumption. Hall describes how like a bricolage is Black culture in the diaspora but marking Black identities nevertheless.

> Selective appropriation, incorporation, and rearticulation of European ideologies, cultures, and institutions, alongside an African heritage . . . led to linguistic innovations in rhetorical stylization of the body, forms of occupying an alien social space, heightened expressions, hairstyles, ways of walking, standing, and talking, and a means of constituting and sustaining camaraderie and community. ("What" 290)

There are clearly political implications in such construction of identity and community. This political work is not restricted to hip-hop nor to African diasporas, of course. Victor Hugo Viesca says that Chicano/a identity is formed through popular culture and music as well, for "popular culture and especially popular music functions as a vital marker of the changing shape of Chicano/a identity" (479).

I argued earlier that American identity in particular is liable to flux and instability. Our preoccupation with style as a marker of race is one more reason for that fluctuation. As noted earlier, though, the facts of racial history in the United States belie a myth of totally free identity invention, just as those facts expose a myth in which the default American identity is always White. American identities have always and must always be constructed in relation to issues of race at least, as well as other dimensions of humanity, such as, gender and class. That those racial issues are often disguised and are sites of struggle is another reason why American identities are fluid. Wynter comments, "When you take the fictitious construct of American whiteness and place it back-to-back with the true transracial nature of America, in principle and in blood, you get the two differently charged poles from which the cultural energy of American identity flows" (15). This is true, as has been noted, in the face of a myth of Whiteness as a default. Wynter continues, "The institution of whiteness requires dissociation from much of the essence of the American experience, if not the human experience. Whiteness is about racial purity; we are relentlessly mixed" (22). There are clearly styles through which the different versions of White identity (e.g., Appalachia, Italian, old-money East Coast, Valley Girl) are bodied forth. Hence, the conditions for construction of identity peculiar to America make identity especially constructed and imaginary in the face of historical facts about race. In important ways, the need to constantly renegotiate and adjust identities so as to escape the absurdities created by our racial contradictions makes American identities fluid.

Gender and sexuality constitute another terrain on which identity is created through style in consumption. If it is true, as Butler maintains, that "what we take to be an internal essence of gender is manufactured through a sustained set of acts, posited through the gendered stylization of the body" (*Gender* xv), then that stylization is largely performed through stage props widely available in the market. Mort argues that men's magazines equate style with the construction of masculine identities through purchases: "Purchasing decisions we understood to be intimately bound up with decisions made about the self. . . . Men were defined as members of a group with shared interests and problems. It was the rituals of consumption which bridged the individual and collective modes of address" (77). There is a coherence, according to Butler, of the stylistic performances that make a gender identity, for "gender is not a noun, but neither is it a set of free-floating attributes, for we have seen that the substantive effect of gender is performatively produced and compelled by the regulatory practices of gender coherence" (*Gender* 33). We know which styles mean which gender, and, according to Butler, we constitute that gender in ourselves by performing within that repertoire, or we perform transgressive gender identities but necessarily in reference to the same style code. Gendered identity is constituted by, it does not precede, stylization, for "gender is always a doing, though not a doing by a subject who might be said to preexist the deed" (*Gender* 33). Identity is the product of repeated stylizations over time: "Gender is the repeated stylization of the body, a set of repeated acts within a highly rigid regulatory frame that congeal over time to produce the appearance of substance, of a natural sort of being" (*Gender* 43–44). The same could be said, by extension, of other dimensions of identity.

If gender is a constructed component of identity, then so, too, is the related dimension of sexuality. Butler refers to gay and lesbian appropriations of heteronormative styles as proof, not of some original heterosexual identity but of the constructedness of all sexuality: "The 'presence' of so-called heterosexual conventions within homosexual contexts as well as the proliferation of specifically gay discourses of sexual difference, as in the case of 'butch' and 'femme' as historical identities of sexual style, cannot be explained as chimerical representations of originally heterosexual identities" because there are no such original identities. Instead, "the replication of heterosexual constructs in non-heterosexual frames brings into relief the utterly constructed status of the so-called heterosexual original" (*Gender* 41). Jon Stratton traces the history of such a performed construction of gender in noting the construction within capitalism of sexuality in the eighteenth and nineteenth centuries: "The allying of the homosexual with the female took place at the same time that the female body was becoming fetishised. The distinction between the active male and the passive female, which was central to this fetishistic order, was also mapped on to the heterosexual-homosexual division" (129). All sexualities, in other words, are constructed and have histories. In a paradoxical example, Walker notes how often she is "accused" of not being a lesbian on the basis of her "femme" style, although she would claim that identity (xi–xvi). Her own identity claims would seem to run counter to the examples of construction through style, but, of course, the attributions of heterosexuality that she draws support the idea that identity is stylized, for the attributions are based on style.

I have explored the idea that identity is constructed, and that it is constructed through style. I have shown the political implications of such construction on the edges of our exploration. It is now time to confront directly some claims that identity is specifically a matter of politics and is struggled over. Michel de Certeau observes, "The fragmentation of the social fabric today lends a *political* dimension to the problem of the subject" (xxiv). The implication will be, of course, that the styles that create identity are instruments of that political struggle.

## Social and Political Struggle through Style

This section shows how political *struggle* is carried out through style, beginning with an examination of the idea of *identity politics*, in which one sees that identity is not only a matter of style but of political alignment and opposition. Globally, politics is increasingly being played out on a terrain of style. Global politics is enabled through the shared language of style. I argue that late capitalism encourages this sharing of style as a global political language, for that furthers commodification. Style as the terrain and language of political struggle will be illustrated in examples of subcultures, the urban context, the body, generational differences, race and ethnicity, morality, and class struggles. Style as a ground of political struggle will be illustrated in detail through cycles of excorporation and incorporation. Finally, this section concludes by arguing that the ascendancy of style as a political language means the gradual reduction of a long tradition of verbal, expositional, argumentative discourse as the hallmark of political and democratic discourse.

The term *identity politics* is familiar to all. Whillock comments that today "identity politics supplants the traditional political mantra of 'the common good' in exchange for what is good for a particular group" (10). Yet, it may be more accurate to say that identity politics does so in the open, replacing history's specious calls to further "the common good" that turned out only to be the good of a particular group who enjoyed hegemony at the moment. I believe that those most likely to bemoan the rise of identity politics because it is potentially divisive are those whose identities connect to groups who used to enjoy the most a lack of challenges to the groups' political dominance. Or to be blunt, straight, White males with economic security are most likely to elevate the pointy nose at the idea that identity might be a site of instability and struggle. To point out that there may be many common goods or that the truly common is smaller than usually thought is an act of political struggle, and understanding that truth is a necessary step toward realization of some kind of truly fair and just common good.

Simply to assert an identity is a political statement because it is a claim of visibility and presence against a social and political structure in which denial of visibility has so often been a power ploy. Walker argues that the visibility that comes with the public assertion of identity is itself political.

> Demanding visibility has been one of the principles of late-twentieth-century identity politics, and flaunting visibility has become one of its tactics. . . . In the face of silence and erasure, minorities have responded with the language of the visible, symbolizing their desire for social justice by celebrating identifiable marks of difference that have been used to target them for discrimination. (1)

And, of course, what term fits the flaunting of "identifiable marks" so as to achieve visibility more than *style*?

I have observed this before, but let me return to the simple truth that to establish an identity can mean establishing a division in relation to those with different identities. Bauman notes that "'identity' means standing out: being different, and through that difference unique—and so the search for identity cannot but divide and separate" (16). Of course, having an identity does not mean being unique, it means being aligned with a social category if not community; but Bauman is correct in pointing to the beginnings of social struggle in the construction of identity in that identity is always also *not being among those people over there.* This has, of course, likely always been true in history, but several scholars suggest that identity is increasingly a site of power struggles and thus politics. As John Hartley claims, "Citizenship is now struggled over in the name of identity, not territory" ("Frequencies" 11).

Examples of identity and style as a political ground of struggle abound. Scholars have observed the obvious—that identity formed in terms of race is a site of political struggle. Crane states that racial and religious minorities and other marginalized groups more often use style to express identity (172); of course, their marginalization makes such stylistic expression of identity always already an act of political struggle. To make oneself distinct as part of a marginalized group is to claim the visibility that, as observed above, is a political claim. Crane refers to studies showing that Black households spend more on clothing, especially for adolescents, and that Black adolescents are more likely than Whites to do so (172, 191–92). The styles expressed in that way are likely to be read as marking their identities as distinct from other races. Those who ground and express their identity in the signs of one race (or religion or sexuality and so forth) will likely see themselves as aligned against those who identify with another. A more complex twist on the matter is suggested by Wynter, pointing to the centuries-old racial mixing of Americans both culturally and genetically, which creates racial identity as a site of struggle within the subject. "Americans are people who look in the mirror of identity and," he observes, "confounded by the truth, make up their own reflections in an effort to reconcile their social contradictions" (35). The mixing and instability of American racial identity makes it especially a site of political struggle over identity.

Gender and sexuality are elements of identity for which style is a political battleground. Alexander Doty finds the idea of "queerness" to be inherently political because it challenges category systems of gender and sexuality that have undergirded past oppressions: "Ultimately, queerness should challenge and confuse our understanding and uses of sexual and gender categories" (xvii). This works because "what queer reception often does . . . is stand outside the relatively clear-cut and essentializing categories of sexual identity under which most people function" (15). Queerness introduces instability and, thus, struggle into the politics of sexual identity. Think of the ways in which gender or sexual *confusion* may be created with political effect by the strategic manipulation of style so that one's whirling mother, as David Bowie sang in "Rebel, Rebel," cannot tell if one is "a boy or a girl." Similarly, Butler argues that effective feminist strategies are those that are subversive of received categories: "The critical task for feminism is not to establish a point of view outside of constructed identities . . . [but] to locate strategies of subversive repetition enabled by those constructions" (*Gender* 187–88).

Clothing can be a style battleground between generations. "My father used his clothes to pass along culture to me," Seabrook recalls. "I, in turn, used clothes to resist his efforts" (58). When Seabrook observes that "in hip-hop as on MTV, the politics of identity were happily married to the poetics of consumption" (76), he is identifying one of his sites of resistance to his father in that political struggle. Not only clothes but also other purchased commodities become moves in political struggle, and Seabrook notes that reliance on style to engage in identity politics is more likely to happen among the young (94).

Identity politics and entertainment often coincide, as stylized claims of identity are managed through choices of music, concerts, film, and so forth. Hartley observes, "A combination of identity politics and entertainment media has grown up in the private sphere, and is now sustaining the most vibrant areas of media innovation and expansion" ("Frequencies" 9). One may think of music specifically identified with the young during the Vietnam War or with the working class during the rise of globalization (as in Country and Western) to see the confluence of identity politics and elements of style.

Identity is an important terrain on which political battles are fought with style. But it is not the only dimension of style's political importance. Consider how style—with its attendant components of image, narrative, floating signs, simulation, consumption, and so forth—is an important site of political struggle even beyond issues of identity.

Hariman equates style and political power in observing that in politics, "Relations of control and autonomy are negotiated through the artful composition of speech, gesture, ornament, décor, and other means for modulating perception and shaping response. In a word, our political experience is *styled*" (2). Michel Maffesoli argues that the political forces structuring social groups today are based on a desire for affiliation rather than on reason and that the basis for their affiliation is the display of similar styles: "These aggregations no longer owe anything to rational programming, but rather rely on the desire to be with similar-minded people, even if it means excluding those who are different" (33).

Style, a major preoccupation of politics these days, is political through its contribution to the construction of identity. Next examined are the ways style is political through its contribution to the construction of social groups and the relationships among them.

If style is a site of political struggle, then the globalization of style—through global markets and global entertainment and information networks and experimentation with styles across cultures—means that to some extent, global politics converge. Political moves expressed through style are at any rate understood for what they are globally; hence, the resistance of many Third World leaders to an influx of Western styles into their cultures, for style carries politics with it. Ritzer observes that the world is now increasingly consuming in the way Americans do (173). If it is true that there is politics in such consumption, we might speculate as to whether the world then shares more of the same political struggles, albeit likely inflected through the cultural system of each locale.

Politics today is less and less instrumental, that is, attempting to do or to change matters, Maffesoli states. Instead it is "communitarian," attempting to draw benefits and create community in given situations of pre-existing entitlements and empowerments (9). Such a politics is surely at the structural level referred to earlier. This situates politics at the heart of group relationships across societies. The styles associated with those social groups have political impact. Milner observed, "For [Max] Weber, status groups are defined in relation to a specific style of life, a specific notion of honour" (69). He also says that collective identity and action today develop on a class basis: "This is a finding that has been confirmed by almost all large-scale, quantitative research into the subject" (104). The instruments used to express that identity and action are increasingly stylized ones. Whether main groups of affiliation are class, as Milner posits, or some other human demographic, style is political because it defines groups as different from one another, defining the terms of difference as well. "The concern with fashion, presentation of self, 'the look' on the part of the new wave of urban *flâneurs*," Featherstone says, "points to a process of cultural differentiation which in many ways is the obverse of the stereotypical images of mass societies" (97), which assumed a dull conformity. Postrel describes such differentiation across classes as complex: "Individuals do not simply imitate their social betters or seek to differentiate themselves from those below" (11–12). On the other hand, Featherstone describes a process in which upper classes use style for precisely such a purpose: "The introduction of new tastes, or inflation, results when lower groups emulate or usurp the tastes of higher groups, causing the latter to respond by adopting new tastes which will re-establish and maintain the original distance" (88).

For style to be the instrument or the terrain of political struggle, either in terms of identity or among groups, the meanings of style must be widely shared and regularized—which was observed earlier in thinking of style as a language. A fruitful way to think of style as a language is to think of it as a system of meaningful commodities put to use in social organization. Mary Douglas and Baron Isherwood stress the meaningfulness of consumption, a major dimension of style: "The patterned flow of consumption goods would show a map of social integration" (xxii), a map I contend would be a chart of political struggle, alignment, and opposition. If political struggle is thought of as carried out first on a map of consumption, with matters of class, race, gender, and so forth ordered by consumption, then politics will be seen operating widely in a culture—and operating through style.

Consumption, Douglas and Isherwood say, "is the very arena in which culture is fought over and licked into shape" (37), and given the close link between style and consumption, the same claim might be made then for style. Mort argues that the politics of Thatcherism in the United Kingdom was sustained by a discourse of consumerism that, of course, included questions of style and aesthetics.

> In Britain, the success of "Thatcherism," especially at the level of popular politics, drew attention to the sustained use of the languages of consumption. The rhetoric of the marketplace, which equated the freedom to spend money with broader political and cultural freedoms, was identified as a key part of this political vocabulary. (5)

Seabrook makes a similar argument that the old distinctions between High Culture and Low or mass culture, which politically empowered privileged classes, have disappeared. In that old distinction, "the difference between elite culture and commercial culture was supposed to be a quality distinction" (27). But commercial culture is swallowing up all other social category systems, a development that is one and the same as an engrossment with style: "The old distinction between the elite culture of the aristocrats and the commercial culture of the masses was torn down, and in its place was erected a hierarchy of hotness" (28), clearly a reference to style and stylishness. Because this making of distinctions is fraught with political consequences, it illustrates the role of style as the ground of political struggle. Crane makes a similar argument: "In 'consumer' fashion, which has replaced class fashion, there is much more stylistic diversity and much less consensus about which is 'in fashion' at a particular time. Instead of being oriented toward the tastes of social elites, consumer fashion incorporates tastes and concerns of social groups at all social class levels" (134–35). Consumer fashion, a major element of style, is thus a terrain of political struggle precisely because it has encoded within it on the same turf the interests of all social groups.

All groups, the disempowered as well as the empowered, express claims to power and to political alignment in aesthetic judgments that are keyed to style. Hebdige, studying the ways in which many marginalized subcultures articulate political refusals stylistically, argues that "the meaning of subculture is, then, always in dispute, and style is the area in which the opposing definitions clash with most dramatic force" (3). Who are the young, punks, Goths, or gang members? Answers from the street and from the boardroom are expressed in a language of style. The challenges that subcultures pose to established power are crafted on a terrain of style, Hebdige says, for "the challenge to hegemony which subcultures represent is not issued directly by them. Rather it is expressed obliquely, in style" (17).

De Certeau claims that urban life is especially fruitful for both asserting and resisting power in everyday life, and much of that struggle would be through manipulation of style (94–95). Established residents as well as new arrivals in cities display styles attempting to control the complex urban environment, and they are controlled by the styles they confront. Sharon Zukin contends that people in cities work off styles of architecture to construct identity, for "the endless negotiation of cultural meanings in built forms—in buildings, streets, parks, interiors—contributes to the construction of social identities" (81). It is the proximity of symbols of both domination and resistance in the city and of the multiplicity and complexity of meaning in readily available signs that makes the city such a fruitful site for identity construction. Zukin notes the increasing importance of the aesthetic in the service economies of cities: "It is notable that as cities have developed service economies, they have both propagated and been taken hostage by an aesthetic urge" (81). She describes the construction of symbolic terrain in cities today: "The symbolic economy thus features two parallel production systems that are crucial to a city's economic growth: the production of space, with its synergy of capital investment and cultural meanings, and the production of symbols, which construct both a currency of commercial exchange and a language of social identity" (82). Zukin's references to the aesthetic and to symbols bespeak style as the instrument for political work.

Body styles, Fiske maintains, may either reinscribe norms of hegemonic power or resist them: "The relationship between the body beautiful and the body ugly, between the healthy and the unhealthy, the well and the badly dressed, the groomed and the unkempt, the muscular and the flabby are social relationships of norms and deviations, and therefore political relationships aimed at naturalizing in the body the norms of those with most power in the social formation" (*Understanding* 92). As one example of a body style that may be subversive, he notes, "Being defiantly fat can, therefore, be an offensive and resisting statement, a bodily blasphemy" against empowered and established norms of style (*Understanding* 93).

Seabrook related that he and his father waged a generational battle on the terrain of clothing. Fashion has often been described as a political battleground, which, of course, is the focus of Hebdige's examination of subcultural refusals of hegemony (Barnard seconds Hebdige's view of punk as a critique of the dominant aesthetic and, thus, political). Crane sees clothing as political discourse: "In any period, the set of clothing discourses always includes those that support conformity to dominant conceptions of social roles and those that express social tensions" (100). Barnard agrees: "Fashion and clothing, then, may be understood as weapons and defenses used by the different groups that go to make up a social order, a social hierarching, in achieving, challenging or sustaining positions of dominance and supremacy" (41). Therefore, as Barnard claims, "fashion and clothing are the scene of the various moving battles in which meanings and identities are fought over," which, of course, are central to politics today (102). The fragmentation of the public today contributes to making fashion a political battleground, Crane says, as different groups struggle over meaning: "Meaning is not, as Baudrillard claims, disappearing from media texts and consumer goods such as fashion; instead they are interpreted in contradictory ways by increasingly fragmented publics" (172). One political move fashion enables in that struggle is to define or challenge class positions: "Fashion and clothing, as cultural phenomena, may now be understood as practices and institutions in which class relations and class differences are made meaningful" (Barnard 42).

The politics of race is often carried out on a terrain of style. Leland opines that race in the United States is seen either as biologically determined or as "infinitely permeable," and if the latter, then race is seen "as style" (164). Whether race is seen as style or as marked by style, the connections between racial groups and styles of clothing, movement, entertainment, food, and so forth are a symbolic economy of which nearly everyone is aware and which we continually reinscribe. Majors and Billson describe the style of "cool pose" as a political strategy among African American males, being a response to a history of oppression (2 3). Kitwana describes rap music as "now one of the most powerful forces in American popular culture" (195), a stylistic force that has been harnessed for political ends: "Because of rap, the voices, images, style, attitude, and language of young Blacks have become central in American culture" (196), and as noted above, visibility is both a means and an end of politics.

Because politics is here discussed broadly and not only as electoral politics, it is worth observing the extent to which style and consumption are moralized, almost always with political implications. Vivian provides a clear overview of the process.

> Evidently, contemporary political investments reflect a momentous change in political values. The cohesive sentiment of community now competes with the leadership of elected representatives; the collective fruits of the present trump the progressive vision of an improved future society; the *perception* of immediate needs and desires spurs collective action more than the promise of civic *representation*. Consequently, the style of current social and political formations . . . supports an aesthetic rather than a civic morality. (232)

Yet, it is then on that terrain of aesthetic morality and, thus, style that political struggles are engaged. Unsure of our religious underpinnings and suspicious of traditional politics, style has become the new basis for moral judgments.

This moralization of style is a process with ancient roots in American culture, for, Ritzer discusses, "Although the early Calvinists required signs of success in order to help them determine whether they were to be saved, later Calvinists sought evidence of their good taste. Good taste was linked to beauty and beauty to goodness" (116–17). Such an economy of taste and morality sets style up to be a battleground of social judgment. Seabrook says, "Taste is the ideology of the tastemaker masquerading as disinterested judgment" (24). As an example of where such ideology is used, he cites "the American cultural hierarchy . . . a hierarchy of power that used taste to cloak its real agenda" (32). Crane gives an example of where such power would be exercised in referring to uniforms and dress codes as forms of control, and, of course, these are more "official" means of exercising politics through style (67–68). One may think of the history of African American music in the United States as an example of a culturally identified style that was judged by empowered Whites to be less tasteful than other genres—with clear political consequences.

The confluence of morality and style can occur on a large scale of city planning, an exercise that politically engages class and race. Zukin states that "visibility in forms of the built environment, in public art, art galleries, museums and studios, emphasizes the moral distance from old, dirty uses of space in a manufacturing economy" (82). It is not hard to see how that moral distancing is likewise directed toward the poor and marginalized, who must still live in cities and districts still tainted by that industrial grime. Because the very poor are susceptible to charges of being unpleasing aesthetically, the moralization of style can be an instrument of domination. When bell hooks remarks that "the poor are demonized" in the media, it will usually be assisted if not effected through aesthetic depictions (*Where* 72). Of course, this politics of domination may have little different final effect than other means of domination, nor are the dominated without resources for refusing marginalization on those very terms of style.

The moralization of style is helped by the stylization of morality. "The tendency in modern Western societies," Featherstone maintains, "is for religion to become a private leisure-time pursuit purchased in the market like any other consumer culture lifestyle" (113), which should be evident from examining today's popular, high-production value megachurches. Pause to consider Bauman's claim to the contrary, that aesthetics and morality are not linked today: "One thing which the aesthetic community emphatically does not do is to weave between its adherents a web of *ethical responsibilities*, and so of *long-term commitments*" (71). Although Bauman has a point, what aesthetics does is to support the moral judgments we make of groups who are aesthetically different from one's own. Responsibility and irresponsibility, commitment and aversion, then develop their own logics and rationales, secured by an aesthetic that says who "our" people are or are not. Ethical responsibility can then be nurtured atop a stylistically secured base.

The moralization of style occurs in large part through a process of Othering, of making those who are in competing social groups seem to be strange, different, and wholly beyond our pale. Bauman argues that the way we differentiate ourselves from others and make judgments of them, surely a process with political implications, is through aesthetics or style. He claims that postmodern human relations "promote a distance between the individual and the Other and cast the Other primarily as the object of aesthetic, not moral, evaluation; as a matter of taste, not responsibility" (33). One way to keep the Other, or subaltern, within a net of control and connection is to order one's consumption so as to consume the signs of the Other. Paul A. Cantor succinctly describes the process in referring to multiculturalism: "The ideology of multiculturalism has a tendency to aestheticize the issue of difference, focusing on ethnic variations in costume or cuisine. Dealing with purely cultural differences—phenomena such as folk dances or folk songs—it is easy to celebrate differences, because nothing vital is at stake" (58). One can then feel connected to the Other without feeling vulnerable. In her book *Black Looks: Race and Representation*, hooks describes this as the act of "Eating the Other" (21–40). It is a process that allows us to feel through consumption that we control the Other while keeping our distance. She argues that in recent years, "Spheres of advertising that had always ex-cluded poor and lower-class people had no trouble mining their culture, their images, if it would lead to profit" (*Where* 65). It is a process with a long history in this country, as when Whites would go slumming to hear Afri-can American jazz and blues, consuming the music and thus feeling some sense of control without ever truly connecting with African Americans on a meaningful basis. Henry Yu describes the process as "exoticism," which allows dominant groups to coexist with Others: "Embracing the foreign na-ture of ethnicity rather than sending foreigners packing, cultural pluralists have replaced nativism with exoticism" (203), and he uses as an example the Othering of Tiger Woods as he began to gain dominance in what had been the White-dominated sport of golf.

Fashion is one example in which empowered classes have "eaten the Oth-er" with political implications, Ritzer says, for "haute couture that caters to the leisure class has adopted fashions that come 'from below,'" and he gives dining out as an example of the process: "The 'white' businessman entertain-ing clients at an inexpensive Thai restaurant . . . is consuming ethnicity while displaying his cultural capital—familiarity with exotic ethnic food" (213). David Theo Goldberg identifies a similar process in sports spectatorship: "Today commodity racism finds its principal expression in and through the hyperconsumptive spectacle of sports" (39).

Focusing now more narrowly on a process that illustrates the potential of style as a site of political struggle particularly well, I would sum this up under the rubric of cycles of *excorporation* and *incorporation*. Think of he-gemonic, mainstream, commercial culture as a sort of monolithic entity for a moment, although, of course, it is not always that in reality. In any system of dominance, some will be marginalized, oppressed, and disadvantaged. A recurring strategy for the marginalized is to appropriate a sign of their marginalization and to turn its meaning, to make of that sign a means of refusal of disempowerment. This process can be referred to as excorporation, pulling out (ex) of mainstream commercial culture a sign of oppression and turning it. This goes on so long as the group's appropriation of that sign does not become too popular, too widespread. When it does, the sign and, if possible, the group who appropriated it must be neutralized and in some way *incorporated* back into mainstream culture. The chief way this is done in late capitalism is by making the excorporated sign cool or desirable and then marketing it. Fiske describes the cycle explicitly.

> Excorporation is the process by which the subordinate make their own culture out of the resources and commodities provided by the dominant system, and this is central to popular culture, for in an industrial society the only resources from which the subordinate can make their own subcultures are those provided by the system that subordinates them. There is no "authentic" folk culture to provide an alternative. (*Understanding* 15)

Fiske then describes the process of incorporating dangerous signs back into that system, largely through commodification (*Understanding* 15–16). Postrel describes a cycle in very similar terms to Fiske's (98–99).

A classic example of excorporation is the Christian cross, that instrument of shame and torture that was a key sign of the early oppression of the Church. The sign was excorporated and turned, becoming a defiant symbol of the Church. Of course, as the Church itself became empowered and dominant, the cross was incorporated, no longer the sign of an oppressed group but now a representation of power and respectability, until today one hardly remembers its scandalous origins.

I begin this exploration of this cycle in agreement with Milner's observation, "Hegemony is thus never in principle either uncontested or absolute, but is only ever an unstable equilibrium ultimately open to challenge by alternative social forces" (50). There are always both domination, with attendant oppression, and resistance. The cycle should be understood in terms of Barnard's distinction between refusal and reversal: "Refusal is the attempt to step outside of the offending structures and reversal is the attempt to reverse the position of power and privilege that operate within those structures" (129). Excorporation is an attempt to counter if not reverse disempowerment, but it does so precisely by pulling certain signs out from the offending structure rather than by working within the structure.

While a sign is excorporated, it is not necessarily then a part of popular culture, because it becomes during that phase of the cycle the peculiar mark of a marginalized group. The sign in its excorporated state is strange, even offensive, to the mainstream. In reincorporation, the sign becomes part of popular culture, today usually through commodification. Because incorporation involves the snatching back of signs that have for a while been the "property" of oppressed groups, Fiske argues, "Popular culture is the culture of the subordinated and disempowered and thus always bears within it signs of power relations" (*Understanding* 4–5). Another way to put this is to say that popular culture and, thus, style always have their origins in pain, whether near or distant.

In opposition to Fiske, Sean Nixon sees popular culture as imitative of higher social classes: "It is emulation, the desire to follow the habits and lifestyles of your social betters, which, above all, accounts for the cascading of new propensities to consume and new levels of consumption through the social body" (28). One need only look at the extent to which the shelves of popular culture are stocked with the signs of previously marginalized groups, such as, gays, lesbians, and African Americans to question Nixon's assumption. One might also turn to Barnard's critique and refusal of Georg Simmel's and Thorstein Veblen's similar "trickle-down" theories of fashion dispersal (130). Crane, in attacking Simmel's version of this "top-down" model prefers a "bottom-up" model "in which new styles emerge in lower-status groups and are later adopted by higher-status groups" (Fiske 14). Leland takes a similar view in describing the origins of hip fashion: "Hip fashion does not mean having the right clothes, but being able to work the language, which bubbles up from the streets and thrift stores, not down from the design houses" (46).

As noted with Fiske above, excorporation is always the turning of a sign, of some kind of cultural material that is provided by the social and economic system of domination. Excorporation is a guerilla raid on signs of oppression. As Fiske says, "Popular culture is the art of making do with what the system provides" (*Understanding* 25). Elsewhere, he uses the idea of "popular discrimination" to describe the process by which local cultures are made by appropriation of available material, for "popular discrimination begins with the choice of which products to use in the production of popular culture and then passes on to the imaginative linking of the meanings and pleasure produced from them with the conditions of everyday life. . . . The popular is functional" ("Popular" 216).

The process of strategic appropriation and excorporation is also noticed by de Certeau, who distinguishes between "strategies," which are the exercise of power by the strong, and "tactics," which are "an art of the weak" (35–38). It is interesting from the point of view of rhetoric that de Certeau sees Aristotle's rhetorical system as one of empowered strategies and the Sophists' methods as tactics that "perverted, as he [Aristotle] saw it, the order of truth" (38), although of course the Sophists were in play before Aristotle. De Certeau also finds parallels of strategies and tactics with grammar and rhetoric: "Whereas grammar watches over the 'propriety' of terms, rhetorical alterations . . . point to the use of language by speakers in particular situations of ritual or actual linguistic combat" (39). As examples of tactics, he suggests "dwelling, moving about, speaking, reading, shopping, and cooking" (40), the stuff of everyday life that turns and uses available signs.

De Certeau argues, "The tactics of consumption, the ingenious ways in which the weak make use of the strong, thus lend a political dimension to everyday practices" (xvii) and sounds exactly like Fiske in saying that in popular culture, "People have to make do with what they have" (18). As an example of such making do, de Certeau describes "la perruque," which "is the worker's own work disguised as work for his employer," a common industrial subterfuge paralleled by symbolic appropriations and reworkings across the cultural spectrum (25). "The actual order of things," de Certeau says, "is precisely what 'popular' tactics turn to their own ends, without any illusion that it will change any time soon" (26). Excorporation is part of the larger process of everyday subversion de Certeau describes, in which "order is tricked by an art. Into the institution to be served are thus insinuated styles of social exchange, technical invention, and moral resistance, that is, an economy of the *'gift'* (generosities for which one expects a return), an esthetics of *'tricks'* (artists' operations) and an ethics of *tenacity* (countless ways of refusing to accord the established order the status of a law, a meaning, or a fatality)" (26).

For every act of excorporation by which the marginalized turn a sign of their oppression there is incorporation, the use of mainstream power to co-opt those excorporated signs. Slayden and Whillock relate, "Acts of resistance and populism—graffiti provides one example—are routinely censored and silenced through commercial assimilation" (x). If I may be allowed a personal example, back in the late 1960s, young people seized upon the "establishment's" expectation that one should be neat and well dressed as a sign of oppression. Clothing was excorporated by rebellious youths who wore it until holes developed rather than buy new garments—and when holes did develop or when those of us who were in our adolescence outgrew our clothes, we simply patched them or extended hems with the gaudiest pieces of unmatched cloth we could find, to make sure people knew we were not doing our commercial duty by buying new clothing regularly. Alas! these acts of excorporation lasted just long enough for someone to figure out that such a style could be marketed, and pretty soon our incorporated, harlequin-patched clothing was being sold, newly manufactured, down at the department store. This is the situation described by Bauman: "The styles once practiced by marginal people in marginal time-stretches and marginal places, are now practiced by the majority in the prime time of their lives and in places central to their life-world; they have become now, fully and truly, lifestyles" (26). Butler blames "repetition" for the co-optation of the subversive but especially repetition through the kind of commercialization that creates most incorporation: "Subversive performances always run the risk of becoming deadening clichés through their repetition and, most importantly, through their repetition within commodity culture where 'subversion' carries market value" (*Gender* xxi).

Hebdige likewise points to commodification as the instrument of incorporation: "As the subculture begins to strike its own eminently marketable pose, as its vocabulary (both visual and verbal) becomes more and more familiar, so the referential context to which it can be most conveniently assigned is made increasingly apparent. Eventually [it] can be incorporated, brought back into line" through the market (93–94). This was certainly true of the subcultures he studied, such as, punks and Rastafarians, whose shocking gear and clothing were soon found for sale in chic boutiques. Hebdige makes it clear that the cycle of excorporation and incorporation is one of style: "The creation and diffusion of new styles is inextricably bound up with the process of production, publicity and packaging which must inevitably lead to the defusion of the subculture's subversive power" (95).

A similar process happens with excorporated music, eventually, Glenn C. Geiser-Getz argues: "Threatening forms of musical expression are sometimes neutralized in a powerful consumer culture through commodification, in which the offending symbols are rendered profitable and relatively harmless to the dominant culture" (254). S. Craig Watkins claims a kind of excorporation and incorporation cycle for hip-hop as well: "Throughout its early history, hip hop amassed most of its appeal by maintaining an aura and edge that placed it in opposition to the cultural mainstream. . . . In the end, hip hop did not simply join the mainstream; in effect, it redefined the very meaning and experience of the mainstream" (126). This is surely a mark of power and success but also of incorporation. How excorporated can hip-hop be today when you can buy it at Wal-Mart?

Clothing, as noted, can be part of this cycle of excorporation and incorporation. Barnard argues that jeans have been used as a way to step out of class distinctions, refuse a disempowered status, and mark marginalized identities (133–34). On the other hand, "However, almost at the same time as they were becoming a sign of opposition to class identities and positions, jeans were starting to be appropriated or incorporated by the system that they were being used to criticize" (135). We might think here of old, frayed, ripped jeans worn in defiance of boardroom expectations by the poor who would never make it to the boardroom anyway—and then that one may purchase, for quite a high price, new, frayed, ripped jeans at local malls. Barnard also notes a similar cycle for unlaced sneakers and sagging pants (140). These were once the fate of those who had been jailed. Laces and belts were confiscated so they could not be used as weapons. Of course, the young, the poor, the urban, and the non-White person might see no belts and no laces as signs of unfairly high rates of incarceration. Appropriating those signs of oppression and turning them, sagging and unlaced sneakers began their fashion life on the streets as an excorporated defiance of a system that unfairly jailed African Americans, Latinos, the young, and the poor. Now, of course, such styles are all the rage, and enormous pants or sneakers designed to have the laces removed may be found in any suburban mall. This latter example brings us to Kitwana's point that African American culture has often been implicated in the excorporation-incorporation cycle. He refers to highly visible mainstream African American culture and to local street cultures: "The commercialized element of this cultural movement and the off-the-radar one fuel each other. The underground element provides a steady stream of emerging talent that in turn gets absorbed into commercialization" (200). Zukin refers to the commodification of racially marked commodities in the city: "Ethnicity is both promoted and reviled in neighborhood shopping streets, which can equally become symbolic centers of solidarity or resistance" (89). One may think here of street styles that defiantly excorporate mainstream signs, played out on sidewalks in front of shops that are selling (incorporating) last year's defiant style to the tourists. One may think of shopping streets that are either stigmatized or celebrated as where Latinos or Asians go to shop.

Camp style often involves the cycle of excorporation and incorporation. Camp has often been understood as an instrument of political struggle against an often-oppressive establishment. Matias Viegener describes "gay punk fanzines":

> These publications promote a kind of festive combat: they employ style to decenter a totalizing cultural hegemony. Style in this formulation involves a reterritorialization, a vocabulary stolen from the master, which functions to rehearse and sarcastically resolve cultural contradictions. On the one hand, style generates a mark of difference, a code visible only to the initiated. On the other, it signals a certain refusal. (238)

David Bergman argues that camp can only work in the context of a privileged structure of empowerment (12). Camp then excorporates signs of disempowerment from those structures and turns them to the advantage of gay and lesbian communities (Ross 58). Camp's turning of a wide range of signs is read as poor taste, yet it celebrates such interpretations. As Andrew Ross explains of camp, schlock, and kitsch, "What is important is their persistently subordinate relation to the dominant culture, by which they are defined as examples of 'failed taste'" (62).

The process of excorporation and incorporation is an ancient one. Think of various ethnic slurs that were excorporated and turned and if done so successfully, then incorporated back into mainstream culture—think of the journey that the term *nigger* has made from offensive slur to, in the form of *nigga*, a term of solidarity and kinship, which one now finds incorporated through commodification in nearly every hip-hop tune one hears. The term *queer* has likewise seen a journey from insult to a "turned" celebration of difference—and now it is becoming completely incorporated back into respectability as learned and reverend dons publish academic journals and put on conferences of Queer Studies. Of course, style runs throughout the whole cycle, as the excorporated sign is made a part of the style of the marginalized group, and mainstream stylization of the sign as a commodity is a sure sign of its reincorporation.

Other styles cycle in and out of excorporation and incorporation. Leland comments, "Hip . . . shuttles ideas and language between the criminal underworld and aboveground society. It translates crime as an aesthetic" (224), largely through continually turning mainstream signs to its own purpose and then putting that appropriation on sale at the mall. Another example of such excorporation is given by Marcel Danesi: "punk" culture seized upon spiked dog collars as an instrument of oppression given that the spikes were originally worn pointing inward, to cause pain should a dog resist the lead. The punks literally turned the collars inside out, the spikes protruding, and wore them as an excorporated style of accessory (47). The other side of the cycle then is "the process of incorporation or containment" as described by Fiske above (*Understanding* 15). Before long, spiked dog collars were on sale in young-misses sections of department stores.

Some signs may refuse incorporation, signs that stutter back and forth in incomplete cycles of excorporation and incorporation. To some extent, the word *nigger* has this characteristic. It can be excorporated only as the already turned word *nigga*. The original term continues to be such a sign of oppression, it continues to carry so much damaging meaning that it cannot be fully turned in excorporation nor completely incorporated (as in hip-hop lyrics). Les Back, Michael Keith, and John Solomos argue that graffiti as such cannot be fully incorporated after its subversive creation: "All graffiti are narrative in that they attempt to tell alternative stories about places.

These stories, at their most basic, signal the failure of the public sphere to incorporate them" (98).

The last part of this chapter explores in more depth the summary conclusion that for many people, style is the terrain on which politics is conducted today. Political discourse today is less and less the sending of primarily verbal messages to targeted audiences and is more and more a matter of stylistic performance. In this way, we say who we are, what roles or offices we are fit for, with whom we align, and with whom we do not. To understand why candidates get elected, why bills are passed, and how power is struggled over, we will increasingly need to examine style as political.

The state of discourse in politics today is explained in a quotation from an analysis by Peter M. Kellett and H. L. Goodall Jr.

> A modernist view of communication supports a view of power that is derived from a perceived unity of social and political manifestations in modern philosophy, commodity capitalism, and scientifically driven technologies. Such a view of power privileges a "sovereign rational subject" who is conceived of as an autonomous, disembodied, individualistic Self. . . . [But] modernist standards of public speaking, argumentation, discussion, and debate also promote elite forms of discourse; only the most well-educated, argumentatively trained, and eloquent members of a community . . . are entitled to practice it. (159)

The alleged democratic nature of deliberative public speaking is and for a long time has been a bill of goods sold to the academy. The ability to get up and give a speech, thumb hooked in the vest pocket (or to design a political advertisement or to write a cogent letter) has never been an ability nor an opportunity vouchsafed everyone within a given democracy. Women and foreigners could not speak in democratic Athens. Daniel Webster, John Caldwell Calhoun, and Henry Clay debated gloriously while African slaves were silenced in that forum. That highly verbal and disputatious academics celebrate this kind of discourse as the epitome of political communication is no wonder, but it is self-serving. Today, people are less interested in and less skilled at that kind of discourse than ever. People do politics but in different ways. They do it through style. As Matias Viegener concludes from studying punk style, "its extreme stylization tells us that politics is intimately laced with both aesthetics and everyday life" (241). And the politics of cultural struggle is likewise carried out in popular culture, for as Hall argues, "the struggle over cultural hegemony . . . is these days waged as much in popular culture as anywhere else" ("What" 287).

A key instrument of the political power of popular culture and of style lies in the centrality of signs, images, and, above all, in meaning, for control over meaning is control over politics. Raiford Guins and Omayra Zaragoza Cruz make this point: "Most profoundly, however, the intellectual shifts that pressed toward a reckoning of the popular have sought to understand how it is a site of struggle where the ability to create meaning is recognized as a significant form of power" (9). This political power from image, meaning, and sign is also noticed by Hall: "It is only through the way in which we represent and imagine ourselves that we come to know how we are constituted and who we are. There is no escape from the politics of representations" ("What" 291).

It is not conventional government and its patterns of communication that are politically powerful today, Bauman argues, but rather the "life strategies" that are enacted in everyday life, and that would surely include style. He claims, "The context in which moral attitudes are forged (or not) is today that of life-politics, rather than social and system structures; that, in other words, the postmodern life strategies, rather than the bureaucratic mode of management of social processes and coordinating action, are the most consequential among the factors shaping the moral situation of postmodern men and women" (33). Vivian likewise argues that new politics today encourage increased interaction with others based on changing, local models rather than a single "constitutional" model, and those changing, local models are often based on style (233).

As one example of where the politicization of everyday life has gone hand in hand with the stylization of everyday life, Mort contends that style became a site of political action in Britain beginning in the late 1980s, where "style was projected as the site of a protracted struggle over new forms of politics" (25). Style, especially through images, can be subversive and resistant, a way of refusing unequal distributions of power. Stuart Ewen and Elizabeth Ewen note, "In a society predicated on the marketing of images, images become a weapon of resistance," and the authors point to life-styles specifically designed to scandalize respectable power (182). Clothing is one such site of resistance, for they contend that "today there is no fashion: there are only fashions. The diversity of revolt has been translated into a diversity of markets" (186). Note the implication that it is precisely the political function of fashion that has caused its diversification. Of course, fashion may also be imposed on people as a way to demand conformity. Thus, "today's fashions offer the weapons of resistance and compliance in one, ready to wear" (187).

There are repeated references to commercialization above and below in examples of the merger of style with politics. Of course, commodification is key to style, and Nixon likewise observes the same political impact of struggles carried out through style.

[C]ommercially produced goods and services have the capacity to intervene in and shape particular lived cultures through their capacity to mould subjective identities and shape social habits and routines. Commercial enterprises—be they advertising agencies or retailers—can be thought of in this sense as articulating cultural projects or missions every bit as transformative in their ambitions towards specific populations as those pursued by social reformers and policy-makers. (35–36)

People who acknowledge the political power of popular culture, and especially its central feature of style, will agree with Leland that "an integrated pop culture today, in other words, tokens economic and political change tomorrow" (79). Several examples of the effectiveness of the politics of popular culture and, hence, of style may be examined. Jack Babuscio argues of camp style that "camp can be subversive—a means of illustrating those cultural ambiguities and contradictions that oppress us all" (28). On a related note, Doty argues for the widely liberating consequences of spreading queerness through the culture, for "when cultural texts encourage straight-identified audience members to express a less-censored range of queer desire and pleasure than is possible in daily life, this 'regression' has positive gender-and-sexuality-destabilizing effects" (4).

Watkins claims a great deal of political impact for hip-hop, which, as noted already, is highly implicated with style: "The intersection between hip hop and politics has empowered a generation of youth to believe that they not only have a right but maybe even an obligation to make a difference in the world" (164). That political action was embodied explicitly in style as expressed by young political activists, for "when they did address city and state officials, they did so in the style, vernacular, and character of hip hop" (182). Watkins offers the example of Detroit Mayor Kwame Kilpatrick, who "was touted as American's hip-hop mayor," and one may think of Russell Simmons's activism and the Rock the Vote campaign in the election of 2004 at least. Watkins is also cognizant of the negative political impact of some hip-hop, for "the woman-hating inclinations in corporate hip hop have become so common, they appear ordinary" (211).

Goldberg argues that sports fandom, which is certainly connected to style in terms of dress, decoration, language, and entertainment commitments, has come to replace traditional patriotism for many: "Supporting one's team today has taken the place of what it was once like supporting one's country, right or wrong" (34). Back, Keith, and Solomos argue that graffiti and other transgressive treatments of space can be a form of making political demands: "The appropriation of city spaces as alternative 'spaces of representation' was as much a part of the populism as the aesthetic of graffiti art itself" (75).

Another form of political struggle through style that will be familiar to many has to do with the political implications of cosmetics, dress, and adornment, especially for women. Lesa Lockford argues,

> The elusive ideal . . . requires massive expenditures on cosmetics, adornments, and—in extreme cases—surgery, as well as rigorous exercise and diet. [On the other hand] . . . a woman can raise her consciousness and stand against the dominant culture's tyranny by refusing to perform traditional femininity. This is precisely what many feminists have done when they choose, for example, not to wear makeup, feminine dresses, or high heels or to enact other traditionally feminine behavior. (7)

Women's issues are also addressed politically through style on other fronts. Lockford notes that "the discourse on inappropriate body size is often accompanied by the taken-for-granted assumption that the body is unruly and in need of disciplining and that we are helpless to control it on our own" (30). Representation of women in general is a political terrain, not least because such representations present and encourage certain styles. Lockford argues that "gender ideology is defined and perpetuated by commercially generated images of women" (31) in advertisements for products that will go to makeup style, and, therefore, which styles have what effects on women will be a site of contestation.

On the other hand, forms of traditional politics are increasingly moving in the direction of popular culture, turning more into style and less into traditional modes of deliberation, as witnessed by the de rigueur appearance of presidential hopefuls on evening comedy-skit shows and late-night talk shows during campaigns. Or as Baudrillard argues for other forms of politics, "Now tests and referenda are, we know, perfect forms of simulation: the answer is called forth by the question, it is design-ated in advanced. *The referendum is always an ultimatum*: the unilateral nature of the question, that is no longer exactly an interrogation" (*Simulations* 117). Political referenda, and we may say elections as well, are increasingly becoming forms of entertainment as much as or more than political deliberation. Baudrillard addresses another political phenomenon, opinion polls: "The political sphere entirely loses its specificity when it enters into the game of the media and public opinion polls, that is to say into the sphere of the integrated circuit of question/answer" (*Simulations* 124). Traditional politics loses its specificity because it merges with popular culture. At this writing, evening "news" shows on television are full of call-in "surveys" in which one may "vote" for one opinion or another, already given to the caller, and for many that is what voting has become. This puts people in the position described, again by Baudrillard: "It is no longer necessary that anyone *produce* an opinion, all that is needed is that all *reproduce* public opinion" (*Simulations* 126). If there is any truth to Baudrillard's claim that "power, too, for some time now produces nothing but signs of its resemblance. And at the same time, another figure of power comes into play: that of a collective demand for signs of power," then we should note how much like style is his description of politics, with its reduction to signs (*Simulations* 45).

Baudrillard certainly takes extreme positions whenever he writes, but others have also noted the shift of traditional politics into popular culture and style. Seabrook refers to "presidential politics . . . where the job is not so much to lead as to entertain and divert" (5–6), which is done, of course, through style. Zukin refers to urban politics and argues that control over image is a major goal of such struggles: "To ask 'whose city?' suggests more than a politics of occupation; it also asks who has a right to inhabit the dominant image of the city" (81). Image is struggled over because it expresses rules and power, as Zukin argues: "Visual artifacts of material culture and political economy thus reinforce—or comment on—social structure. By making social rules legible, they re-present the city" (81). Even if one argues that significant power exists beyond the image, the image will nevertheless be a site of political struggle as a representative of such power. Zukin refers to the style of imposing buildings: "Thus the symbolic economy of cultural meanings and representations implies real economic power" (82).

Vivian argues that "the form and function of a particular style of politics cannot be apprehended without surveying the communicative or symbolic modes by virtue of which it is engendered and disseminated" (233). The same may be said for the apprehension of a politics of style. We now need a way to understand how style works rhetorically as a ground of politics, a theory to explain how style persuades, and a method to guide the critical analysis of texts of style. This is the task of the next chapter: to organize a rhetoric, a scheme of the kinds of "communicative or symbolic modes" in which style today undergirds our persuasive relationships with one another.

# 4

# A Rhetoric of Style for the Twenty-first Century

> Style in oratory must not be identified with life-style; the for-
> mer is merely an adjunct of the latter.
> —Quentin Crisp, *How to Have a Life-Style*, 103

Style is central to everyday life, identity, social organization, and the politics of the twenty-first century. The previous chapter examined important components and linkages to style such as aesthetics, commodification, systematicity and language, and image. This chapter proposes a rhetoric of style.

By *a rhetoric*, people usually mean one or more of three nonexclusive ideas. A rhetoric can be a handbook or guide for *practice*. One might consult such a rhetoric to find out how to engage in persuasive or influential practices. Bookstore shelves are full of such rhetorics, offering the public advice on how to give speeches, construct business presentations, and so forth. The purpose of a rhetoric of practice is improved *performance*. Second, a rhetoric can be a *theory* of how persuasion works, a systematic statement of the ways in which influence operates in particular circumstances. Clearly, a rhetorical theory can be closely interconnected with a guide to rhetorical practice, and in principle, a theory is always adaptable to practice even when the theory does not offer practical advice for implementation of principles. The purpose of a rhetorical theory is improved *systematic understanding* of how rhetoric in general works in the world. Third, a rhetoric can be a *critical method* of analysis. Techniques of noticing are systematically explained so that the reader may be empowered to see the workings of rhetoric in new ways. The purpose of a rhetorical critical method is improved *focused understanding*, or *appreciation*, of particular rhetorical events or of more importance, *types* of such events. Of course, a method for observing how rhetoric works easily turns into a theory or a handbook for practice or a guide for critique, so these three senses are not exclusive.

This chapter deals with the second and third sort of rhetoric attempts to explain the major structural components of a rhetoric of style and how those components work to produce influence—and—explain how to look for those mechanisms of influence in the media and in everyday life. Most rhetorics warn the reader against using them in too linear a way, and this is no exception. One needs perforce to begin with one point and follow it with another, but that structural requirement of writing should not be taken as the logical sequence by which one would either think about or analyze real examples of the rhetoric of style. The process of understanding and critiquing any sort of rhetoric is as complex as is the doing of rhetoric, so a rhetoric should be sensitive to that complexity, and readers of rhetorics should avoid assuming that the linearity of writing implies a linearity of process. The theoretical elements covered here often doubleback on each other, an earlier point assuming the existence or influence of a later point, and vice versa. Let me also say that this rhetoric of style is not meant to deny the validity of other rhetorics. The rhetoric of style is increasingly important in our world. But if someone has in view a rhetorical practice that is not subsumable within this rhetoric, a practice that seems better informed by other rhetorics (e.g., Aristotelian, Burkean), then such a person should use another rhetoric for practice, understanding, and critique.

To begin, then: There are five structural components to a rhetoric of style: primacy of the text, imaginary communities, market contexts, aesthetic rationales, and stylistic homologies. Each component has a substructure with clear connections to other components. Let us leap into the fray with a discussion of the first component.

## Primacy of the Text

Elsewhere, I have defined a text in this way: "*A text is a set of signs related to each other insofar as their meanings all contribute to the same set of effects or functions*" (*Rhetoric* 34). The text may be understood as the principal component of the rhetoric of style, as it is of the rhetoric of popular culture. We live in a world of texts, of signs, and of images. Texts are the ground of much of interaction as physical proximity fades in importance as a medium of connection to others. Texts are increasingly the focal point of the public sphere, so much so that John Hartley observes "how pervasive the textualisation of public life has become" (*Politics* 2). Increasingly, we socialize, shop, gather information, and engage in many of life's functions through texts online, on television, and even when encountering strangers in public places. At this writing, young people interact with each other by collecting friends on MySpace or Facebook when they are not text-messaging each other furiously. Younger people construct virtual igloos and invite their online friends to come over and socialize on www.clubpenguin.com. Older people play poker, discuss motorcycles, fight the Civil War, and read each other's blogs on a multitude of Internet sites. In most of these circumstances, the text is the main thing or the only thing we have that mediates among us.

In traditional rhetorics, texts respond to preexisting real circumstances (Bitzer). Without denying the real or a construct thereof, I claim that for most people today, many preexisting circumstances are in reality in the form of a preexisting text. This is because the exigencies that draw rhetorical responses, especially in public rhetoric, are increasingly represented in texts rather than experienced directly. Texts are generated by most people not in response to a real war in one's backyard (for the United States, Europe, Japan, and so forth, and, of course, this may change) but in response to texts of a war—in response to a widely circulating text that a political figure or candidate produced—or in response to mediated texts of war but usually not in response to some immediately and directly experienced reality connected to that war, figure, or candidate.

Texts are primary sites for the construction of identity and social affiliation. In a performative world of unstable communities and identities, people create texts to say who they are and to call out to others. Identity and social allegiance merge with texts, which is not to say they become only texts but that all the real stuff of class, race, gender, sexuality, and so forth becomes continuous with texts. Texts become the port by which those real dimensions of life are accessed. And it is by going to shared texts, such as, film, television, and the Internet, that people find common ground. As I will show, texts are thus the grounding for imaginary communities.

Texts are complex and polysemous, both discrete and diffuse. They are nodal: what one experiences here and now is a text, but it may well be part of a larger text extending into time and space. Texts tend to grow nodes off themselves that develop into larger, more complex but related texts. The texts we present to others by which they read us are likely to extend in time and space and to be part of larger social and political texts in which one personally does not appear. A critic's choice of what to call a text is always therefore strategic rather than materially given. This is especially true of a rhetoric of style, which is a continuous series of nodal displays and readings scattered throughout everyday life and media and linked to other nodes of texts created by other people and groups.

If texts are primary, then values, motivations, allegiances, identities, communities, and intentions can be read off a text. That is true largely in a culture of textuality, but that is the culture we have. Texts facilitate the creation of different meanings, values, motivations, allegiances, identities, communities, and intentions in people but not simply or unidimensionally. The critic reading a text proposes meanings, values, motivations, and the like that the text facilitates and—this is quite important—uses methods to keep the critic "honest," to show that a given reading is not idiosyncratic or fanciful but is based on a redundancy, multiplicity, and convergence of signs within the text that can be shown to facilitate the reading. In other words, if a critic identifies a given style as conservative, the critic must show many—the more the better—signs that mean "conservative" in the style and that will be understood to be readily readable in that way by the critic's own audience. The critic does not assume that such a reading exhausts the text, especially in its nodal nature as it chains out into experience. But the more the reading can be shown to obtain as the text chains out, the more valid is the reading off the text.

A rhetoric of style is primarily textual, because style is the text we all wear on our backs like a shell. Style is explicitly designed to be a text to be read and noticed by others. A population, a world, trained to notice style in others is one trained to notice texts. A world based on image, on floating signs, is one based primarily in texts. Certainly, a simulational world is primarily textual, as lack of direct referentiality and a closed loop of textuality are key to simulation. A world of performative rhetoric is primarily textual. The act performed is key with the potential to create the identity of the one performing it.

Another way to get at the primacy of the text in a rhetoric of style is to look at attention and effort. Today, people pay attention to the styles they project in their person, at home, and in public. Style is crafted and strategic even if it is crafted out of awareness—it is not accidental or happenstance. The aestheticization of everyday life is an engrossment in style and thus also in the texts of personal appearance, home décor, and so forth. Likewise, people are aware of the styles of others, reading off those styles socially useful information about class, sexuality, and so forth. If style is a preoccupation with people today, then it is a textual preoccupation as people are concerned with signs that are available to be read in public.

## Imaginary Communities

In traditional rhetoric, the audience is material and real. It is a specific group of people, perhaps locally concentrated or perhaps widely dispersed. The traditional audience may not be personally known to the rhetor, but its existence is assumed to occur prior to the appearance of rhetorical texts, and some characteristics are known in advance —otherwise traditional rhetoric could scarcely proceed.

But in the rhetoric of popular culture today and especially in the rhetoric of style, the audience is not as strong a precondition for rhetoric. Indeed, very often, the audience is an effect of rhetoric, it is a consequence of presenting a text. An audience may even be a sign of success. This is especially true in circumstances of new technology, for, Hartley observes, "A technology cannot call a public into *action* before that public has been called into *being*, and the establishment of a community of readers around a new communicative technology takes time" ("Frequencies" 9). If one puts up a Web site, for instance, it is unlikely that thousands of people are waiting at their computers for that text, saying to themselves, "When, O when, will Gertrude put up that Web site?" Gertrude puts up the Web site and then an audience forms, and the number of hits or visits to the Web site becomes a measure of the success of the site. The rhetoric of style likewise creates its own audience in that sense that people notice and attribute meanings to displayed styles. The public displays of styles are like magnets moving through the world, attracting whoever resonates with the style, attracting those whose own styles seem consonant with the one displayed.

It is in the connection to imaginary communities that the political dimensions of a rhetoric of style may be seen. John Fiske argues, "The politics of a cultural form lie in its social mobilizations rather than in its formal qualities" (*Understanding* 165), perhaps another way of saying politics is as politics does. How does a rhetoric of style do both political and personal work in the social mobilization that is an imaginary community?

Texts connect with imaginary communities in stylistic rhetoric. I mean imaginary in two ways. First, the community that is connected to the text (as audience, as reference point, as producers of the text, and so forth) is nearly always manifested through texts, and in that sense, the community must be imaged or imagined. Even a material flesh-and-blood audience must usually be imagined, encoded in image and sign, before it can be a party to rhetoric. In courts of law, parties must be represented: plaintiff and respondent, state and accused. Even if one acts as one's own attorney, one represents oneself. In a sense, people's interactions with others are the same, especially in a rhetoric of style. This is in part because, as noted earlier, our world is becoming primarily textual, and we engage audiences, communities, and groups by engaging their representations or signs. If the president goes on television to rail against the Afghans, for most Americans the Afghans are imaginary. That is not to say that they don't exist, but they must be materialized in sign and image—we must imagine them for them to be party to that rhetoric. Most people rarely encounter material Afghans in the flesh. Hartley observes, "It is the public that turns out to be a fabrication, while talking pictures are, in this respect, the only reality there is" (*Politics* 33). But the president is imaginary also, for most people encounter him only as an image, and his staff and handlers are likely to be hard at work presenting him in texts as a very particular kind of image. However, even if we encounter a flesh-and-blood, material president, we encounter a representation of a complex of realities, as are we in our own complexities.

Hartley notes the inherently imaginary, representational nature of democracy today among dispersed citizens: "Democracy is conducted through representations circulated in public even though no public (no *demos*) assembles in one place to constitute and govern itself. The process of abstracting and representing politics has gone so far that the public itself is now circulated as a representation, in the form of public opinion, which is an industrially produced fictionalization of citizenship" (*Politics* 36). Note that for Hartley, the imaginary nature of democracy stems from the primarily textual nature of citizens as representations.

A reciprocal implication of this first sense of the imaginary is that the person creating a text or a node of a text is imaginary also. This first sense of the imaginary is seen clearly in the rhetoric of style. By imagining who we are and who are the others to whom we want to speak through style, we construct the schemes of signs and images that present a representation of ourselves to others as we have image-ined them. And as audience members we are called to in terms of subject positions that we can or cannot assume so as to align or not with the images of others. Style is the medium in which this socially charged process of imagination takes place, and thus we construct, call to, and respond to imaginary communities.

A second sense of imaginary here is the idea that rhetoric calls into being audiences, publics, and communities. Bradford Vivian argues for the constructedness of all parties to discourse: "In a postmodern *épistémé*, the self is not so much an autonomous agent who exists prior to the influence of social and political relations as it is an embodiment of certain capacities for agency formed at their intersection" (234). People with, for instance, deep, conservative religious and political convictions are not all waiting in a room someplace for someone to come address them. There are indeed real people with such convictions, but for the most part, they are scattered, diffused through a social fabric that is colloidal, composed of similar vast diffusions of demography, ideology, and so forth. Even as diffused, such a collation may not think of itself as a community prior to being called that by a text. Hartley observes, correctly, "It is no longer certain what the public is, or where to find it" ("Frequencies" 9). The president in an election year begins ending all his speeches, interviews, and press conferences with requests that people pray for the United States of America. The president has then imagined what a public would be that is friendly to his party's election chances and has called them into being. People who are shot throughout the social fabric cohere around that text and become a public. The same may be said of appeals to immigration reform, gun control, or any issue one may think of: while individual bodies are material, publics, audiences, and communities are today largely imagined and called forth through imaging and signing. Their coherence is imaginary and symbolic as publics, audiences, and communities.

Dick Hebdige imagines the rise of subcultures in this way, called forth discursively as a rhetorical response, "each subculture representing a distinctive 'moment'—a particular response to a particular set of circumstances" (84). David Theo Goldberg gives an example of a radio audience called into existence by a text: "Sports radio fashions a clientele, filling the unconscious with desires less and less of its own making. It molds subjects as seekers of spectatorial excitement, instant gratification, consumers of newly fashioned and packaged merchandise" (38). Note the power and range of influence attributed to the texts of sports radio in creating and "filling" such an audience.

The concept of subject positions, reviewed earlier, is one way to understand how individuals and communities alike are constructed in relationship to texts. James Donald stresses the political implications of that taking of a position in the imaginary: "The citizen is always becoming-a-subject. . . . Taking up a position within the symbolic, because it is to occupy a necessarily empty position which makes it possible to articulate a need as desire, always entails a sense of loss. It produces a sense of subjectivity as lack that motivates the compulsion to heal the wound of modern culture" (179). If the citizen is becoming, then the citizen is constructed. Simon Frith argues that imaginary forms constrain but also free the construction of individual identities: "But if identity is always somehow constrained by imaginative forms, it is also freed by them: the personal is the cultural" (122). It is in imaginative forms that we assume but also change our being, and that has the potential to be liberating.

Calling an imaginary community into being need not imply intentionality, nor need it imply a clear starting point. An imaginary community coheres around a text, the textual being primary, and does so without the conscious intention of anyone for that to happen. The coherence may not have occurred within memory nor even all at once. One may think of imaginary communities that cohere around "cult classic" films, musical groups, or television shows. Individuals may do particular things to perpetuate such communities, but their initial inception need not have been intentional, nor need it be clear when such a thing occurred. This is especially true when texts are nodal, chaining out in time and space rather than happening discretely. One may think of the cult status of *The Rocky Horror Picture Show* or *The Big Lebowski*, each of which has communities of fans with distinct rituals, but it would be hard to say that those communities were specifically planned at a particular moment, even if ongoing efforts (nodal texts of festivals, revivals, and so forth) keep the communities cohering around the texts. Judith Butler notes that imaginary communities called into being around texts or textual practices can also dissolve as such "dialogic structures" dissolve: "Moreover, when agreed-upon identities or agreed-upon dialogic structures, through which already established identities are communicated, no longer constitute the theme or subject of politics, then identities can come into being and dissolve on the concrete practices that constitute them" (*Gender* 21–22).

It is around texts of style that many communities cohere today. A stylistic performance or text appears, and around it communities form. Exciting communities perpetuate themselves by propagating texts of style that ground the communities. Such communities may or may not have been imagined previously by those performing the styles, but the communities are imaged and image-ined into existence through the performance of the style. Sometimes, kinds of stylistic performance and imaginary communities have been congealed together for so long it is difficult to trace what came first, so a model of evolving texts at the core of imaginary communities that evolve in response may be most appropriate. It is the connection between style and individual and social identity that makes a rhetoric of style so cohesive for imagined communities.

Imaginary communities can be quite powerful. The engrossing online simulation *Second Life*, Chicago Bears fans, and Episcopalians are but a few examples of imaginary communities with great power over members. The communities are pulled together by texts, especially texts of the rhetoric of style, but then the texts created in the name of the imaginary community have great cohesive power. They exert a strong pull to display style of one sort or another. This is one reason why people of stigmatized groups display risky styles, for to imagine a community of which one is a part is to acknowledge and to feel the symbolic demands of that community, regardless of cost. This is true for everyone, not just the stigmatized, for if the stigmatized are called to display a style that may give them trouble, it is equally true that the nonstigmatized are strongly called to display signs that are hegemonically consonant with their imaginary communities. One implication of this power is that an imaginary community can be controlling and dogmatic, constraining and limiting the subjects and identities that form in alignment with them—but largely if such a community is not understood to be, in fact, imaginary by those enrolled in it.

Imaginary communities can also be (although they need not be) extremely democratic, and nowhere is this better seen than in the communities that appear and disappear on the Internet. Called together entirely around online texts, such communities are entirely discursive, held together by the imaginations of those involved. John Leland notes, "The Net . . . is an operating system that does not need alphas. It defeats authority. Its consensuses are micro—*within* subgroups rather than *between* them" (337). Hartley argues that today's popular media generally are the site where publics are created: "Television, popular newspapers, magazines and photography, the popular media of the modern period, are the public domain, the place where and the means by which the public is created and has its being" (*Politics* 1). If this is true, then we should expect from the constantly evolving nature of those media and the every-half-hour churning of programming that the imaginary communities created there would be especially transient. A highly and obviously changeable, imagine-able, and transient community is inherently less likely to be the basis for entrenched dogma and control.

## Market Contexts

Rhetoric today takes place largely in market contexts, and the rhetoric of style is ideally suited to help us understand that. Bakari Kitwana observes that "we live in an age where corporate mergers, particularly in media and entertainment, have redefined public space. Within this largely expanded public space, the viewing public is constantly bombarded by visual images that have become central to the identity of an entire generation" (9). Note that public space and the public are generally thought of as elements of rhetoric, yet Kitwana places them within the market. Market contexts especially help us to understand the rhetoric of style. Signs of rhetorical importance today include words but go far beyond words to include other symbolic systems, such as, goods. Goods have the meaning they do for people in a global economy largely because those goods are also commodities, having entered a market system. And if those goods have meanings not originally derived from markets, the meanings nevertheless enter the market merged with goods, that is to say, the market incorporates them.

Increasingly, commercial rhetoric is the rhetoric of politics, social interaction, and religion. Sean Nixon argues, "Advertising and the wider commercial field have acquired a new centrality and salience to economic and cultural life in the last decade and a half or so. Certainly, developments within the commercial domain have been central to recent accounts of social and cultural change" (3). Jean Baudrillard sees this merger as developing over a long period: "All through the 19th and 20th centuries political and economic practice merge increasingly into the same type of discourse. Propaganda and advertising fuse in the same marketing and merchandising of objects and ideologies" (*Simulations* 125). Featherstone thinks of shoppers as audiences, the latter usually a rhetorical term: "Shopping is rarely a purely calculative rational economic transaction to maximize utility, but is primarily a leisure-time activity in which people become audiences" (103). Notice his reference to pleasure, or the entertainment value of the market. Hartley likewise notes a collapse and conflation of entities, such as, publics, consumers, and audiences, who are normally kept distinct: "People are simultaneously addressed as publics and audiences, citizens and consumers, and the media of democracy have expanded into areas previously thought of as belonging to the private sphere and to commercial entertainment" ("Frequencies" 9). He sees politics "expanding" into commerce, but one might as well call that entering into the contexts of commerce. Lisa Lowe and David Lloyd argue similarly that nowadays "politics, culture, and the economic form an inseparable dynamic" (130). And Jon Stratton sees the whole cultural field becoming commercialized: "The realm of ideas and fantasy has now been commodified and integrated into a totalizing capitalist system which is driven by consumption" (15). Note that his reference to "ideas and fantasy" invokes the imaginary and asks us to think of imaginary communities as thriving within market contexts.

The market context is the frozen floor of meanings upon which rhetoric dances today. It is largely impervious to rhetorical means to change it. An important reason for this conflation of consumers and citizens is a shift in power from the state to the corporation. As Paul A. Cantor notes, "In the face of global economic forces, individual nation-states are increasingly compelled to allow markets to dictate their policies rather than dictating policies to markets" (197). The novels of William Gibson depict such a world in the near future, when the state is practically a branch office of global corporations. The market context seals off its base of power in late capitalism. Rhetorical attacks on the market will be turned into pleasurable commodities, slogans on shirts, action-adventure movies, entertainment, or items one can buy that carry a pleasurable little frisson of naughtiness from the time past when those signs were used to storm the gates. This may be cause for despair, but late capitalism has figured out how to seal its roots from being dug up, and that's the way it is.

Rhetoric, including political rhetoric, is now largely carried out in these market contexts, or, as Hartley observed, "Citizen-formation is now undertaken by chain stores" ("Frequencies" 9). He implies that as President George W. Bush reminded the nation after 9/11, it is a civic duty to shop. But a market context need not be entirely reactionary. George Ritzer likewise discusses different models of being a consumer, including the "victim" and the "rebel," and concludes with "consumer as citizen," which is actually a socially conscious, progressive stance toward politics carried out in market terms, such as, purchasing green products and so forth (65–66). Similarly, Stuart Ewen refers to "the new *consumer democracy*, which was propelled by the mass production and marketing of stylish goods . . . founded on the idea that symbols and prerogatives of elites could now be made available on a mass scale" (32). This implies that a style that democratizes previously elite goods can be progressive.

Michel de Certeau reminds us that a market context can supply people with the means to create small triumphs of appropriation in everyday life, and so the study of the rhetoric of style within market contexts should consider such appropriations: "These ways of reappropriating the product-system, ways created by consumers, have as their goal a therapeutics for deteriorating social relations, and make use of techniques of re-employment in which we can recognize the procedures of everyday practices" (xxiv). Such techniques would include the cycles of excorporation and incorporation within the market context that were presented earlier. A refusal of empowered interests can be expressed in the uses one makes of everyday goods in the construction of style.

If a person or a community is involved in the global network of markets that is late capitalism, then the market serves as a superordinate rhetorical context. The market is a mechanism for spreading sign systems and their meanings internationally. For that reason, a rhetorical system that makes use of the market is relatively international and stands a good chance of being understood more widely than do other rhetorical systems. Such a system is the rhetoric of style. African presidents wearing Western suits—American hipsters wearing restyled Mao jackets—African Americans wearing African clothing—Moscow teenagers wearing football, soccer, and rugby jerseys from overseas—all these people are speaking the language of a rhetoric of style that the market makes certain that people around the world understand. To be sure, local cultural differences bend these meanings but not so much that a core of shared meanings does not remain.

A global system of style is a global system of rhetoric. Pierre Bourdieu argues that globally, cultural systems are merging with markets: "The autonomy of the worlds of cultural production with respect to the market, which had grown steadily through the battles and sacrifices of writers, artists and scientists, is increasingly threatened" (37). "Cultural mass production" is now the epitome of globalization as music, films, and television are distributed around the Earth, and so the cultural and the commercial merge, he argues (77). Cantor agrees: "American globalization first and foremost takes the form of a globalization of culture" (25), and, of course, that means through the market.

The rhetoric of style is accessible to the critic who is likewise engaged in that global marketplace of style and its sign systems, as are nearly all of us. The critic is advised to be a student of popular culture so that he or she may learn from the marketplace—that is to say, from films, pop music, sporting events, and so forth—what the elements of style mean and how they call to imaginary communities. We may think of the market as selling texts, which in the rhetoric of style are then taken into one's own subjectivity and performed in connection with imaginary communities. Each individual's reenactment of one part of the rhetoric of style is the recreation of a node of a text that the market advertises widely—or the individual is appropriating and then turning the signs of such texts for political purposes in particular imaginary communities—and to the extent that such excorporation is successful, it will shortly be reincorporated back into the market.

## Aesthetic Rationales

Any rhetoric must answer the question of what it is that people encounter in texts that moves them. A rhetoric explains how it is that the stuff of texts connects to human thinking, motives, and being such that people are influenced. Such an explanation we might call a rationale for rhetoric, following Donald C. Bryant's definition of rhetoric as "the rationale of informative and suasory discourse" (14). Rhetorics in the past have identified appeals to human faculties and psychology (George Campbell) to reason, emotions, and personal appeal (Aristotle) to motives (Kenneth Burke)—the list is a long one. In each case, rhetorics present their distinctive rationales for how texts create their effects.

A rhetoric of style predominates in a world engrossed with aesthetics, and so an aesthetic rationale is such a rhetoric's chief explanation for effects. What counts as a good reason to decide or act varies from one age to another; in the current age, what counts as a good reason is often that which is aesthetic. Such a rationale need not exclude appeals to reason, motives, and so forth, but it holds that such appeals are likely to succeed or not more for their aesthetic values than for adherence to rules of logic, psychology, or other rationales. Reasons, motives, and so forth are *activated aesthetically* in a culture that is aesthetically dominated, as is ours. Looking back to the ideas of texts and the creation of imaginary communities, Vivian discusses the formation of group identities in terms of the aesthetic dimensions of the text, including texts of rhetorical style:

> The manner in which group identities cohere or disperse according to an aggregation of symbols, rituals, or other aesthetic phenomena . . . constitutes the rhetoric of postmodern style. . . . The dissemination of a particular style is manifested in the material relations, or the communal bonds of sentiment that it either establishes or disrupts. (238)

And, as he notes, those material relations are grounded largely in the aesthetics of the performed text, which is the rhetoric of style.

An aesthetic rationale is manifested, first, in the primacy of aesthetic forms of expression and aesthetic criteria for judgments and decision. Such a rationale is in contrast to the expositional discourse of traditional rhetoric, as described by Neil Postman. Vivian argues explicitly that this is the case for a rhetoric of style: "In this context, rhetoric encompasses something other than transparent or autonomous communication. It is an aesthetic (rather than conceptual) rhetoric; an affective (not rational) communication; a collective (instead of individual) expression" (237). This does not mean that "the beautiful always wins," although it does mean that in some cases. Robert D. Hariman, in studying political style, notes that "the greater problem here is . . . how modern societies have become unduly defenseless against aesthetic manipulation" (10), a defenselessness that Hariman, nevertheless, believes can ultimately be overcome through education and awareness. If the beautiful always wins, then we need to learn how to manipulate beauty, or the appearance of beauty, if that is not a redundancy. An aesthetic rationale is not attuned to issues of what is "true," although if anyone is so attuned, then that person is advised to make the truth look stylish—which is really not much better or worse, I think, than the advice to make the truth look rational (whether it is or not). Les Back, Michael Keith, and John Solomos note the political power of graffiti, an aesthetic form that may or may not be seen as beautiful, but certainly it is a form with its own rationale, for "graffiti writing invokes a technology of communication that is neither entirely logocentric nor merely symbolic, but instead creates a regime of communication that refigures the public sphere" (75). An aesthetic rationale might call for a somber, ugly, violent, or decayed textual aesthetic, depending on the effect being created. People accustomed to the rhetoric of style are well attuned to judgment based on the aesthetic impression they and others create.

Aesthetic rationales fit today with market contexts. Virginia Postrel refers to a design ideology, but she might just as well be talking about ideology in general or rhetorics in general: "If modernist design ideology promised efficiency, rationality, and truth, today's diverse aesthetics offers a different trifecta: freedom, beauty, and pleasure" (9). We should note that design aesthetics are usually for the purpose of selling, and so an aesthetic rationale fits with the market contexts of a rhetoric of style. Peter M. Kellett and H. L. Goodall Jr. also argue for a connection between market contexts and a relative shift away from expositional discourse: "Without warrantable argument as a discursive foundation for civil discourse, we move from being 'citizens' in a modern sense to 'consumers' in a postmodern one" (161). When we decide less on the basis of argument, then the remaining bases for appeal  aesthetics, style, feeling, and so forth—tend to be mechanisms of the market. Kitwana notes that the highly marketed aesthetic form of "rap music has given young Black males a primary avenue through which to access public space" (87), and, of course, it has done so through an aesthetic rationale embodied in the music.

An important dimension of an aesthetic rationale is pleasure, and here the aesthetic rationale also connects to the market contexts, for pleasure is likewise key to the rationale of hyperconsumption. Pleasure and aesthetics come to govern even public decisions, for as Zygmunt Bauman argues, "One may say that in popular perception the duty of the postmodern citizen . . . is to lead an enjoyable life. To treat subjects as citizens, the state is obliged to supply the facilities deemed necessary for such life" (34), which would surely include venues for shopping and for entertainment. We should note Postrel's observation that one of the first things that Afghan women did after the Taliban was overthrown was to buy multicolored burkas (ix–x), clearly an indication of the important connection between politics and pleasure.

An aesthetic rationale is manifested in narrative values, such as, narrative coherence, character development, conflict and resolution, and so forth (Fisher). Texts, to the extent that they tell a story, must tell a good one. People decide for or against propositions based on whether they are backed by a plausible narrative. Style tells stories about people, whether in terms of dress, décor, movement, or other element. A living room decorated in a Southwest rustic style tells a consistent story; it may or may not be a story one likes, but it has an effect. Someone going down the sidewalk wearing a ballerina tutu, a German helmet from World War II, and skates is not offering a consistent story, and that impression created through style will succeed or fail relative to that incoherence (depending on the effect desired).

The narratives of aesthetic rationales may be organized and searched for by the critic in familiar genres and forms of narrative patterns. Butler argues, for example, that *parody* is a political strategy for undermining gender categories (*Gender* 186), and parody is, of course, a well-established discursive form with its own narrative integrity. Today's electronic media contribute to a replacement of expositional forms with narrative forms, a very common form being *conflict*. Bourdieu argues that television is "always inclined to confuse a rational dialogue with a wrestling match" (22), and by wrestling match, I believe he means narrative forms of conflict, agonism, and struggle. We may think here of the extent to which so much coverage of political news is cast in terms of who is winning or losing rather than in terms of policy or utility.

An aesthetic rationale is manifested in quality of image, what is compelling or not, pleasing or shocking, attention-getting, and so forth. Much work has been done lately on the image, or the visual dimension of rhetoric and communication (including Jessica Evans and Stuart Hall, Cara A. Finnegan, Hariman and John Louis Lucaites). Specific rationales of how images persuade, therefore, abound, so no elaborate details need be given here. Clearly, the rhetoric of style is largely concerned with the visual and with the effects created by managing the image. Fiske gives the somewhat dated example of video arcades, of course, a highly visual entertainment, as a site where meaningful political work is done: "[V]ideo arcades are popular, particularly among subordinated males . . . because they can be used to think through, to rehearse in practice, the experiential gap between the masculine ideology of power and performance and the social experience of powerlessness" (*Understanding* 139). Playing in a video arcade can be (or was) part of youth life-styles. Hartley agrees that politics today is often carried out through a visual aesthetic rationale: "Pictures . . . are also the form in which democracy is diffused and disciplined" (*Politics* 3). He argues that images are both records and instruments of political struggles: "Pictures are objective traces of socio-semiotic struggles (conflict), allegiances (consensus), and ideologies (sense-making practices), right across the spectrum from big-deal public politics to intimate personal culture" (*Politics* 29). The aesthetic rationale of those games, then, can be a speculative instrument for thinking about power and, therefore, an adjunct of rhetoric.

Clearly, some are skeptical about the rhetorical and political efficacy of the aesthetic. Referring to the performative, which, of course, is often carried out on an aesthetic dimension, Henry A. Giroux argues that "the issue is still open regarding how the performative can have some purchase in terms of social action or contribute to producing new forms of identity and politics while simultaneously developing a political and ethical vocabulary for creating the conditions of possibility for a politics and pedagogy of economic, racial, and social justice" (193–94). Although there is not the space here to respond in detail to concerns that the aestheticization and stylization of rhetoric destroys politics, I do want to point to some analyses that suggest otherwise. Hartley argues that we need to attend to the frequency cycles of events and suggests that what seems to be a dissolution of the public sphere may be a change in frequencies: "For those who worry about the decline of public service media, the commercialization of the public sphere, and the evacuation of the public domain, perhaps the problem is one of frequency. People are responding to different speeds of public communication, but this doesn't necessarily mean the end of democracy. It's speeding up, not dumbing down" ("Frequencies" 10). The traditional cycles of campaigns, elections, social movements, and so forth, in other words, take time. Politics can be played out in quick flashes in the rhetoric of style, in aesthetics, and through today's quick-cycling communication media.

## Stylistic Homologies

A final structural component to the rhetoric of style is stylistic homologies. Noted earlier was that a homology is a formal resemblance across different texts, actions, objects, and other orders of experience. I also suggested earlier that what gives coherence to any given style is just such a homology. Our sense of "a style" is a sense of a formal link across texts, actions, objects, and orders of experience tying them together. A style may be thought of as a formal system of signification. Such systems are composed of the possibilities of meaning in a wide range of signs joined together by the possibilities for combination in a formal structure. Think of an Edwardian style in manners, dress, decoration, and so forth. Each sign in that system of signification has a range of possible meanings, and the system itself is indeterminate, because it would be impossible (as for most such systems) to specify exactly and exhaustively which signs compose the system.

Although texts have *primacy* in a rhetoric of style, it may be said that homology has *centrality* in unifying a style as a coherent discourse. The signs within a stylistic system have a wide but not an infinite range of meanings. The meanings of a style's signs are, therefore, similar to what Graeme Turner described for the signifying system that is a film: "On the one hand, the audience's readings of a film occupy a theoretical field of almost infinite possibility; on the other hand, in practice we find that while the audience's readings may differ, they will still be contained within a relatively discrete range of possibilities" (144).

The signifying system that is a style is held together by formal properties such that one could look at a new article of dress, for instance, newly designed, and identify it as Edwardian. If the style is homological across a very wide range of experience, we might speak of patterns of human relations, of economic organization, or of international affairs as following the same form that we call Edwardian. Some American presidents, to reference another style system, have been accused of conducting foreign affairs as if they were "cowboys," which bespeaks the unfolding of a homology or formal pattern beyond the original referents of prairie and tumbleweed, schoolmarms and outlaws. Such homologies are facilitated by the nodal nature of texts.

The presence of a set of signs found in a performance of stylistic rhetoric tends to bring to the fore meanings of those signs that triangulate or cohere through the style that orders them. How and whether the meanings of signs cohere are, of course, often described as ideology, and here also we may turn to those who have noted the multiplicity and contradictions in that concept. So we might say that the gravity that pulls together an Edwardian style is its ideology that works homologically. Turner, likewise, argues that "the culture's ideological system is not monolithic but is composed of competing and conflicting classes and interests, all fighting for dominance" (155). So a critic might also compare the ways in which different stylistic performances call out different ideologies through strategic combinations of signs, and

showing the struggle of competing significations may be an important critical task. As Fiske argues, "The role of the critic-analyst, then, is not to reveal
the true or hidden meanings of the text, or even to trace the readings that
people make of it; rather, it is to trace the play of power in the social formation" (*Understanding* 45). We might say that texts could not have primacy,
especially a highly nodal text dispersed across time and space, were there
not homologies to congeal signs into texts with ideological import.

To explore the stylistic homologies of a rhetoric of style is in a sense to
explore the repertoire of signification for a given enactment of that rhetoric.
A given style is a repertoire of signs as well as the homological glue that binds
them together as a style. From such a repertoire, the performer of a rhetoric
of style chooses a set of signs to create a text or a node of a text, being careful
to choose stylistic signs the meanings of which generally converge. The sense
of convergence is given by the range of possible meanings within a cultural
context that each sign has and by the homological attraction creating unity in
a style. Or perhaps the performer goes for a strategic incongruity, still making
use of the sense of possible meanings and the homological gravity of the style,
the violation of which is what creates the sense of incongruity. Rhetorics of
style are then read in the same way, the reader relying on triangulating the
plausible meanings generated by the signs and the homological cohesion or
incongruity of the style(s) displayed. An aptitude for reading form must be
developed in the critic. Mere facts alone will not reveal homologies. As de
Certeau argues for the study of everyday practices, "statistical investigation
grasps the material of these practices, but not their *form*" (xviii).

It is in recognizing and participating in stylistic homologies that imaginary communities and their subjects cohere around texts. A homology calls
to such communities, and those for whom that integrating form feels like
who they are, for whom it resonates with their imagined alignments will
respond. In this way, one of several gay styles, for instance, pulls an imaginary community together around the many nodes of a text of performed gay
styles—and the same may be said of straight styles or of any other homologically gravitated matrix of text and community.

## Charts and Schemes

Those who learn a rhetoric and attempt to use it in criticism or teach it in
classes often love charts and schemes and for good if perilous reason. Such
instruments organize our thoughts, clearly show the main elements of the
rhetoric, show interconnections, and are well adapted to the multiple-choice
test. This chapter concludes with just such a chart that explains the main
points of a scheme of a rhetoric of style given below. Similarity in terms from
one main element to another should suggest points of interconnection and

complexity in the scheme. Some of these connections are suggested for the substructure under each main element of the chart as explained in succeeding lists, with the connections presented in abbreviated form in italics in the text. These lists are not meant to be a comprehensive and conclusive scheme of connections, merely to suggest the interdependence of each element. I hope that this method of presentation of the tables will avoid the peril to which I alluded above, which is that the critic or student takes a scheme as a set of simple marching instructions for going straight through a study or a paper. One cannot possibly "do" all of the connections suggested in a given study,

---

**Primacy of the text**

- textual world
- bases for identity and community
- nodal texts
- convergence, redundancy, and triangulation of meaning
- reading off of the text
- images and floating signs

**Aesthetic rationales**

- aesthetic bases for decision and judgment
- culture of aesthetic engrossment
- aesthetic bases for identity and social organization
- pleasure and desire
- narrative rationale
- performance
- images

**Stylistic homologies**

- systems of signs and meaning
- unity of styles
- wide range of texts in system
- coherence of communities and subjects around forms

**Imaginary communities**

- effects of discourse
- facilitation by new technology
- coherence around style
- coherence around texts
- representation of communities and subjects by texts
- creation of communities and subjects by texts
- calling forth of motives, actions, and values by communities

**Market contexts**

- insulation from change
- merger of state, culture, and market
- shift of signs and images to commodities
- pleasure and desire
- possibility for struggle
- uses of everyday life
- excorporation and incorporation
- uses of goods as languages, systems of signs
- grounding of community and identity by commodities
- global rhetorical system

and let me repeat, these are not all the connections that could be made. So a critic using this rhetoric will need to use his or her judgment as to which elements and connections best help to reveal the text of style. A rhetorical criticism of style should be imaginative, sensitive to its subject matter, and, well, stylish. I hope the chart is taken as heuristic only and a summary of main elements of a rhetoric of style.

The chart begins with the five major elements of a rhetoric of style and some of the main substructures within each. The order in the chart is arbitrary, but going counterclockwise from the upper left and ending in the middle, the elements are in the order presented earlier in this volume. *Stylistic homologies* is placed as the element in the middle so as to represent the centrality of that concept. For the lists under the elements and the lists throughout the text of this chapter, I begin what may seem like an exercise in "ringing the changes" on the bells. For each item under each major element, I suggest some connections to items under the other major elements. The connections are brief, but a little more detail is included in the lists in the text. The reader would be correct in noting that there are connections that I do not describe. My aim is not to be exhaustive, which would be a book in itself, but to suggest the complexity of this rhetoric and how interconnected the elements are. Because the connections are reciprocal, discussion of each succeeding list is shorter than discussion of the ones before it because connections were already suggested. Accordingly, no list is given in the main text for connections to stylistic homologies because some connections to that element were already suggested in all the other lists. In the main text, the connections, which are listed under each of the major elements, are in italics; the connections are just some that could be made.

## Connections from and to Primacy of the Text
**Primacy of the text (italics indicate some connections)**
### textual world

- imaginary communities: *effects of discourse; coherence around styles; coherence around texts; facilitation by new technology*
- market contexts: *insulation from change*
- aesthetic rationales: *aesthetic bases for decision and judgment*
- stylistic homologies: *systems of signs and meaning; wide range of texts in system*

### bases for identity and community

- imaginary communities: *representation of communities or subjects texts; creation of communities and subjects by texts*

- market contexts: *grounding of community and identity by commodities*
- aesthetic rationales: *aesthetic bases for identity and social organization; culture of aesthetic engrossment*
- stylistic homologies: *coherence of communities and subjects around forms*

## nodal texts

- imaginary communities: *representation of communities and subjects by texts; creation of communities and subjects by texts*
- market contexts: *uses of everyday life*
- aesthetic rationales: *performance*
- stylistic homologies: *wide range of texts in system*

## convergence, redundancy, and triangulation of meaning

- imaginary communities: *effects of discourse; coherence around styles; coherence around texts*
- market contexts: *shift of signs and images to commodities*
- aesthetic rationales: *aesthetic bases for decision and judgment; narrative rationale; images*
- stylistic homologies: *systems of signs and meaning*

## reading off of the text

- imaginary communities: *calling forth of motives, actions, and values by communities*
- market contexts: *possibility for struggle; uses of goods as languages and/or as systems of signs; global rhetorical system*
- aesthetic rationales: *aesthetic bases for decision and judgment; performance*
- stylistic homologies: *systems of signs and meanings; coherence of communities and subjects around forms*

## images and floating signs

- imaginary communities: *representation of communities or subjects by text;, creation of communities and subjects by texts*
- market contexts: *pleasure and desire; global rhetorical system*
- aesthetic rationales: *pleasure and desire*
- stylistic homologies: *wide range of texts in system*

The first subcategory under *primacy of the text* is the idea that we live in a *textual world*. This connects to the subcategory under *imaginary communities*, which says that audiences and other communities are the *effects of discourse*, because such effects assume texts in place before the formation of groups that receive them. Texts are clearly primary if imaginary communities *cohere around texts* but also if such communities *cohere around styles*, for styles are made public in texts and as texts. The extent to which imaginary communities are *facilitated by new technologies* illustrates the primacy of the text, for what these technologies do is to bring more compelling texts, of higher quality and appeal, into more people's lives and, thus, provide the core around which communities cohere.

The idea of a textual world connects to the idea that *market contexts* are *insulated from change. Insulating* the market context within which rhetoric works is a matter of having people operate within a textual environment, responding to what is created in those texts, rather than to look "directly" in any sense at material conditions. The idea of a textual world is connected to the *aesthetic bases for decision and judgment* that are key to *aesthetic rationales*. This is because aesthetics is presented and nurtured in texts, and such nurturing occurs more easily in a highly textualized world. Finally, a textual world arises from the *systems of signs and meanings* that are part of *stylistic homologies*, the text being a temporary assemblage of the signs and meanings that cohere into styles. Clearly, a textual world also engages the *wide range of texts in the system* that is a subset of stylistic homologies, as people move from a preoccupation with one text after another.

The second subcategory under *primacy of the text* is that such texts form the *bases for identity and community*. The connections suggested by this subcategory are clear. Obviously, that characteristic connects to the subcategories of *imaginary communities* in which *communities and subjects are both represented by* and *created by texts*. If texts form the bases for identity and community, then we should note that many of those texts are composed of commodities, and that connects to the idea that *commodities ground community* under *market contexts*. A text that features high aesthetic values will, as is suggested under *aesthetic rationales*, be the *bases for identity and social organization*. If texts are primary, then the *aesthetic engrossment* with texts would lend itself to such texts becoming the basis for identity and community as aesthetically engrossing texts demand social attention and involvement. It is also clear that this subcategory connects to the subcategory of *stylistic homologies*, which holds that *communities and subjects cohere around forms*, for the form is a dimension of a text that holds great attractive value in calling communities together.

The third subcategory of textual primacy has to do with *nodal texts*. When the element of *imaginary communities* holds that *communities and subjects are both represented by* and *created by texts*, it is likely that nodal texts serve this function. Rarely do all subjects and communities encounter a given master text at once, a text so central and powerful that by itself, it causes communities to cohere around it. Instead, it is nodal texts chaining out in connection in everyday life that form the bases for community formation. Thus, naturally, the idea of nodal texts connects to the *market context* idea of *uses in everyday life*, for the appropriation of commodities in the fabric of daily existence is nodal. In these everyday market contexts, the *aesthetic rationales* of *performance* take place, as people enact nodal texts in the passing series of moments that form everyday life. And because this must necessarily entail a wide range of performances in many different contexts, the idea of nodal texts connects to the idea of a *wide range of texts* as grounding *stylistic homologies*.

Studies of primal texts depend on the critical methods of *convergence, redundancy, and triangulation of meaning* as critics point to a number of meanings of signs that come together in texts. Such convergence should then support claims under *imaginary communities* that communities are *effects of discourse*, for if communities cohere around style and cohere around texts, there must be a coherence of meaning in those texts that allows them to do so. The community that is an effect of a text is then held together by meanings that hold together in the text. Components of a text, such as, signs and images, may find such coherence in terms of their participation in a *market context* as a system of signs, and so the sense in which *signs and images become commodities* in that market context is one of convergence. The idea of convergence finds a lot of connection with *aesthetic rationale*, for such a rationale is a *basis for decision and judgment* and cannot do so unless the meanings of aesthetic signs come together to enable focused decisions. The *narrative* dimension and the *performance* dimension of the aesthetic rationale likewise require a coherence of meanings to create cohesion and order. And clearly, if stylistic homologies are based on systems of signs and meaning, coherence of signs and meanings is part and parcel of systems.

The ability to *read off of texts* is a subcategory of the primacy of texts. To read off of texts, one must be confident in the efficacy and reality of the meanings, even if complex and multiple, that are found there. Such confidence lets one conclude that *motives, actions, and values are called forth* by *imaginary communities* in the texts that the communities produce, as a step beyond the process by which the *communities form around previous texts*. To read off of texts, one will usually identify more than one possible reading—indeed, being sensitive to the possibility of *struggle* over a wide range of facilitated meanings is key, and this supports the idea of struggle in everyday life that we find under *market contexts*. Goods and commodities are parts of texts created by communities that articulate those motives, actions, and values. I have argued that these motives that can be read off of texts increasingly converge internationally because goods and the styles they support are more and more a *global rhetorical system*. Therefore, *goods form a kind of language or system of signs* that facilitate the reading of those meanings within the global rhetorical system. Because texts under *aesthetic rationale* create *aesthetic bases for judgment and decision,* the critic may assume that carefully supported meanings that are read off of texts provide such a basis. Shared knowledge of such meanings and values that may be read off of a text also form the basis for *performance,* for if we could not reliably read off of texts, we could not count on our own or others' performances being understood. We can reliably read off of texts if there are, as *stylistic homologies* have it, *systems* of signs and meaning, the systematicity of which generates confidence in reading texts. And *communities and subjects cohere around texts* precisely because the texts can be read off of in reliable ways, such that we can rely on the communities and subjectivities formed.

The final subcategory of the primacy of the text is the prevalence of *images and floating signs* in a rhetoric of style. It is because so many signs float away from an original, real context that in *imaginary communities* today, *communities and subjects are both represented by* and *created by texts*. It is the flexibility and changeability of such floating signs and images that allow the connection of imaginary communities to texts, for otherwise, communities would be less imaginary and signs less flexible in representing and creating them. Images and floating signs are major sites of *pleasure and desire* in *market contexts,* as they facilitate the ability of people to play with meanings not materially connected to their real existence. It is these images and floating signs that compose the *global rhetorical system* of market contexts, for signs and images that may float away from original contexts are more easily understood on their own terms by people internationally. We find *pleasure and desire* as a subcategory also of *aesthetic rationale,* and floating signs and images connect to that concern for the same reason that they do in market contexts. When we think of texts in terms not only of floating signs but also of images, we are thinking of quite a *wide range of texts in a system,* which is a subcategory of *stylistic homologies.*

## Connections from and to Imaginary Communities

Remember that as we explore some of the connections from *imaginary communities* to the other elements, we are not discussing connections to the primacy of the text, because those were mentioned above. Some connections between the primacy of the text and imaginary communities have already been discussed above.

**Imaginary communities (italics indicate some connections)**

**effects of discourse**

- market contexts: *grounding of community and identity by commodities*
- aesthetic rationale: *aesthetic bases for identity and social organization*
- stylistic homologies: *coherence of communities and subjects around forms*

**facilitation by new technology**

- market contexts: *merger of state, culture, and market; pleasure and desire*
- aesthetic rationales: *culture of aesthetic engrossment; pleasure and desire; images*
- stylistic homologies: *wide range of texts in system*

**coherence around style**

- market contexts: *grounding of community and identity by commodities*
- aesthetic rationales: *aesthetic bases for decision and judgment*
- stylistic homologies: *unity of styles; coherence of communities and subjects around forms*

**coherence around texts**

- market contexts: *shift of signs and images to commodities*
- aesthetic rationales: *narrative rationale; performance; images*
- stylistic homologies: *coherence of communities and subjects around forms*

**representation of communities and subjects by texts**

- market contexts: *shift of signs and images to commodities; possibility for struggle; uses of everyday life; grounding of community and identity by commodities*
- aesthetic rationales: *aesthetic bases for identity and social organization*
- stylistic homologies: *systems of signs and meaning; coherence of communities and subjects around forms*

### creation of communities and subjects by texts

- market contexts: *grounding of community and identity by commodities*
- aesthetic rationales: *bases for identity and social organization*
- stylistic homologies: *coherence of communities and subjects around forms*

### calling forth of motives, actions, and values by communities

- market contexts: *possibility for struggle; excorporation and incorporation; grounding of community and identity by commodities*
- aesthetic rationales: *culture of aesthetic engrossment; aesthetic bases for decision and judgment*
- stylistic homologies: *systems of signs and meaning; unity of styles*

The first subcategory of imaginary communities is that they are *effects of discourse*. If an imaginary community is an effect of discourse, then an important part of that discourse will be commodities within a *market context*. Goods are ways of communicating. Therefore, the contention that *commodities ground community and identity* as discussed within market contexts will connect to the idea that communities are the effects of discourse. Another important part of the discourse that creates communities is its *aesthetic rationale*, and so this subcategory connects to the claim that *aesthetics is the basis for identity and social organization*, identity and society being effects of aesthetic discourse. And an imaginary community that is an effect of discourse will certainly be, within *stylistic homologies*, a community of subjects that *cohere around forms*, for forms order discourse.

The second subcategory of imaginary communities is that they are facilitated by *new technology*. It is new technologies that contribute to the *merger of state, culture, and market* within *market contexts*, for these previously distinct spheres converge through technology that puts them all together and on the same footing in making politics entertaining and entertainment politically powerful. New technologies are precisely what enable an *aesthetic engrossment* within *aesthetic rationales*, as better-mediated experiences of film and television fascinate audiences with greater power. Such engrossment works by appealing to *pleasure and desire*, and the engrossment is often enabled by the excellence of the *image* that is aesthetically constructed. New technologies are found, as explained in *stylistic homologies*, across a *wide range of texts* and could not be so powerful, integrative, and engrossing were that not true.

Imaginary communities, in the third subcategory, *cohere around style*. This connects to the claim in *market contexts* that *commodities ground com-*

*munity and identity.* A product or brand can be the textual and stylistic core around which communities come together and in which people find a sense of identity. Similarly, part of the *aesthetic rationale* is that people use *aesthetics as bases for decision and judgment.* The style that others, such as, politicians, neighbors, potential friends, and so forth, display, thus, becomes a *basis for decision and judgment,* and one such decision is whether to join in the imaginary communities cohering around that style. The *unity of style* provides the symbolic basis for such cohesion as part of *stylistic homologies. Communities and subjects cohere around forms,* and the form is what is at the center of a style that is far-flung across experience, widely distributed enough to provide a basis for cohesion.

Imaginary communities also *cohere around texts,* a slightly broader category than just that of style. In connecting this to *market contexts,* we might look at the claim that *signs and images become commodities.* It is in becoming a commodity that signs and images become not only texts but also specifically the kind of texts around which imaginary communities can cohere. Some textual elements may be recognized in the *aesthetic rationale* subcategories of *narrative, performance,* and *images.* Imaginary communities come together because they are called to by narrative or by the ongoing performances of public and private figures or because of key, powerful images. Texts produced through those means are the core of such coherence. Similarly, when the claim is made under *stylistic homologies* that *communities and subjects cohere around forms,* we must recall that forms are at the heart of texts, structuring them, and it is often the form in texts that provide the basis for community coherence.

*Communities and subjects are represented by texts* in the next subcategory of imaginary communities. This connects to several of the subcategories of *market contexts. Signs and images become commodities* in many instances precisely because they come to represent communities and subjects—what was an ordinary phrase or a kind of shoe is turned into commodities exactly because the phrase or shoe represents things, such as, an athlete or a town with cultural capital. Commodities are used in *struggle,* and commodities that represent communities and subjects textually are especially agonistic, as the task of representing people is always politically charged and, thus, a site of struggle. Communities and subjects are represented particularly by the texts of *everyday life,* including the commodities used in everyday life, as food, fashion, entertainment choices and other commodities come to represent imaginary communities and people. In sum, it should be apparent that as *commodities ground communities,* they come to ground those communities in the rhetoric of style. Therefore, as part of *stylistic homologies,* communities and subjects are represented by texts as they *cohere around forms,* for form is often the engine driving the ability of a text to pull an imaginary community around it. Imaginary communities and subjects are represented by manipulation of the resources offered in *systems of signs and meanings,* which must be understood not only within particular communities but also widely, even globally, so that we may know what represents imaginary communities and subjects who are not a part of ourselves.

Similarly, imaginary *communities and subjects are created by texts.* If they are created by texts, some of which are composed of commodities, then as the *market contexts* element has it, *commodities ground community and identity* because they create community and identity. If imaginary communities and subjects are created by texts, the *aesthetic rationale* dimension of those texts claims that *aesthetics is the basis for identity and social organization,* which is certainly true if identity and the social are created in any way by aesthetic texts. And in the same way, the idea that *communities and subjects cohere around forms,* as expressed in *stylistic homologies,* can be understood as saying that imaginary communities and subjects come into being as they so cohere.

The final subcategory of imaginary communities is that *motives, actions, and values are called forth by imaginary communities.* This is true if, as *market contexts* show us, *commodities ground community.* Motives, actions, and values are either expressed in or implemented by commodities, and so as they ground communities, they do so with an effect on motives, actions, and values. Because motives, actions, and values are never simple and are nearly always contested, they become sites of *struggle.* Cycles of *excorporation and incorporation* are also involved in the calling forth of motives, actions, and values, because both excorporation and incorporation are attempts to seize control of meanings and influence motives, actions, and values. An important part of *aesthetic engrossment,* a subcategory of *aesthetic rationale,* is the all-encompassing claim that an aesthetic text can make on life, claiming the ability to influence motives, actions, and values as people become absorbed in aesthetic texts. Because motives, actions, and values are *bases for decision and judgment,* they can function that way on an aesthetic basis as they are generated by imaginary communities in texts. Working through the *systems of signs and meaning* created by stylistic communities, imaginary communities call forth motives, actions, and values, and the *unity of styles* creates a unity of those three that matches the overall logic of *stylistic homologies.*

## Connections from and to Market Contexts

Two sets of connections are left to make for the element of *market contexts,* because some of the links to be made to primacy of texts and imaginary communities have been made already.

## Market contexts (italics indicate some connections)

### insulation from change

- aesthetic rationales: *culture of aesthetic engrossment; aesthetic bases for identity and social organization*
- stylistic homologies: *systems of signs and meaning*

### merger of state, culture, and market

- aesthetic rationales: *aesthetic bases for decision and judgment; culture of aesthetic engrossment; aesthetic bases for identity and social organization*
- stylistic homologies: *unity of styles; coherence of communities, and subjects around forms*

### shift of signs and images to commodities

- aesthetic rationales: *culture of aesthetic engrossment; aesthetic bases for identity and social organization; pleasure and desire*
- stylistic homologies: *systems of signs and meaning*

### pleasure and desire

- aesthetic rationales: *culture of aesthetic engrossment; pleasure and desire*
- stylistic homologies: *wide range of texts in system*

### possibility for struggle

- aesthetic rationales: *aesthetic bases for decision and judgment; aesthetic basis for identity and social organization*
- stylistic homologies: *systems of signs and meanings*

### uses of everyday life

- aesthetic rationale: *culture of aesthetic engrossment; performance*
- stylistic homologies: *wide range of texts in system*

### excorporation and incorporation

- aesthetic rationales: *aesthetic bases for identity and social organization, performance*
- stylistic homologies: *wide range of texts in system*

### uses of goods as languages and/or systems of signs

- aesthetic rationales: *aesthetic bases for decision and judgment; narrative rationale; performance; images*
- stylistic homologies: *systems of signs and meaning*

**grounding of community and identity by commodities**

- aesthetic rationales: *aesthetic bases for identity and social organization; performance*

- stylistic homologies: *coherence of communities and subjects around forms*

**global rhetorical system**

- aesthetic rationales: *aesthetic bases for decision and judgment; culture of aesthetic engrossment*

- stylistic homologies: *systems of signs and meaning; wide range of texts in system*

Discussed earlier was the idea that market contexts are *insulated from change* because in late capitalism the working of the market generally seals itself off from rhetorical interference. This insulation from change is connected in the *aesthetic rationale* to *aesthetic engrossment*. Think of such engrossment as an absorption of public attention in the aesthetic dimensions of texts, more than in underlying structural conditions. Engrossment can function as a deflection of attention from insulated issues. Aesthetics also provides a *basis for identity and social organization*, and late capitalism seems to have co-opted aesthetics enough so that identity and social organization are conducted at a level that ensures the insulation of market contexts. In other words, the fact that we construct identity and social organization in the market is rarely questioned. In terms of *stylistic homologies*, this means that the *systems of signs and meanings* themselves are constructed to deflect attention from the capitalist bedrock. Attempts to question or break that insulated context will not find easy traction with available systems of signs and meanings.

In the market context, we find a *merger of state, culture, and market*. This connects to a number of subcategories of *aesthetic rationale*. If aesthetics are the *basis for decision and judgment*, then making decisions across different modes of state (politics), culture, and the market get put on the same aesthetic footing. *Aesthetic engrossment* is likewise a kind of trope of merger, in which attention to aesthetic matters pulls all other considerations onto its own terrain. Once state, culture, and market are merged, it allows the aesthetic connection to that merger to become the *basis for identity and social organization*. A unified, if shifting, dimension of state, culture, and market becomes an aesthetic basis for such organization. This is abetted by the *unity of styles* within *stylistic homologies*, as styles pull together texts and performances of state, culture, and market. *Communities and subjects cohere* around a merged terrain of state, culture, and market with less fragmentation and more coherence as the process of merging strengthens.

*Signs and images become commodities* in market contexts. The process is connected to *aesthetic engrossment* within *aesthetic rationale*, for the commodification of signs and images is a way of moving them into a market context that is all encompassing. One reason why it is all encompassing is that the market is a major site of *pleasure and desire*, and so everything connected to it is involved in enticing and satisfying people. Hence, through the market, people can find an *aesthetic basis for identity and social organization*, as signs that signal subjectivity and social connection become signs that operate within the market. To do so, signs and images must enter into a *system of signs* described by *stylistic homologies*. The market is a system, and anything that enters into it must become part of a comprehensible system of signification.

*Pleasure and desire* are major engines of the market context. There is a clear connection, then, to *pleasure and desire* within the *aesthetic rationale* as aesthetics becomes commodified. *Aesthetic engrossment* reflects absorption in the lure of pleasure and satisfaction of desire in the market, fueled by the pleasures of aesthetics. This occurs across such a *wide range of texts* that we can easily see the connection to that subcategory of *stylistic homologies*. In the market context, pleasure and desire are fueled aesthetically in as many texts as possible.

The market context contains a possibility for *struggle*, as people use commodities for social and political ends to exercise power over others or to refuse its exercise over themselves. When struggle makes use of *aesthetic rationales*, it becomes connected to *aesthetic bases for decision and judgment*. The ability to affect decisions and judgments through aesthetic means becomes what is struggled over using aestheticized commodities. The outcome of such struggles takes the form of *aesthetic bases for identity and social organization*. As aestheticized goods come to feature some meanings over others, the formation of identity and social organization follows in their wake. What these goods mean comes to be part of *stylistic homologies*, especially *systems of signs and meaning*. Such systems constrain struggle but may also be the outcome of previous struggles as the ability to control systematic meaning is fought over.

Market contexts include the uses of commodities in *everyday life* for rhetorical purposes. This is part of *aesthetic engrossment* within the *aesthetic rationale*, for engrossment occurs when everyday life is caught up around a unitary logic or perspective. *Performance* is also an aesthetic enactment in everyday life, and it frequently makes use of the commodities that are commonly available to people. Thus, a *wide range of texts* incorporated into *stylistic homologies* can be part of this rhetoric of everyday life, encompassing performances and all the aesthetic texts that engross us.

*Cycles of excorporation and incorporation* are a subcategory of market contexts and are played out using goods that move in and out of the market. Such goods serve as the *basis for identity and social organization* within the *aesthetic rationale*. Goods are excorporated to mark the refusal of people and communities to be disempowered, and goods retain some shreds of that connection to the margin when they are incorporated back into the market in their new, turned forms. The excorporation of goods is always a kind of *performance*, making use of what is available to people and turning the meanings of those goods, often in local contexts. Because the cycle can be played out in a *wide range of texts*, the cycles depend on *stylistic homologies* to identify a sign as excorporated and turned or as incorporated and a commodity.

In market contexts, *goods are considered as languages and systems of signs*. It is because goods provide a relatively stable (although, of course, evolving) system of signification that they can serve in the *aesthetic rationale* as *bases for decision and judgment*. We can know what it means and what decisions and judgments we should make when we see a commodity being used in one way or another, and such use often takes the form of performance. Aesthetic *narratives* need not be entirely verbal, of course, and "stories" are often told in that language of commodities. In doing so, people often make *images* of commodities, or they create visual images using goods and the systematic meanings that such goods support. This is clearly consistent with the claim under *stylistic homologies* that there are *systems of signs and meanings* that hold together stylistically, for it is in tapping the symbolic potential of such systems that individual performances of style do their work.

Finally, I have argued that market contexts have created a *global rhetorical system* in which increasingly people engaged in capitalism around the world understand texts created through commodities. Therefore, a rhetoric of style, which relies heavily on the use of goods, will increasingly be understood globally by those enrolled in a global market. Clearly, this connects to the *aesthetic rationale* that holds that aesthetics is a *basis for decision and judgment*, because it becomes the work of that global rhetorical system to spread a shared basis for decision and judgment globally. The process is facilitated by *aesthetic engrossment*, which focuses attention worldwide on the aesthetic dimension that goods can especially body forth. In connection to *stylistic homologies, systems of signs and meanings* that anchor a style are thus shared globally; one may say that it is the logic of styles that is spread in this way. And because such styles are manifested across many goods, many actions, and many media, the systems are spread through a *wide range of texts*.

## Connections from and to Aesthetic Rationale

It remains but to suggest a few connections from the element of aesthetic rationale to the element of stylistic homologies, because some connections to and from all other elements have already been offered.

**Aesthetic rationale (italics indicate some connections)**

### aesthetic bases for decision and judgment

- stylistic homologies: *systems of signs and meaning; wide range of texts in system*

### culture of aesthetic engrossment

- stylistic homologies: *systems of signs and meaning; coherence of communities and subjects around forms*

### aesthetic bases for identity and social organization

- stylistic homologies: *coherence of communities and subjects around forms*

### pleasure and desire

- stylistic homologies: *systems of signs and meaning; wide range of texts in system*

### narrative rationale

- stylistic homologies: *systems of signs and meaning*

### performance

- stylistic homologies: *wide range of texts in system*

### images

- stylistic homologies: *wide range of texts in system*

When I am finished, then, some connections from all of the other elements to the element of stylistic homologies will have been made, and this necessarily incomplete list of connections will be finished.

I have argued that in a rhetoric of style, there are *aesthetic bases for decision and judgment*. Those bases depend upon the *systems of signs and meanings* that are the core of *stylistic homologies*. We make aesthetic judgments based on our sense of such systems, of how styles hang together or not. Those systems stretch across a *wide range of texts*, such that we are often or always making such aesthetic judgments. I have argued that we live in a culture of *aesthetic engrossment*. Engrossment is facilitated by the *systems of signs and meanings* in *stylistic homologies*, for a fixation on aesthetics is encouraged when many different signs and meanings resonate with one another aesthetically. *Communities and subjects cohere around the forms* of style when there is aesthetic engrossment, for certain aesthetic forms are returned to again and again as the basis for community and subject formation.

An important subcategory of the element of aesthetic rationale is that there is an *aesthetic basis for identity and social organization.* Clearly, this is connected to the *stylist homologies* subcategory that *communities and subjects cohere around forms.* It is the form at the heart of style that provides a foundation for the aesthetic construction of self and society. *Pleasure and desire* are key to the aesthetic rationale as well. Pleasure and desire are found in a *wide range of texts* pulled together across *stylistic homologies;* they are nearly indispensable components of any aesthetic rationale. And pleasure and desire must also be implicated in the *systems of signs and meanings* that form stylistic homologies, for they give styles much of their motivating power.

The aesthetic rationale largely incorporates a *narrative* rationale, and narratives are nothing if not systematic. It is the systematicity at the heart of narrative that connects it to *systems of signs and meaning* in *stylistic homologies.* The aesthetic rationale also is embodied in *performance* and makes heavy use of *images.* Both these subcategories connect to the *wide range of texts* through which stylistic homologies are spread.

In sum, I have proposed some major elements of a rhetoric of style: primacy of the text, imaginary communities, market contexts, aesthetic rationale, and stylistic homologies. I have suggested thirty-four subcategories within these five elements. And I have suggested some connections among those thirty-four subcategories. I would certainly be content to regard everything in this chapter as an incomplete system and would welcome further development of elements, subcategories, and connections. In my view, the point is not to be exhaustively complete but to offer a structure that might assist theorists and critics in understanding and critiquing the rhetoric of style. I would caution such scholars not to make too heavy or mechanistic a use of these elements but to use them as inventional prods to saying interesting things about how style works rhetorically. By way of illustration of that goal, the next chapter offers a critique of the way in which style holds together what is often called a "gun culture" in the United States and how attention to style can help us understand some of the appeal and implications of that culture.

# 5

# Gun-Culture Style and Its Rhetoric in the United States

> Political stylists are usually conservatives. This is not because
> tories so often come from the upper classes and have learned
> to speak ever so nice but because conservatism is in its nature
> on the side of style; its object is to erect barriers—to preserve
> forms and rituals.
>
> —Quentin Crisp, *How to Have a Life-Style*, 110

Go to a search engine online, and type in "gun culture." One need not cruise the sites offered for very long to realize that *gun culture* is a term denoting a site of struggle in American society today. It is remarkable how disparately people view those two words. Some praise it, as in the declaration on a Web page that a gun culture is a "culture where guns are recognised as tools, respected but not feared. Where criminals are punished, but the ordinary citizen is trusted" ("Gun Culture"). The Wikipedia entry on author John Ross describes his book: "*Unintended Consequences* is a controversial novel of fiction that mixes real events with fiction. These events portray a continuing oppression of the American gun culture that, the author believes, has occurred since the passage of the National Firearms Act of 1934."

On the other hand, the "British Fear Rise of Gun Culture" is the headline for an online issue of *USA Today* (Hale). On this side of the pond, a Web site connected to *New York* magazine probes "New York's Gun Culture" and wonders "Will Assault Weapons Now Flood New York?" (Bernstein). Historian Michael A. Bellesiles argues that the gun culture is a fairly recent and pernicious development in American history, without the venerable roots in the founding of the nation claimed for it by gun advocates.

It is not hard to see the politics in these comments about gun culture. The criminal is coddled while the "ordinary citizen" is distrusted and oppressed and hence must enlist in a gun culture—or—gun culture is behind a wave of destructive, easily available guns washing over countries around the globe, thus it is a culture to be controlled and contained. This chapter examines the culture from the point of view of style to identify and analyze some interesting rhetorically charged texts.

The word *culture* itself is difficult enough, but in this case, I want to side-step it altogether. I argue that the gun culture, whatever else it may be, is a rhetorical style that carries motives and attitudes in word, gesture, clothing, automobiles, image, and other stylistic elements. To understand gun culture and the political and social work it supports, one must see it as a style. I want to shed some light on this phenomenon that has inspired much public discussion over time.

To support the claim that gun culture is a style, I rely on the theory of the rhetoric of style, which I gave in chapter 4. I want to show in a critical example how that theory may be used methodologically to explain the motives and effects of the styles people display. As noted earlier, methods of rhetorical criticism are often misused by being taken mechanistically, the gears and pistons of the method itself becoming the chief object of contemplation. Here, I want to let that mechanism be seen but as a means not an end, seen to be facilitating a reading of style rather than as the main event. I make use of some of the charts and schemes explained in chapter 4 but will not follow them in lockstep, mechanistically.

Let me say a word about my own position in this matter and about the materials I examine. I came to an interest in actual guns about halfway through life and have since developed that interest. However, I recall watching many a television Western shoot-'em-up in the days of my youth, and as a child, I was rarely without a cap pistol. I dearly longed to be a cowboy when I grew up. Like many who might think of themselves as connected to gun culture in some way, I have a strong sense that some of my identity as a subject has been called into being by an American culture full of images and texts of firearms. Some part of me is an imaginary desperado cohering around a wash of cowboy, gangster, and World War II texts that are readily available in movie theaters and on television.

I am a life member of the National Rifle Association (it's cheaper than renewing your membership each year, plus they gave me a cool leather jacket), but I attend no rallies or conventions, and I generally hang up when they call to ask for money. I do read their magazine when it comes in the mail. If the airport bookstore has them, I might buy other gun magazines to pass the time on the plane. I cannot say that I collect guns because "collecting" bespeaks a discipline and level of expertise that I do not have; however, I have accumulated some of them, and I enjoy shooting them. Every now and then, I will go to a gun show when it is in town or nearby. Sometimes I will go to a gun store and see what's on sale. I have never hunted, although I do not oppose the sport. Finally, I live in Texas, and if there is gun culture anywhere, it is here. Texas has a law allowing legal concealed carry of a pistol, as do most states, but the only possible legal answer to your question, Dear Reader, is no, I am not carrying one now (for if I were, and I told you so, it would no longer be concealed, and that is illegal).

The style that is gun culture is surely embodied in a series of nodal texts and manifests itself here and there in connected texts and performances that display a remarkable consistency of style. As with most styles, one cannot examine every node of such a far-flung text. Here, I use as the basis for my analysis these nodal texts: attendance at a multitude of gun shows in and around greater Milwaukee, Austin, and San Antonio; regular reading of the Usenet group rec.guns, which is a moderated forum open to the public; shopping at firearms stores or at the "hunting" counters of sporting-goods stores in Wisconsin and Texas; and the six most recent issues at this writing of the *American Rifleman* magazine, the chief publication of the National Rifle Association. (Two of the kinds of textual nodes cited here are of the sort that can be examined by the reader: *American Rifleman* and the rec.guns postings. The six issues of *American Rifleman* cited are listed once under the name of the magazine in the References. Because I pull examples from throughout each issue, including advertisements, sidebars, and short blurbs, I simply reference the citation by giving an abbreviation for the magazine, the date, and the page on which the example is found rather than any article title, thus: [*AR*, October, 2006, 2]. To protect the privacy of those posting on rec.guns, I do not list any of that material in the References and cite the postings in the text merely by the date on which they were posted rather than by the poster's name. I have copies of the original material I cite.)

In addition, I rely in this chapter on my own experience of handling and shooting guns at several firing ranges. I believe these sources comprise a wide range of nodal texts that bring to the study the characteristics of being in market contexts, which are aesthetic, online, writing-based, visually based, and personally-locally performative. The style of gun culture certainly chains out into popular media, such as, film and television, and has done so for decades, but I invite the reader to extend this analysis to other such texts.

Let me emphasize what it means to think of the gun culture as a style with rhetorical impact. Any group of gun owners and enthusiasts displays about as much diversity as any other group of people sorted by interest: gardeners, mystery-novel lovers, motorcyclists, and so forth. To say that there is a gun culture is to say that there is a certain style that is commonly found among people. Of course, there are exceptions to what I will claim about gun culture, but it is the style and the mass of people displaying or performing that style who make up the gun culture. The style and mass provide a core of signific'cation, a set of signs and practices with symbolic gravity that draws toward the core an imaginary community and certain subject positions. With these caveats in mind, let me begin.

## A Working-Class Stylistic Homology

It may be passing strange to find a gun enthusiast who is also a poet, but such am I. In *Pedestal Magazine*, an online venue, I published this poem.

### At the Gun Show

These are men, this band of brothers,
who have come to be men
in their own peculiar ways.

These are old white men who know what they know,
learned in trenches, beaches, steam, blood, screams
learned on factory floors and heat cracked pastures.
These men have worn steel-toed shoes,
Red Wings and boots,
big buckled Lone Star belts
for forty years.
These men eat lunches in diners with formica and chrome,
nearly burned nearly weak coffee and chicken-fried steak,
go in Penney's and Sears for checked print shirts,
canvas and denim pants.
Their skin is seersucker.
What they know is a straight country road,
no turnoffs, few driveways, rarely a turnaround.
These men store slights and defeats in the bags
of their wrinkled, seamed faces.
Victories align with the tilt of their jaws.
They have earned the broken angles of their weathered hats.
Their handshakes are firm,
and they mean what they say.
They show you their knives and remember
the Case and the Marble's of days gone by.
They spread out in Barcaloungers
watching the three major networks, or sports.
They go to the Baptist church or the Methodist
with their patient wives, or not,
and have Sunday dinner at Luby's each week.

There is steel in their soft drawls,
the crack of bone in inquiring lookdowns,
the keeping of secrets in looking aside.
They love a good laugh with other men.
These men are masters of the calibers,
learned in stocks and actions, twists and chokes,
their hard creeds are laid out in millimeters
and gauges are their song.

The parking lot is a harbor,
boats bobbing on the asphalt bay under the sun:
four by four, by doublewide, extended and cabbed.
Bumper stickers tell this American tale
in prophecies turned into mantras.

These are the spiced, the chipper, the wives:
blonde-helmeted, Texas Athenas,
behind every good man,
assailing, buck-hardy and friendly.
That's it.

These are the Asians, Hispanics, and Blacks.
These men are defiant and furtive,
the few, the strong, the proud.
Claiming and getting a place as men with men.
Claiming a share of the giving of violence.
Sleekly watched or ignored
as they assert their ways among the laden tables.
They make faint pulses, short ripples as they go
and quickly afterward the churn of middle age and whiteness
closes in upon their wakes.

These are the young men, late teens, earnest boys
strivers in manhood, standing, and power.
Brows knit and lips parted and not-meeting eyes,
smooth muscled, shaven T-shirted military cut,
maybe on leave and maybe signing up,
earnest, self-aware, barely noticed.
Making one-handed catches
of stories and lore, stats and opinions
tossed around just overhead.

Praying over knives, lockbacks
fantasy daggers, throwing stars,
plastic crossbows and blowguns,
the red squirrel's bane,
intently seeking signs among the camo,
the optics and holsters.
These are the young men and boys, who look into mirrors
where others see rows of revolvers and rifles,
shattered pieces of mirrors in among the AK's,
whose bright images are thrown back to them
by steel and oil-rubbed wood,
who move in a dream, weaving desire
among the tables and older men who stand,
talking, displaying, demonstrating,
who pull desire after them like a ribbon of lust,
who call to themselves as they go,
"I want it, I want to be, I will be someday."

Woven through the represented images and experiences of the poem is a clue to what I think is the central stylistic homology in the gun culture: These texts both represent and call to an imaginary community that is *working class*. Gun culture performs a working-class style, its signs will be read as working class, and that is what holds it together, that is what calls imaginary communities and subjects to it, that is the key to how that style organizes communities and subjects. The style supports and generates what might be identified as working-class values and motivations.

The question may arise as to what I mean by working class, much less working-class style. In answer I am going to appeal to your knowledge, Gentle Reader, because as is the case with most styles, the public generally and even globally has been taught how to read and understand this style. It has synonyms: blue collar, redneck, lower-middle class, and so forth. By working-class style, I mean that the signs bear reference to those who work hard jobs involving a fair bit of manual labor, who are paid hourly rather than by salary, who work with their hands, who often do not own the means of production and especially not the means of production for their work—and to those who resonate with signs of those who are described by those characteristics. Signs with those meanings compose the core of a working-class style. As one riflescope ad says to its hard-working imaginary community, although their product makes weekend hunting easier, "When it's time to weather another week at work, though, you're all on your own" (*AR*, September 2006, 5). In other words, the imaginary community cohering around such texts works hard. Articles describing do-it-yourself projects are quite commonly found, and they assume the possession and handy knowledge of tools (*AR*, May 2006, 60), which signals the working class. Many signs in American popular culture are connected to the working class, and often the connection is floating. Pickup trucks, Country and Western music, Jeff Foxworthy and his redneck jokes, biscuits and gravy, labor unions, steel-toed footwear—the list of signs that "say" working class is a long one, but they cohere into a style. If you want a musical, hyperbolic expression of working-class style, go find Ray Wylie Hubbard's excellent album *Delirium Tremolos* and listen to the song "Choctaw Bingo."

Dan Savage gives a glimpse of what this style is *not* when he, a gay, upper-middle class, San Francisco journalist, enters a gun range: "I may not have looked like a gun owner—jeans too baggy, hair too short, gut undetectable" (248), all of which suggests what gun-culture style is by contrast. The style is performed for us, taught to us, on television shows like *Laverne and Shirley, Roseanne, Dog the Bounty Hunter, Blue Collar Comedy Tour,* and so forth. It will not do to cry out that one knows a plumber who wears a suit and tie when not crawling beneath sinks, who reads Shakespeare, lunches on brie and baguettes, and drives a Volvo (see? you understand those things as *not* working-class style, do you not?). Nor will it do to note that physicians and CEOs visit gun shows and ranges from time to time; either they are not part of the gun culture I am describing, or they go to these venues sporting the signs of working-class style. We are speaking of style not reality and of a style that the media has taken pains to teach for many decades now.

This chapter explains how the components of gun-culture style consistently display signs that will likely be read as working class and how the texts displaying that style, therefore, call forth a range of consistent values, motivations, and actions in response. But like any style, like any ideology, gun culture contains some interesting contradictions that are key to understanding how it works rhetorically. First, I argue that gun-culture style contains a contradiction that is peculiar to the working class, which is *a tension between a passion for individuality and self-determination on the one hand, and deference to authority, rules, and laws on the other hand.* Second, I argue that gun-culture style contains a contradiction that is peculiar to the manifestations of the working class, at least in the United States, and that is that we have both rural and urban working class. Much of the performance of gun-culture style is *working-class rural*: overalls, torn jeans, cowboy hats, pickup trucks, hunting firearms, and so forth. Yet, much of the *social threat* for which one might go armed is depicted in a variety of texts as *urban* or *suburban*: home invasions, robberies at business, assaults on the street, strangers at the door, and so forth. Many of the people described as responding to such threats with a quick draw are depicted as urban working class. I conclude with a discussion of the social and political implications of this enactment of gun-culture style.

## Working-Class Style

Gun culture is a style composed of signs that will largely be read as working class. A columnist claims that he and his brethren write about guns so as to "buy shoes for our kids," which bespeaks a no-frills economic status (*AR*, September 2006, 75). Another writer declares, "No gun writer will ever be a millionaire, and my tastes and pocketbook run to the more pragmatic" (*AR*, August 2006, 85). Both these comments imply a simple, dollar-store kind of style. This is not to say that the individuals or groups who cohere around this style are (whatever that means) working class. One cannot tell, and with style, surface is substance. In texts likely to generate and then to be consumed by the gun culture, what comments such as these do, is call to an imaginary community to form around a *style* of working-class performance, narrative, and images.

A parallel might be drawn with the annual motorcycle rally in Sturgis, South Dakota, which is attended by a number of mild-mannered professionals, lawyers, and CPAs and the like, who nevertheless have their roaring Harleys shipped in and who don bad-mother gear during the festivities, becoming part of what is clearly an imaginary community clustering around an outlaw style. Many who are attracted to and who perform gun-culture style are drawn more by signs than by reality. Whether the signs are floating or not, it is clear that those signs say "working class."

Let us examine some texts that evoke a working-class style. On rec.guns, postings often evoke the working class. One solicitation for campaign contributions deferentially asks for "your hard-earned political dollars" (October 11, 2006). People in the gun culture are as often described as "working with more than one rifle or caliber" rather than "shooting" with them (October 11, 2006). An ethos of hard work is created that anchors a working-class style.

References in the gun-culture literature to firearms for "service" or "duty" evoke everyday working-class occupations. Beretta's latest product is identified as a "service pistol" (*AR*, September 2006, 96). An FNH USA pistol is advertised as a "Power Tool" that can be used "for on- and off-duty service" (*AR*, October 2006, 41). The H&K P2000 V3 is described as "a duty gun" (*AR*, June 2006, 58). The military M1917 Lewis gun "saw duty" in wars around the world (*AR*, June 2006, 62). One thinks of service and duty more as descriptors of working-class police officers, fire fighters, or soldiers than of white-collar executives. The gun one buys then becomes consistent with the kind of style that working people might display. A *duty* pistol is stylistically homologous with a service *uniform*.

It is clear that gun culture is pointedly and determinedly working class in its system of signs. At gun ranges, shows, and stores, these signs are readily apparent. Clustered around the outside doors of gun shows are a gang of smokers, puffing away on unfiltered cigarettes, more of them than one, I think, finds outside of tony office buildings in the financial district.

Grooming is working class, varying by locale. Some of gun-culture style works by exclusion, by what it is not: Expensive, stylish haircuts are rarely seen. Hair is either buzz-cut or long and free or in some fabulously dated working-class style like a mullet. One finds longer hair with more braids and beards in Austin, Texas, than one finds in Milwaukee, Wisconsin, the latter featuring more clean-shaven burrheads, but many of the grooming strategies one sees resonate with one of the several styles associated with the working class. Women often have Texas Big Hair, whether they are in Texas or not, or their hair often is long, stringy, and not quite recently washed.

Images in publications advise those subjects cohering around the gun culture as to appropriate styles, and the advice is to get plain, cheap wear. Images often show heavy men with bad haircuts and simple work clothing like t-shirts or collarless, short-sleeved shirts, as in an advertisement for Lee reloading equipment (*AR*, May 2006, 56). An advertisement for the U.S. Concealed Carry Association shows a man and a woman both wearing cowboy hats and faded denim shirts open over a blouse for her and a t-shirt for him. Their faces are lined and weather-beaten, and he sports a scruffy beard (*AR*, May 2006, 59). Another man in denim overshirt and faded cotton undershirt with a beard advertises a vitamin supplement to improve vision (*AR*, May 2006, 73). There can be stylistic crossover between gun culture and other styles, such as, that of bikers, as long as both styles use the system of working-class signs. One storekeeper's poster on rec.guns describes a man who entered his business, a pistol-packing fellow who "looked like a hard core biker." The same poster describes the owner's extensive experience in "biker bars" (October 7, 2006).

Body styles seen at shows, dealers, and ranges will often be read as working class. In the summer when sleeves are short, tattoos may be seen often, which is a case in point concerning the system of signs at work here. Obviously, people of all classes sport tattoos now but the marks retain working-class meanings regardless. I believe one will find heavier bodies, a more corpulent style, among the gun culture. These are not physiques toned in expensive gyms or by taking leisurely walks in the evening with the shi-tzu, these are bodies that work hard and then rest on couches with beer in the evenings. No slim White dukes or Nancy Reagans here. As Anthony Bourdain observed, "How did the age-old equation that poor equals thin and rich equals fat change so that now our working poor are huge and slow-moving, and only the wealthy can afford the personal trainers, liposuction, and extended spa treatments required, it seems, to be thin?" (12–13).

Some body styles show the damage of a hard life more likely experienced in the factory or field than in the corner office: some people are bent, some limping, some stand or sit gingerly. One typical published image shows a sweating, dirty shotgunner whose grimy fingers are heavily taped and bandaged, having suffered some sort of damage recently, perhaps from his own Benelli (*AR*, October 2006, 11). One dealer who frequented Milwaukee gun shows was missing nearly all of his fingers beyond the first knuckle, on both hands. His business—wait for it—was selling knives. I imagine, I hope, that his affliction beset him at work, before he began dealing in those goods.

Clothing typically found where the gun culture congregates also will be read as working class, and here, too, some of this system of style works by way of exclusion, or what it is not. You will *never* find a suit or sport coat, tie, cardigan sweater, and the like in these places. You won't find polished leather shoes. Flashy Hawaiian or guayabera shirts are never seen—too much like vacation, too much associated with those who can afford to go to places where such styles originated. You do find plain, simple, homey clothing, made of denim, khaki, or synthetic fabrics. A photo spread of the 2006 NRA convention shows a lot of buckskin, jeans, baseball caps, and cowboy hats (*AR*, August 2006, 59). Perhaps you will find leather jackets at the range, show, or dealer's, the more creased and worn the better. Overalls and jeans are quite common, often of unfashionable brands generally available at discount stores, often worn with sweatshirts, or worn plaid or checked shirts. The magazine reader is advised to buy clothing on discount from the *Sportsman's Guide*, and some plain clothes indeed are depicted (*AR*, October 2006, 64). In another issue the appeal for the *Guide* is made plain: "Stop wasting your money! Always for Less! (*AR*, August 2006, 41). Younger men and boys often wear "wife beaters" or muscle shirts. It is not at all unusual to find someone in a work-shirt uniform, their last name stitched over a pocket and a company logo on the shoulder. Old t-shirts with faded icons and slogans, nondescript sweat suits, old leather shoes or canvas sneakers are the order of the day. Hats are fairly common, and they are nearly always baseball "gimme" caps or cowboy hats in one style or another.

Images from *American Rifleman* illustrate these elements of working-class style, telling the gun culture what to display, calling to those who will display the style. A man and his young son sit on a concrete city pier (rather than in a pricey boat), fishing; they wear simple clothing and baseball caps

(*AR*, October 2006, inside front cover). A championship pistol shooter wears a gimme cap advertising shooting products (*AR*, August 2006, 21). A rifle shooter at a gun range is wearing the same style of cap with a different logo (*AR*, August 2006, 29). That style appears again in an advertisement for the Outdoor Channel (*AR*, August 2006, 89) and in an ad for Sierra bullets (*AR*, July 2006, 25). Other working-class avatars are represented. Surely, there is no more characteristic icon of the working class than Elvis Presley ("Born poor in a two-room house in Tupelo, Mississippi"), and, sure enough, the Elvis commemorative pistol is for sale at just a touch under two grand (*AR*, September 2006, 3).

The cowboy style is often integrated with working-class style, being a sort of frontier subset. The Yamaha ATV is advertised with photographs of hard-working cowboys roping cattle in a rodeo and with a camouflaged hunter in the woods—"In this arena, ain't nothin' tougher" is declared (*AR*, October 2006, 30–31). *Arena* is a metaphor turning the act of hunting into a melded cowboy/rodeo/working-class experience. An advertisement for Tony Lama boots advises the reader to "look like a cowboy. Work like a maverick," and "Western Work" is the name of the line of footwear offered (*AR*, October 2006, 34). A cowboy hat, jeans, and Western shirt adorn a rifleman in a Ruger ad (*AR*, June 2006, 3).

Voices bespeak the working class. Accents are demotic: in the places I have experienced, accents are plain, honest Midwestern, Southern, or Southwestern. Vocabulary tends to be plain, except when discussing technicalities of firearms. I once went to a gun show with a fellow professor where we found ourselves discussing the "aesthetics" of this or that firearm—and it suddenly occurred to us that *aesthetics* was a word very unlikely to be widely used by those around us in that context. "It ain't easy," complains a homely advertisement for Burris scopes (*AR*, October 2006, 37).

I am not at all saying that those who attend gun shows or go to the range are unlearned or simple. Often, it is quite the contrary—another gun-culture friend of mine (and Mensa member) once pointed out a dealer behind a gun-show table who was likewise a member of Mensa. But the style enacted is of a way of speaking, both in tone and content, that especially bespeaks the experience of people who have over the long haul had little time for idle chatter, who have had hard work to do with their backs and hands, out in the weather. Speech is direct and pointed. Speech is generally reserved—you will hear very few blabbermouths at gun shows or on ranges, many sit silently at their tables or benches, acknowledging your presence or passing with a firm nod and direct eye contact. Small talk is usually about guns or politics—and the politics is uniformly conservative. One rec.guns poster complained of receiving an offensive answer to a question he asked a person who was carrying a handgun. The fellow is admonished by another poster that "you might have been a little too curious for his temperament" (October 8, 2006). People address each other politely: "sir" or "ma'am" is often heard, and as one threads through the crowded aisles of gun shows, one constantly hears apologies for the inevitable shove or bump. Sales are always concluded with a firm handshake and a straight look in the eye. As the science fiction author Robert A. Heinlein is famously and often quoted as saying (e.g., Petrie, Smith), "An armed society is a polite society."

In sum, to enter the gun culture is to enter a world of signs, to permit oneself to become a subject constructed by those signs, a world that revolves systematically and predictably around meanings of the working class. Now, any such system of signs will inevitably entail contradictions, and these contradictions are key to understanding the ideological work done by those signs. Let us examine two sets of contradictions emerging from the gun culture's working class style.

### The First Tension: Individuality and Self-Determination versus Rules, Order, and Deference

To understand this first tension of individuality and self-determination versus rules, order, and deference, it helps to have worked at working-class jobs, as I have. I earned money in my rosy youth by painting buildings, working around farms, shoveling manure (and now I chair a university department), hauling pinball machines, serving as a security guard, and once I had the Dickensian employment of laboring in a grindstone factory. In such work, it becomes clear early on that you have to please the boss to keep your job—and very often, you really *need* to keep that job. Deference to authority must be performed, but it must also be real. This deference becomes engrained through the work and the discourses surrounding the work.

At the same time that one defers to authority for economic reasons, the working-class experience is often one of resentment and defiance of that very authority. It can be oppressive to work in the strict regimen of the factory or field day in and day out. Conditions are harsh, and very little variation from rules, order, and procedures is allowed. Creativity is rarely encouraged. There is the lingering awareness that you work hard, take many physical risks, and make considerably less money than your supervisors so as to enrich someone else. There is resentment against the often-petty exercise of power by those appointed over you. The contradiction between rules, order, and deference on the one hand and defiance of authority and power on the other is broadly enacted in working-class style, both in a wide range of texts and in personal performances. One finds those contradictions in gun-culture style.

Deference to authority in the form of following rules is key to many working-class jobs. If one is in a union, union rules must be strictly followed not only for legal reasons but because they are in one's own class interests. Union or no, most working-class workplaces have strict rules of conduct and procedure. Sometimes these rules are to ensure safe and correct functioning of heavy equipment. Sometimes they are for insurance purposes. Sometimes they are handed down by higher management for what seem no better than whimsical purposes. But rules, order, and strict procedure are inherent to the everyday reality of the working class. Deference to authority thus becomes central to working-class style. One must performance deference daily on the job.

Deference to rules and authority is expressed in the gun-culture literature. Think of these expressions as coaching and modeling a style emphasizing the primacy of rules, a style around which an imaginary community will cohere. "The first rule of gunfighting" is humorously described as "have a gun" (*AR*, September 2006, 87). Gun owners are encouraged to work at "understanding the rules and procedures that must be followed when traveling with firearms and ammunition" (*AR*, October 2006, 88). NRA members are encouraged dutifully "to report suspected security violations" they observe among those who travel with guns (*AR*, October 2006, 94). Citizens who wished to keep their guns in the aftermath of Hurricane Katrina and in the face of police confiscation are described as "law-abiding" (*AR*, October 2006, 12), a term often applied to those who wish to keep guns legally.

In a sense, the Second Amendment to the Constitution itself embodies this first contradiction: "A well regulated Militia, being necessary to the security of a free State, the right of the people to keep and bear Arms, shall not be infringed." While I am very far from being a scholar of Constitutional law, one need not dig very deep here to notice the emphasis on regulations in regard to the militia, as against a right generally granted to and dispersed among the population. On the other hand, the bearing of arms outside of the military or police is necessarily something that people do individually, holding those arms in their homes or on their persons. One can even find this contradiction in that little nugget halfway through the amendment: "free State." One could well argue that to the extent one is "free," then one is not subject to the "State," and to the extent one obeys the "State," then one is not "free."

When one learns to shoot, typically a set of firm rules will be instilled: assume the gun is always loaded—never point the gun at anything one isn't willing to destroy—be sure of one's target and of what lies beyond it—keep one's finger out of the trigger guard until ready to fire. Many a range master or parent drills these rules into novices, and they are indeed important. Were they obeyed, there would rarely be firearms accidents. A gun-culture style is one grounded in rules. But one must not only follow rules, one must perform a style of deference and discipline when in that culture.

When people gather to shoot—whether at organized matches or for individual practice at gun ranges—there is typically a "range master" of some sort who is in charge of enforcing rules. Usually, this individual does so with a ferocious personal style and with good reason. For instance, at some outdoor ranges, especially the more basic and less high-tech sort, cease-fires are called from time to time so that shooters may walk forward from their stations to check or change their paper targets downrange. It is of vital importance that all firearms be put down on the bench and empty with actions open while people are walking toward the targets. The shooter found fiddling with a gun during a cease-fire or breaking any of these rules in any way will incur the wrath of the range master and ostracism from fellow shooters. I have observed that range masters perform styles of near-military rigor and discipline while shooters follow suit by enacting ostentatious deference.

Rules are often enforced at gun shows and stores as well, where the usual practice is to ask the dealer if one may handle a firearm on display, if one may dry fire it (pull the trigger on an unloaded gun), and there is an expectation in testing out the feel of these guns that one does not take aim at anyone. One may well hear something unpleasant from dealers or fellow shoppers if one breaks these rules. Style is an important part of this enforcement of rules, for commands are uttered with vocal force and presence, authority clearly expressed in the loud voice and personal assertiveness of those enforcing the rules.

Postings on rec.guns often evoke rules and proper procedures. Discussions of "reloading," or the home loading of ammunition (which is often a hobby in its own right), are full of forceful or clear statements as to technical specifications. That is a good thing, too, for failure to obey these rules can result in serious accidents. Think of these admonitions as both the online performance of style and modeling for a rule-governed style in an imaginary community. One poster acknowledges the rules others have put down for how far to seat a bullet safely in the case, for instance: "I realize that the bullet needs to be back off the lands just a fuzz" (October 10, 2006). Another poster is offended because another person, in showing him his gun inside a store, "pulled the gun in the store and pointed it at the tanning salon next door" which will be read by disciplined gunners as utterly against accepted safety procedures (October 8, 2006). The person who pulled the gun is chastised by another poster for breaking laws governing concealed carry, describing him as "a stranger who thinks he's beyond CCW [Concealed-Carry Weapon] regulations" (October 8, 2006). Others chime in with similar invocation of broken rules: "To pull it out and wave it around your store is reckless, and shows that this guy is not responsible. If he had wanted to show it to you, he should have asked your permission first, then unholstered it, and safely unloaded it." And in response to a customer's statement that he kept the gun to use on other motorists who crowded him on the road, the same poster continues to cite laws: "To point it at someone for 'unsafe driving' is beyond reckless, it is criminal brandishing. He should face charges for doing that" (October 9, 2006). Another posting on a different topic castigates the family of a recently slain criminal for not teaching their son moral and social rules: "MOMMY is the one who failed her child; didn't teach him right from wrong, and I note the FATHER was not present, mentioned, or commented about" (October 14, 2006).

The first tension within the gun culture's working-class style arises because the culture also includes suspicion, resentment, and defiance of power and authority, the sources of rules. The second half of the paradox of the working class may be understood as resentment of overbearing and unfair authority. Working-class life is often balanced between the need to keep a job and the yearning to tell superiors where that job may be shoved. The poignancy of that paradox is summed up in an advertisement for Leupold riflescopes: "It's okay to break the rules—if you're the one who makes them" (*AR*, October 2006, 28–29). That statement reflects both a yearning to break rules and an awareness that for the most part, one does *not* make them. Another advertisement for a gunmaker declares, "Some attempt to redefine limits. Kimber removes them," expressing a strong yearning to escape the setting of limits (*AR*, August 2006, back cover).

One important way in which this resentment is expressed is in depictions of those who would put restrictions on gun use or ownership. Here especially we can see the working-class nature of gun-culture style. This dimension of style is one of suspicion and resentment of power, epitomized in Charlton Heston's oft-repeated rhetorical challenge to gun grabbers to come take his rifle "from my cold, dead hands," a declaration he often performed in public while waving that weapon defiantly above his head (for an example, see "Heston Guns" from the BBC Web site). Those in favor of gun control are often pictured as "abusive corporate giants" (*AR*, May 2006, 10) or "the liberal media" (rec.guns, October 14, 2006), funded by economically, socially privileged "rich anti-gun donors" (*AR*, September 2006, 16). Wayne LaPierre, NRA executive vice-president, made a point of identifying the enemy as of high economic status in arguing, "New York billionaire Mayor Michael Bloomberg [is] emerging as the kingpin of a renewed culture war against private ownership of firearms" (*AR*, August 2006, 10). In another column, it is noted that Bloomberg spent "$87 million of his own funds" on his election campaign (*AR*, July 2006, 10). Gun grabbers are depicted as having an "elitist mind-set that it's okay to ban guns they don't own" (*AR*, September 2006, 15). A favorite ploy of the gun culture is to identify advocates of gun control as themselves hiring expensive bodyguards or security services to achieve the protection the working class must do for itself, if it can, with less means: Wisconsin Governor Jim Doyle (despised by the NRA for vetoing a concealed-carry bill) and his "henchmen" are described as enjoying "limousines and security details" paid for by ordinary citizens (*AR*, July 2006, 15). If these elites do get in trouble, they have "greedy trial lawyer allies" to help them out (*AR*, August 2006, 10). These lawyers can have you "hauled into civil court" if you defend yourself with a gun, as one rec.guns posting claims (October 14, 2006). Rules of political correctness also infringe on individual rights, as in a complaint from a rec.guns posting: "That's the problem with our PC times. The honest answer never suffices" (October 17, 2006).

Formidable power and privilege are attributed to gun-control advocates. Allegedly antigun New York Senator Charles Schumer is described in one article as a "power broker" who is "orchestrating the senate takeover" by liberals (*AR*, October 2006, 10). U.S. Representative Rahm Emanuel is described as "Bill Clinton's White House gun control czar" (*AR*, October 2006, 10). Powerful antigun opponents are compared to that epitome of evil power, Lord Voldemort from the *Harry Potter* series (*AR*, September 2006, 10). Antigun activists are funded by powerful backers, such as, "New York City dot-com billionaire Andrew McKelvey," who plan to take away the rights of ordinary, "grassroots" gun owners (*AR*, September 2006, 14–15). Another article likewise contrasts well-funded antigun campaigns with "the grassroots, person-to-person efforts of NRA members" (*AR*, May 2006, 10). Overweening corporate or bureaucratic powers are often accused "of heavy-handed tactics against law-abiding citizens" (*AR*, May 2006, 15).

The United Nations is a favorite sinister power agent, working to "ban civilian possession of small arms worldwide," and U.S. officials are depicted as "resolute in not giving one inch of ground to the dictatorships and terrorists" that influence the U.N. (*AR*, September 2006, 10). The connection between the U.N. and social elites is made clear: "And now the United Nations is engaged in a global gun-ban scheme. It is well-organized and well-funded by eccentric anti-gun billionaires" (*AR*, August 2006, 12). The thing to notice about these claims is not the histrionics so much as the ways in which they both perform and coach a style of resentment of authority.

One incident described on rec.guns shows the tension between the gun culture and authority. A roughly dressed fellow came into a mailing store carrying an ill-concealed pistol. The clerk behind the counter reports, "I asked him if that gun was his personal or if it was issued," in other words, if the customer were a law-enforcement officer. The response: "Instantly, he stepped back and gave me a double-take, raised his hands in the air and asked, 'Do I look like a cop?'" (October 7, 2006). Evidently, the customer, being rather ragged, did not look like any such a thing, but note the offense he evidently took at being taken for an officer, and note that his denial draws a sharp distinction between authority and his down-home style of clothing. In sum, gun culture performs stylistically the common working-class tension between deference to, yet resentment of, power and authority. Although most people experience that tension to some extent, the working class is especially likely, socially and politically, to find such a conflict immediate and poignant.

### The Second Tension: Rural Work Contexts and Urban Threats

Gun-culture style is heavy with the enactment of working class personae and especially a *rural* working class. The style bespeaks working the land. As an ad for hunting binoculars says, "Agriculture is big in this part of Colorado and the deer seem to step right out into the fields" (*AR*, September 2006, 43). Personal performances and the proliferation of images of the rural working class are a key part of gun-culture style, both in person and through representations. If you go to a gun show, you will find the parking lot absolutely full of heavy pickup trucks, panel trucks, and 4x4s, all of them enormous. I park my little silver two-door coupe among them and feel as if I am in the bottom of the Grand Canyon. I have no way of knowing how many of these vehicles do actual rural work, but there simply cannot be that many ranchers and farmers in this world. It is a working-class style being enacted, a style that has subsumed any distinct reality. The pickup truck connection to the gun culture is made clear with the inauguration of the "Ruger Ram," which is "a promotional concept vehicle" that is a Dodge Ram pickup truck outfitted by the Ruger firearms company (*AR*, May 2006, 30). As with clothing, automobile styles that one does *not* find in gun-culture style are often telling. Gun publications rarely or never advertise for street automobiles like sedans. You are much more likely to find tests of the Polaris X2 off-road vehicle (*AR*, July 2006, 30–31). These are some of the key signs around which this imaginary community coheres. And I believe it is important to understand gun culture as an imaginary community, real people who are drawn to a sense of community through style, who are constructing their own sense of identity from the symbolic resources available in gun stores and gun shows and on the shooting range.

Personal appearance, as noted above, displays signs of the working class but also specifically of the rural working class. Skin is weathered and often bespeaks years of smoking and of outdoors work. Boots are common, and they also are unlikely to be new and shiny but will show bona fide years of hard outdoor exposure. The gimme caps show a high percentage of logos for agricultural implements or seed companies.

Images in *American Rifleman* repeat a rural, outdoors theme. "Harness your tractor's power to eliminate ugly brush piles" shouts an advertisement for the DR Chipper (*AR*, June 2006, 37), not the sort of thing that afflicts them in SoHo. An advertisement offers "The Winning of the West Tribute Rifle" accompanied by old-fashioned drawings of rural, Old West scenes (*AR*, October 2006, 5). One image advertising the Henry rifle shows a man in cowboy attire sleeping on the grass by a campfire and another man in a fringed Western jacket (*AR*, October 2006, 5). Scenes of the outdoors with wildlife are quite common, as in an advertisement for Marlin rifles featuring a moose by a mountain stream (*AR*, June 2006, 21).

Hunting plays an important part in gun-culture style, and, of course, hunting is perforce a rural experience. People are sometimes dressed in hunting camouflage at gun shows, ranges, or dealers. Photographs of hunters with downed animals abound in publications. Stories of hunting experiences are widely exchanged. Overheard conversations revolve around hunting trips past or recent, preparations for future trips, and preferences for gear and firearms in that activity. Posts in rec.guns often show a familiarity with hunting, as in this reference to a Winchester rifle, to "the 92, of course, not being capable of taking the big boys" (October 12, 2006), such as, bear.

Hunting is depicted as the utilitarian task of putting food on the table, as a way to stretch the family dollar, rather than simply as an exciting sport. The reality that it can be hard, outdoor work is celebrated. An advertisement declares, "It's 32°. It's sleeting. It's a great day for a Knight," and the image is of a hunter in heavy camouflage firing a blackpowder rifle in the deep, snowy woods (*AR*, October 2006, 1). Another image is a drawing of a hunter taking aim in a vast, outdoor scene, peering through the Simmons riflescope that is on offer (*AR*, October 2006, 7). The Franchi shotgun is described as ideal "if I needed a light gun to drag through grouse and woodcock cover," clearly a reference to rural work (*AR*, October 2006, 79). On rec.guns, one often finds references to hunting in a rural environment, as in the claim, "I live in south Texas and do not plan to hunt very far away. I will mostly be targeting deer and hogs" (October 22, 2006). Another poster advocates using the .270 cartridge "if you're sticking with deer and hogs" or switching to the .30–06 "for elk and bear" (October 23, 2006). The .30-06 is recommended "for deer or elk" by another hunter (October 23, 2006). An extended hunting story is told of "the second in command of the CDC [Centers for Disease Control] in Alaska" who was in Alaska deer hunting "with a .270 when he was confronted by a Brown bear. His body was found by the Coast Guard . . . under brush, half eaten" (October 23, 2006).

A theme bespeaking the rural working class that one finds from time to time especially in gun magazines is that guns and their accessories are tools meant for work, specifically "chores" or related tasks. The Surefire flashlight is offered for Father's Day as "something he'll carry and use and get a kick out of for years . . . [for] camping, fishing, hiking, hunting, disaster prepared-ness or, just changing a tire in the night" (*AR*, June 2006, 13). These terms and the kind of work the tools are described as useful for all bespeak a rural working-class style.

A whole class of rifles is known as the "varmint rifle," such as the Sav-age Model 12, offered to readers specifically as a tool to kill rural pests (*AR*, October 2006, 72–73). The 6 mm Remington cartridges are described as containing "more practical varmint bullets and are my choice for coyotes" (*AR*, September 2006, 54). A rec.guns posting discusses ways "to double the usage of my .308 as a varmint rifle for coyotes" (October 23, 2006). Another one claims of the .30-06 cartridge and rifle, "With the right ammo, it's enough gun to handle anything from varmints (assuming you don't mind the 'red mist' factor on the little ones) to grizzlys [*sic*]" (October 22, 2006), also fea-turing the gun as a versatile tool.

Guns are not the only rural working-class implements mentioned, for one may find a DR field-and-brush mower advertised as a way to "clear and main-tain meadows, pastures, roadsides, fencelines, walking paths with ease!" (*AR*, October 2006, 97). A rec.guns post uses the language of tools in describing one rifle as "a superior club to a handgun" (October 12, 2006). Another poster is "trading up" and is primarily interested in tools, looking for "a new Leather-man e307x pocketknife" (October 11, 2006). One poster makes an explicit link between tools and hunting with a familiar expression, describing a pistol just purchased for "tooling around in the woods with" (October 9, 2006).

If a rural working-class style is widely performed, there are, on the con-trary, many signs in gun-culture style that bespeak a context of urban threat. "A *violent* crime occurs every *23.1* seconds. How will you protect your *loved ones* when they become a target?" asks an advertisement for a political-ac-tion group (*AR*, September 2006, 92). Any gun store, range, or show will have a good representation of firearms that carry meanings of the city and its dangers. Black or gleaming semiautomatic pistols, AR-15 "black rifles," or AK-47s, whether military surplus or newly made for the civilian market, carry meanings of urban combat and threat; one can purchase the *American Rifleman Guide to Black Rifles* (*AR*, August 2006, 31). We learn these urban references from the media, such as, film, television, and popular music (es-pecially hip-hop), which is full of visual and verbal advice about the kinds of guns that might threaten us. The style that is coached by this vision of urban threat is one of constant vigilance and watchfulness, a suspicion that every passing stranger or knock at the door could mean an attack—and that, of course, is not the same as the laid-back, rural style that is also part of the gun culture.

Each issue of *American Rifleman* begins with a section called "Armed Citizen," full of brief extracts from newspapers around the country of incidents in which armed citizens successfully defended themselves, their families, and their properties from assault by showing or shooting their own weapons. The great majority of these anecdotes are from urban or town settings. Very rarely is a story told of the farmer who grabbed his hunting rifle to defend the lonely, isolated ranch. People in these reports are in their homes or places of business in a city, town, or suburb when someone tries to break in or to rob them. Rarely is a motive for the assault given, unless it is obviously a robbery. Overwhelming rage, lifelong criminal addiction, and a passion for destruction are more often attributed to these assailants. The expectation of constant threat is thus coached in the culture.

For example, in one issue (*AR*, October 2006, 8), an intruder breaks into a home to steal the keys to a local bank, bespeaking a dense, urban setting. One story is of a "burglar with a violent and lengthy criminal record" who bursts into a Denver home, and another story is of a man returning to his urban Detroit home to confront "a masked gunman waiting in his garage" (*AR*, October 2006, 8). Another Detroit resident awakes to find his cash being counted in his kitchen by a stranger, whereupon the resident draws a pistol and holds the stranger for police (*AR*, July 2006, 8). In Houston, a homeowner confronts "two armed teens up to no good" and shoots them, while another resident wounds a "phony utility worker" who sought to gain access to his home in the same city (*AR*, September 2006, 12). Yet another Houston intruder is shot by a homeowner after running through six yards, bespeaking an urban or suburban setting (*AR*, August 2006, 8). Houston must be a remarkably violent city, as some such confrontation is reported in most of the "Armed Citizen" columns: one resident is confronted at the door by thugs armed with tire irons, and another homeowner is met by robbers as he enters his house—both incidents end when the homeowners shoot their assailants (*AR*, July 2006, 8). Beyond the "Armed Citizen" column are references to police gun confiscations that "left the good people of New Orleans defenseless against free-ranging criminal predators" who supposedly surround us in urban settings, barely suppressed by the thin blue line of the police (*AR*, October 2006, 10).

Rec.guns postings tend to describe urban threats to safety and security. One person declares, "Only gangsters and criminals carry a gun to intimidate others. Good citizens carry them to defend themselves and others from grave harm" (October 9, 2006). Another posting reports, "Shots were also exchanged between the suspect and a detective in a residential area" of his city (October 13, 2006). In a lengthy posting, one person reminisces "about how many cops I've known that were killed on the job" during his career as a deputy sheriff, and the contexts he recites are largely urban or suburban (October 18, 2006).

Thus, gun-culture style coheres around and calls to motivations of threat and danger as an omnipresent factor in the urban experience. I think a strong implication of such a depiction is that the urban social context itself, especially a heterogeneous one full of strangers and Others, is threatening. Gun-culture style is relaxed in the great outdoors, on guard in the alleyways. The conflict between those two contexts remains unresolved in gun-culture style.

As noted before, to say that the gun culture has a contradictory style is no sort of negative criticism at all. Every style with ideological impact has contradictions because ideology is contradictory. Contradictions can be windows into some interesting implications of an ideology and hence of a style, and that is true of gun culture.

In a sense, the two contradictions observed here overlap—they merge in their implications and resonances. The yearning for freedom and lack of restrictions is resonant with the rural milieu, in which one can often do as one likes without the censure of neighbors or the police. The city and suburbs are a place of closer scrutiny and judgment from others. Go outside and fire a shotgun in the country, and then do so in town, and see what the differing results are in terms of rules and regulations versus freedom from constraints. Even if a game warden may be nearby, hunting is in many ways the essence of free movement with tremendous power literally in one's hands. To be in the city is to be bound around by authority and law. The two contradictions touch each other in the opposition between *powerful agency* on the one hand and *frustrating constraints* on the other.

That tension or opposition may be summed up in one image or figure: *the loaded gun that is never used.* Gun owners will often have such a thing somewhere: in the car, tucked under a shirt, locked in a gun cabinet, under the bed, and so forth. It could well be argued that such a gun is, in reality, being used even if never fired, for it stands in readiness to do so, for better or worse, and that is what the gun owner wants it for. On the other hand, such a weapon might be described as the gun that is all loaded up with nobody to kill. That image, embodying the tension between the readiness for action and the constraints against action, sums up the conflicted ideology of the gun-culture style. More than many other styles, it is one of repressed agency, of shackled power—and the political impact is to perpetuate a hegemony that has kept the working class in just such a position.

The working class is practically by definition an exploited demographic in late capitalism. The hegemonic power structure that keeps working-class people subjugated is served by many strategies. The tension between agency and constraint that underlies the contradictions shown in this chapter in gun-culture style is a major means of that subjugation. Gun-culture style may, thus, be seen as part of a wider effort to preserve an exploitive class structure. Subjects within that style may know they are being subjugated but feel limited means to refuse their disempowerment. That is much of the social and political work that gun-culture style does, that is to say, such is the rhetoric of gun-culture style.

Should the revolution come, should jack-booted thugs go out to confiscate weapons, the gun culture might be the first to cry defiantly, "Come and take it." It might also be the first to roll over, to give in to authority from a lifetime of being coached to do that very thing. The free-ranging and independent agency of the hunting field might prevail, or the culture might roll up into besieged, encircled urban dwellers, packing heat to answer the door for every pizza delivery. But one need not be so histrionic as to pose a revolution, for the working class must face these tensions every day. Foremen and supervisors come to pry creativity and self-respect from the warm, living hands of those who labor every day, while personal freedom and safety are threatened by the unsafe conditions and unfair regulations of working-class workplaces every day. In replicating these tensions, gun-culture style may well be coaching the working class to continue living with them as well.

# Postface, with an Imaginary Etymology

> If sophistication is a matter of being in control of our primary
> reactions, we may now be sophisticated.
> —Quentin Crisp, *How to Have a Life-Style*, 173

I began with a preface. It seems at least as logical as it is whimsical to end
with a postface. This has been a book about putting on a good show, creating a persona, projecting a style. Therefore, I could wish that the etymology
of *preface* were different from what it actually is, because it would affect the
meaning of the bogus term *postface*—indeed, it would affect the meaning of
the whole book. *Preface* is taken from the Latin *praefātiō*, a saying before-
hand, based on the Latin *fātum* or utterance—how utterly predictable. A
postface must then be a saying afterward—well, of course. How I wish both
terms were derived instead from *faciēs*, meaning face or facial. But in style,
we can make things up as long as they look good, so let's do.

A preface would then be what comes before the face, and a postface would
come after the face. Ah, the face: the epitome of surfaces, the thing that is
only beautiful down through the skin, that playground of style, that instrument of dissembling. The book in between would then be but a face, a screen,
a mask, a persona—and it is not hard to find a real etymology of "sounding
through" for *persona*, as in what the performer does in speaking through
a mask that is worn in a performance. In a sense, the current volume is the
style I am performing for the reader, and it is the mask I wear. As is the case
with so much style today, this is all of me that most of you will ever encounter. For all practical purposes, for most of you, this bookish face *is* me. The
surface, this face, is my substance. Yet, if you have made it this far, perhaps
you do not think that the mere face I have worn has been inconsequential.
And who are you, Gentle Reader, as you construct yourself momentarily
around this book? With what style do you read me and compose imaginary
objections or praises in your head? Is your style as reader inconsequential
because it is a style?

Inconsequentiality, inauthenticity, mere skin: such is the nature of many complaints that may linger about my treatment of style here. Many may feel that at the end of the day, style remains but a surface and that a world increasingly engrossed in style is going to hell on a scholarship. The reader may still be refusing my earlier collapse of substance into style. This concern is real and has validity, and it deserves several responses here at the end of my argument.

First, we need to heed the lessons of history and be careful. Each era looks to a golden past—often a recent past—and compares it to its own age, whose members see as a cesspool of degeneration. Their children will see the world in just the same way. It is hard to see where we are as we move through history and impossible to see where we are going. The generations after us, afflicted with the same anxieties, will feel the same way and envy us in our frozen blocks of time, all our virtues and vices reduced to a few sentences in the history books. This is especially true when it comes to changes sponsored by new technologies. Every new technology is feared, is compared unfavorably to the one before, and is misunderstood, especially in the early years of its inception. We simply have fewer anxieties about computers, for instance, now than we did during their introduction into the global market and culture.

And at any rate, it is impossible to turn back a wave of global cultural change fueled by commerce and technology. If people around the world are obsessed with style because we are being driven to hyperconsume so as to support late capitalism, if technology is coming to make style and its sister, entertainment, more and more engrossing, if ways of thinking are shifting from the verbal, expositional, and demonstrative toward a more aesthetic mix—well, get over it. That's the way it is going to be.

Our task is more to understand than to bemoan. I am convinced that once a brave new world of stylistic discourse, rhetoric, and politics becomes the usual thing for people, it will start to seem like the right thing. What is key is to know how this globally spreading system of signification works and to understand our place in it. I believe that this book and others like it are important in helping people to move toward that understanding.

You will have noticed that each section of this book begins with an epigram by Quentin Crisp, that grand eccentric self-described as "one of the stately homos of England," that marvelous old master of style who paid dearly for his craft (e.g., going about in exquisite drag back in the days when Merry Olde England tolerated no such thing). The epigram for this postface is what I want to conclude with for it connects our scary new world of style with the ancient rhetorical tradition. Crisp reminds us that the history of rhetoric is a long session of talky argument, rounded with a style.

Rhetorical theory in the twentieth century experienced a rediscovery and rehabilitation of the ancient Sophists. Works by Susan Jarratt and Edward Schiappa (*Beginnings*) are but two strong examples of first-rate scholarship suggesting that the Sophists were not the knaves and dunces so often depicted by Plato in several dialogues, an infamy that later generations often accepted uncritically. This new understanding of the Sophists sees them as teachers who refused what would become, under Plato, a separation between thinking and doing, theory and political engagement, reason and aesthetics. The Sophists taught a way of merging wisdom with action, of employing thought in political agency, and of seeing all human faculties as joined together in addressing human problems—and that includes style, aesthetics, and reason. Is this not what we need today? Is this not a vision of how people think in a world so strongly influenced by the market and by aesthetics yet not devoid of reasoned thought? Other thinkers throughout history have glimpsed this possibility for the unity of human faculties in Sophistic rhetoric. Cicero in *De Oratore* attacks Plato precisely for splitting thinking and doing, rhetoric and philosophy, blaming him for "that divorce, as it were, of the tongue from the heart, a division certainly absurd, useless, and reprehensible, that one class of persons should teach us to think and another to speak, rightly" (3.16). Amen to that. Yet, perhaps in our era, that divorce has been annulled, and in style, we might see a better marriage of what it means to be human. Might we see such a reconciliation in today's political consultants who teach both what to say and what tie to wear? In today's advertisements that tell you what a product is for and entertain you for twenty seconds?

Throughout his book on the Sophists and sophistication, Mark Backman argues that we have become Sophists today, and I close by endorsing his view. The Sophists encouraged self-consciousness, an awareness of how one could change the world, how one was perceived by others, and most important, how such perceptions could be managed to bring about desired results. Our rhetoric today is a Sophistic rhetoric, our problems and joys are addressed through a discourse of style that subsumes all signs, images and narratives, clothing and argument. It is fitting that late capitalism, for all its faults, teaches that rhetoric to an expanding global network of connected consumers/audiences/publics for in that way also artificial barriers and divisions are dissolved. The rhetoric of style is new, and it is old, and it is how we communicate in our world today.

*References*
*Index*

# References

Ackroyd, Peter. *Dressing Up: Transvestism and Drag: The History of an Obsession.* London: Thames, 1979.

Adorno, Theodor W., and Max Horkheimer. "The Culture Industry: Enlightenment as Mass Deception." Miles, Hall, and Borden 95.

Alansari, Bader. "The Relationship between Anxiety and Cognitive Style Measured on the Stroop Test." *Social Behavior and Personality: An International Journal* 32 (2004): 283–94.

Allport, Gordon. *Personality, a Psychological Interpretation.* New York: Holt, 1937.

Althusser, Louis. *Lenin and Philosophy and Other Essays.* Trans. B. Brewster. New York: Monthly Review, 1971.

Ambady, N., M. Hallahan, and B. Conner. "Accuracy of Judgments of Sexual Orientation from Thin Slices of Behavior." *Journal of Personality and Social Psychology* 77 (1999): 538–47.

Ambady, N., M. Hallahan, and R. Rosenthal. "On Judging and Being Judged Accurately in Zero-Acquaintance Situations." *Journal of Personality and Social Psychology* 69 (1995): 518–29.

*American Rifleman.* Fairfax, VA: National Rifle Association. May–October 2006.

Archer, Dane, and Robin M. Akert. "Words and Everything Else: Verbal and Nonverbal Cues in Social Interpretation." *Journal of Personality and Social Psychology* 35 (1977): 443–49.

Aristotle. *The Rhetoric and Poetics of Aristotle: Modern Library Edition.* Ed. Edward P. J. Corbett. Trans. W. Rhys Roberts and Ingram Bywater. New York: Random, 1954.

Babuscio, Jack. "Camp and the Gay Sensibility." Bergman 19–38.

Back, Les, Michael Keith, and John Solomos. "Reading the Writing on the Wall: Graffiti in the Racialized City." Slayden and Whillock 69–102.

Backman, Mark. *Sophistication: Rhetoric and the Rise of Self-Consciousness.* Woodbridge, CT: Ox Bow, 1991.

Barnard, Malcolm. *Fashion as Communication.* 2nd ed. London: Routledge, 2002.

Baudrillard, Jean. *The Ecstasy of Communication.* New York: Semiotext(e), 1987.

———. *Simulations.* New York: Semiotext(e), 1983.

Bauman, Zygmunt. *Community: Seeking Safety in an Insecure World.* Cambridge, UK: Polity, 2001.

———. "From Pilgrim to Tourist—or a Short History of Identity." Hall and du Gay 18–36.

Becker, Carol. "The Art of Subversive Image Making." Slayden and Whillock 103–12.

Beitel, Mark, Elena Ferrer, and John J. Cecero. "Psychological Mindedness and Cognitive Style." *Journal of Clinical Psychology* 60 (2004): 567–83.

Bellesiles, Michael A. *Arming America: The Origins of a National Gun Culture.* Brooklyn: Soft Skull, 2003.

Benjamin, Walter. *Illuminations.* Trans. Harry Zohn. Ed. Hannah Arendt. New York: Schocken, 1968.

Bergman, David, ed. *Camp Grounds: Style and Homosexuality.* Amherst: U of Massachusetts P, 1993.

Bernstein, Jacob. "New York's Gun Culture." *New York.* 1 October 2006 <http://newyorkmetro.com/nymetro/news/people/columns/intelligencer/9920/>.

Bitzer, Lloyd F. "The Rhetorical Situation." *Philosophy and Rhetoric* 1 (1968): 1–14.

Blair, Hugh. *Lectures on Rhetoric and Belles Lettres.* 1783. Philadelphia: Zell, 1860.

Bourdain, Anthony. *The Nasty Bits: Collected Varietal Cuts, Usable Trim, Scraps, and Bones.* New York: Bloomsbury, 2006.

Bourdieu, Pierre. *Acts of Resistance: Against the Tyranny of the Market.* Trans. Richard Nice. New York: New, 1998.

Brummett, Barry. "At the Gun Show." *Pedestal Magazine.* December 2004–February 2005. 1 October 2006 <http://www.thepedestalmagazine.com/Secure/content/cb.asp?cbid=4545>.

———. "A Counter-Statement to Depoliticization: Mediation and Simulational Politics." *Nordicom* 26 (2004): 111–20.

———. *Rhetorical Homologies: Form, Culture, Experience.* Tuscaloosa: U of Alabama P, 2004.

———. *Rhetoric in Popular Culture.* 2nd ed. Thousand Oaks, CA: Sage, 2006.

———. *The World and How We Describe it: Rhetorics of Reality, Representation, Simulation.* Westport, CT: Praeger, 2003.

Bryant, Donald C. *Rhetorical Dimensions in Criticism.* Baton Rouge: Louisiana State UP, 1973.

Buie, Sarah. "Market as Mandala: The Erotic Space of Commerce." Miles, Hall, and Borden 26–28.

Burke, Kenneth. *A Grammar of Motives.* Berkeley: U of California P, 1962.

———. *Language as Symbolic Action.* Berkeley: U of California P, 1966.

Butler, Judith. *Gender Trouble: Feminism and the Subversion of Identity.* New York: Routledge, 1999.

————. "Performative Acts and Gender Constitution: An Essay in Phenomenology." *Performing Feminisms*. Ed. Sue-Ellen Case. Baltimore: Johns Hopkins UP, 1990. 270–82.

Campbell, George. *The Philosophy of Rhetoric*. Carbondale: Southern Illinois UP, 1963.

Cantor, Paul A. *Gilligan Unbound: Pop Culture in the Age of Globalization*. Lanham, MD: Rowman, 2001.

Cashmore, Ellis. "America's Paradox." Guins and Cruz 159–67.

Cicero, Marcus Tullius. *De Oratore (On the Orator)*. Trans. E. W. Sutton and H. Rackham. Cambridge, MA: Loeb, 1942.

Coates, Nigel. "Brief Encounters." Miles, Hall, and Borden 221–23.

Coelho, Denis A., and Sven Dahlman. "Comfort and Pleasure." Green and Jordan 321–32.

Crane, Diana. *Fashion and Its Social Agendas: Class, Gender, and Identity in Clothing*. Chicago: U of Chicago P, 2000.

Crisp, Quentin. *How to Have a Life-Style*. Los Angeles: Alyson, 1979.

Danesi, Marcel. *My Son Is an Alien: A Cultural Portrait of Today's Youth*. Lanham, MD: Rowman, 2003.

Davila, Joanne, Sara J. Steinberg, Lorig Kachadourian, Rebecca Cobb, and Frank Fincham. "Romantic Involvement and Depressive Symptoms in Early and Late Adolescence: The Role of a Preoccupied Relational Style." *Personal Relationships* 11 (2004): 161–79.

Debord, Guy. "The Commodity as Spectacle." Guins and Cruz 109–14.

de Certeau, Michel. *The Practice of Everyday Life*. Berkeley: U of California P, 1984.

Deutsche, Rosalyn. "Alternative Space." Miles, Hall, and Borden 200–203.

Donald, James. "The Citizen and the Man About Town." Hall and du Gay 170–90.

Doty, Alexander. *Making Things Perfectly Queer: Interpreting Mass Culture*. Minneapolis: U of Minneapolis P, 1993.

Douglas, Mary, and Baron Isherwood. *The World of Goods: Towards an Anthropology of Consumption*. London: Routledge, 1979.

du Gay, Paul. "Organizing Identity: Entrepreneurial Governance and Public Management." Hall and du Gay 151–69.

Evans, Jessica, and Stuart Hall. *Visual Culture: The Reader*. London: Sage, 1999.

Ewen, Stuart. *All Consuming Images: The Politics of Style in Contemporary Culture*. New York: Basic, 1988.

Ewen, Stuart, and Elizabeth Ewen. *Channels of Desire: Mass Images and the Shaping of American Consciousness*. 2nd ed. Minneapolis: U of Minnesota P, 1992.

"Famous Scotts: Sir Walter Scott (1771–1832)." 1 July 2006 <http://www.rampantscotland.com/famous/blfamscott.htm>.

Featherstone, Mike. *Consumer Culture and Postmodernism*. London: Sage, 1991.

Finnegan, Cara A. *Picturing Poverty: Print Culture and FSA Photographs.* Washington, DC: Smithsonian, 2003.

Fisher, Walter K. "Narration as a Human Communication Paradigm: The Case of Public Moral Argument." *Communication Monographs* 51 (1984): 1–22.

Fiske, John. "Popular Discrimination." Guins and Cruz 215–22.

———. *Understanding Popular Culture.* Boston: Unwin, 1989.

"French Headscarf Ban Opens Rifts." 11 February 2004. BBC. 1 July 2006 <http://news.bbc.co.uk/1/hi/world/europe/3478895.stm>.

"French Muslims Fear 'State within State.'" 12 February 2004. BBC. 1 July 2006 <http://news.bbc.co.uk/2/hi/europe/3482641.stm>.

Frith, Simon. "Music and Identity." Hall and du Gay 108–27.

Gabler, Neal. *Life the Movie: How Entertainment Conquered Reality.* New York: Knopf, 1998.

Gallaher, Peggy E. "Individual Differences in Nonverbal Behavior: Dimensions of Style." *Journal of Personality and Social Psychology* 63 (1992): 133–45.

Geiser-Getz, Glenn C. "Worlds at GWAR: Celebrations of Juvenile Resistance in Post-Punk Pop." Slayden and Whillock 247–66.

Gibson, William. *Count Zero.* 1986. New York: Ace, 1987.

———. *Mona Lisa Overdrive.* New York: Bantam, 1988.

———. *Neuromancer.* New York: Ace, 1984.

Giroux, Henry A. "Performing Cultural Studies as a Pedagogical Practice." Slayden and Whillock 191–202.

Goldberg, David Theo. "Call and Response: Sports, Talk Radio, and the Death of Democracy." Slayden and Whillock 29–42.

Goodman, Ellen. "Clothes Make the Candidate." *Austin American-Statesman* 30 July 2007: A11.

Gramsci, Antonio. *Selections from the Prison Notebooks.* Trans. Quentin Hoare and G. N. Smith. New York: International, 1971.

Green, Bill. "Pleasure with Products: Beyond Usability." Green and Jordan 2–5.

Green, William S., and Patrick W. Jordan, eds. *Pleasure with Products: Beyond Usability.* New York: Taylor and Francis, 2002.

Grewal, Iderpal. "Traveling Barbie: Indian Transnationality and New Consumer Subjects." Guins and Cruz 168–83.

Guins, Raiford, and Omayra Zaragoza Cruz, eds. *Popular Culture: A Reader.* London: Sage, 2005.

"Gun Culture." Gun Culture.1 October 2006 <http://www.gunculture.net/>.

Gunns, Rebekah E., Lucy Johnston, and Stephen M. Hudson. "Victim Selection and Kinematics: A Point-Light Investigation of Vulnerability to Attack." *Journal of Nonverbal Behavior* 26 (2002): 129–58.

Hale, Ellen. "British Fear Rise of 'Gun Culture.'" August 6, 2001. *USA Today.* 1 October 2006 <http://www.usatoday.com/news/world/2001/08/07/guns-usat.htm>.

Hall, Stuart. "Introduction. Who Needs 'Identity'?" Hall and du Gay 1–17.

———. "Notes on Deconstructing 'the Popular.'" Guins and Cruz 64–71.

———. "What Is This 'Black' in Black Popular Culture?" Guins and Cruz 285–93.

Hall, Stuart, and Paul du Gay, eds. *Questions of Cultural Identity*. London: Sage, 1996.

Hariman, Robert, and John Louis Lucaites. "Performing Civic Identity: The Iconic Photograph of the Flag Raising on Iwo Jima." *Quarterly Journal of Speech* 88 (2002): 363–92.

Hariman, Robert D. *Political Style: The Artistry of Power*. Chicago: U of Chicago P, 1995.

Hart, Roderick P. *Modern Rhetorical Criticism*. Glenview, IL: Scott, Foresman, 1990.

Hartley, John. "The Frequencies of Public Writing: Tomb, Tome, and Time as Technologies of the Public." MIT Communications Forum. 1 July 2006 <http://web.mit.edu/transition/subs/hartley.html>. Excerpt of *Democracy and New Media*, ed. Henry Jenkins and David Thorburn. Cambridge: MIT Press, 2003. Chapter 16.

———. *The Politics of Pictures: The Creation of the Public in the Age of Popular Media*. London: Routledge, 1992.

Hatfield, Gordon Toi, and Patricia Steur. *Dedicated by Blood: Renaissance of Ta Moko*. Auckland, New Zealand: Hunter, 2003.

Hauge-Nilsen, Anne-Lise, and Margaret Galer Flyte. "Understanding Attributes That Contribute to Pleasure in Product Use." Green and Jordan 257–70.

Hebdige, Dick. *Subculture: The Meaning of Style*. London: Methuen, 1979.

"Heston Guns for Fourth NRA Term." BBC. 20 May 2001. 1 October 2006 <http://news.bbc.co.uk/1/hi/entertainment/1341315.stm>.

hooks, bell. *Black Looks: Race and Representation*. Boston: South End, 1992.

———. *Where We Stand: Class Matters*. New York: Routledge, 2000.

Jameson, Fredric. "Reification and Utopia in Mass Culture." Guins and Cruz 115–28.

Jarratt, Susan C. *Rereading the Sophists: Classical Rhetoric Refigured*. Carbondale: Southern Illinois UP, 1991.

Jordan, Patrick W. "The Personalities of Products." Green and Jordan 19–47.

Kälviäinen, Mirja. "Product Design for Consumer Taste." Green and Jordan 77–95.

Kanemasa, Yuji, Junichi Taniguchi, Ikuo Daibo, and Masanori Ishimori. "Love Styles and Romantic Love Experiences in Japan." *Social Behavior and Personality: An International Journal* 32 (2004): 265–82.

Karp, Jennifer, Lisa A. Serbin, Dale M. Stack, and Alex E. Schwartzman. "An Observational Measure of Children's Behavioural Style: Evidence Supporting a Multi-Method Approach to Studying Temperament." *Infant and Child Development* 13 (2004): 135–59.

Kellett, Peter M., and H. L. Goodall Jr. "The Death of Discourse in Our Own (Chat) Room: 'Sextext,' Skillful Discussion, and Virtual Communication." Slayden and Whillock 155–89.

Kitwana, Bakari. *The Hip Hop Generation: Young Blacks and the Crisis in African American Culture.* New York: Basic, 2002.

Kracauer, Siegfried. "The Hotel Lobby." Miles, Hall, and Borden 145–48.

Lacan, Jacques. *Ecrits: A Selection.* Trans. Alan Sheridan. New York: Norton, 1977.

Leland, John. *Hip: The History.* New York: HarperCollins, 2004.

Lippmann, Walter. *Public Opinion.* New York: Free, 1997.

Lockford, Lesa. *Performing Femininity: Rewriting Gender Identity.* Walnut Creek, CA: AltaMira, 2004.

Long, Scott. "The Loneliness of Camp." Bergman 78–91.

Lowe, Lisa, and David Lloyd. "Introduction to the Politics of Culture in the Shadow of Late Capital." Guins and Cruz 129–46.

Maffesoli, Michel. *The Contemplation of the World: Figures of Community Style.* Trans. Susan Emanuel. Minneapolis: U of Minnesota P, 1996.

Majors, Richard, and Janet Mancini Billson. *Cool Pose: The Dilemmas of Black Manhood in America.* New York: Touchstone, 1992.

Miles, Malcolm, Tim Hall, and Iain Borden, eds. *The City Cultures Reader.* London: Routledge, 2000.

Milner, Andrew. *Class.* London: Sage, 1999.

Mort, Frank. *Cultures of Consumption: Masculinities and Social Space in Late Twentieth-century Britain.* London: Routledge, 1996.

Newton, Esther. "Role Models." Bergman 39–53.

Nixon, Sean. *Advertising Cultures.* London: Sage, 2003.

Norman, Donald A. *The Design of Everyday Things.* New York: Basic, 1988.

———. *Emotional Design: Why We Love (or Hate) Everyday Things.* New York: Basic, 2004.

Noyes, Jan, and Richard Littledale. "Beyond Usability, Computer Playfulness." Green and Jordan 49–59.

Nugent, Benjamin. "Who's a Nerd, Anyway?" *New York Times Magazine* 29 July 2007: 15.

Overbeeke, Kees, Tom Djadjadiningrat, Caroline Hummels, and Stephan Wensveen. "Beauty in Usability: Forget about Ease of Use!" Green and Jordan 9–17.

Petrie, John. "John Petrie's Collection of Robert A. Heinlein Quotes." 1 October 2006 <http://jpetrie.myweb.uga.edu/Heinlein.html>.

Plato. *Gorgias.* Walter Hamilton, Trans. Middlesex, UK: Penguin, 1960.

Postman, Neil. *Amusing Ourselves to Death: Public Discourse in the Age of Show Business.* New York: Penguin, 1985.

Postrel, Virginia. *The Substance of Style: How the Rise of Aesthetic Value Is Remaking Commerce, Culture, and Consciousness.* New York: HarperCollins, 2003.

Reinmoeller, Patrick. "Emergence of Pleasure: Communities of Interest and New Luxury Products." Green and Jordan 125–34.

Richards, I. A. *The Philosophy of Rhetoric*. London: Oxford UP, 1936.

Ritzer, George. *Explorations in the Sociology of Consumption: Fast Food, Credit Cards, and Casinos*. London: Sage, 2001.

Robertson, Pamela. "'The Kinda Comedy That Imitates Me'; Mae West's Identification with the Feminist Camp." Bergman 156–72.

Rose, Nikolas. "Identity, Genealogy, History." Hall and du Gay 128–50.

Rose, Tricia. "A Style Nobody Can Deal With: Politics, Style and the Postindustrial City in Hip Hop." Guins and Cruz 401–16.

Ross, Andrew. "Uses of Camp." Bergman 54–77.

Rossi, Aldo. "The Collective Memory." Miles, Hall, and Borden 172–73.

Rutsky, R. L. *High Techne: Art and Technology from the Machine Aesthetic to the Posthuman*. Minneapolis: U of Minnesota P, 1999.

Rybczynski, Witold. *The Look of Architecture*. New York: Oxford UP, 2001.

Sasaki, Ken-Ichi. "For Whom Is City Design: Tactility versus Visuality." Miles, Hall, and Borden 36–33.

Savage, Dan. *The Seven Deadly Sins and the Pursuit of Happiness in America*. New York: Penguin/Plume, 2003.

Schama, Simon. *A History of Britain 1, 3000 B.C.–A.D. 1603: At the Edge of the World?* London: BBC, 2000.

Schiappa, Edward. *The Beginnings of Rhetorical Theory in Classical Greece*. New Haven: Yale UP, 1999.

———. *Defining Reality: Definitions and the Politics of Meaning*. Carbondale: Southern Illinois UP, 2003.

Seabrook, John. *Nobrow: The Culture of Marketing, the Marketing of Culture*. New York: Vintage, 2001.

Slayden, David, and Rita Kirk Whillock, eds. *Soundbite Culture: The Death of Discourse in a Wired World*. Thousand Oaks, CA: Sage, 1999.

Smith, L. Neil. "Robert Heinlein Remembered." The Heinlein Society. 1 October 2006 <http://www.heinleinsociety.org/rahandme/lneilsmith.html>.

Stearns, Peter N. *American Cool: Constructing a Twentieth-century Emotional Style*. New York: New York UP, 1994.

Stengle, Jamie. "Dallas Man Presses City for Ban on Baggy Pants." *Austin American-Statesman* 2 September 2006: D5.

Storey, John. *An Introduction to Cultural Theory and Popular Culture, 2/e*. Athens: U of Georgia P, 1998.

Stratton, Jon. *The Desirable Body: Cultural Fetishism and the Erotics of Consumption*. Urbana: U of Illinois P, 2001.

Trebay, Guy. "Campaign Chic: Not Too Cool, Never Ever Hot." *New York Times* 22 July 2007, sec. 9: 1–2.

Turner, Graeme. *Film as Social Practice*. 3rd ed. London: Routledge, 1999.

"Unintended Consequences." Wikipedia. 1 October 2006 <http://en.wikipedia.org/wiki/John_Ross_%28author%29>.

Viegener, Matias. "Kinky Escapades, Bedroom Techniques, Unbridled Passion, and Secret Sex Codes." Bergman 234–56.

Viesca, Victor Hugo. "*Straight Out the Barrio*: Ozomatli and the Importance of Place in the Formation of Chicano/a Popular Culture in Los Angeles." Guins and Cruz 479–94.

Vivian, Bradford. "Style, Rhetoric, and Postmodern Culture." *Philosophy and Rhetoric* 35 (2002): 223–43.

Walker, Lisa. *Looking Like What You Are: Sexual Style, Race, and Lesbian Identity*. New York: New York UP, 2001.

Watkins, S. Craig. *Hip Hop Matters: Politics, Pop Culture, and the Struggle for the Soul of a Movement*. Boston: Beacon, 2005.

Wheaton, Sarah. "Latest Campaign Issue? One Candidate's Neckline." *New York Times* 28 July 2007: A11.

Whillock, Rita Kirk. "Giant Sucking Sounds: Politics as Illusion." Slayden and Whillock 5–28.

Willis, Paul. "Symbolic Creativity." Guins and Cruz 241–48.

Wilson, Gregory S., Mary E. Pritchard, and Jamie Schaffer. "Athletic Status and Drinking Behavior in College Students: The Influence of Gender and Coping Styles." *Journal of American College Health* 52 (2004): 269–74.

"Writing Scotland, a Journey through Scotland's Literature: Walter Scott." BBC. 1 July 2006 <http://www.bbc.co.uk/scotland/arts/writingscotland/ learning_journeys/tartan_myths/walter_scott/>.

Wynter, Leon E. *American Skin: Pop Culture, Big Business, and the End of White America*. New York: Crown, 2002.

Yu, Henry. "How Tiger Woods Lost His Stripes: Post-Nationalist American Studies as a History of Race, Migration, and the Commodification of Culture." Guins and Cruz 197–209.

Zhang, Li-fang. "Thinking Styles: University Students' Preferred Teaching Styles and Their Conceptions of Effective Teachers." *Journal of Psychology* 138 (2004): 233–53.

Zondag, Hessel J. "Just Like Other People: Narcissism among Pastors." *Pastoral Psychology* 52 (2004): 423–38.

Zukin, Sharon. "Space and Symbols in an Age of Decline." Miles, Hall, and Borden 81–91.

# Index

**Barry Brummett** is the Charles Sapp Centennial Professor in Communication and is the chair of the communication studies department at the University of Texas at Austin. He is the author of *Rhetorical Dimensions of Popular Culture, Contemporary Apocalyptic Rhetoric, Rhetoric of Machine Aesthetics, The World and How We Describe It,* and *Rhetorical Homologies.* He edited *Landmark Essays: Kenneth Burke and Reading Rhetorical Theory* and is the author or coauthor of several textbooks.

## DATE DUE